DISCONTINUOUS DISCOURSES IN MODERN RUSSIAN LITERATURE

Discontinuous Discourses in Modern Russian Literature

Edited by
Catriona Kelly
Christ Church, Oxford

Michael Makin
*Professor of Slavic Languages and Literatures
University of Michigan*

and

David Shepherd
*Department of Russian Studies
University of Manchester*

Palgrave Macmillan

ISBN 978-1-349-19851-1   ISBN 978-1-349-19849-8 (eBook)
DOI 10.1007/978-1-349-19849-8

© Catriona Helen Moncrieff Kelly, Michael Laurence Makin
and David George Shepherd, 1989

Softcover reprint of the hardcover 1st edition 1989

All rights reserved. For information, write:
Scholarly and Reference Division
St. Martin's Press, Inc., 175 Fifth Avenue, New York, N.Y. 10010

First published in the United States of America in 1989

ISBN 978-0-312-01996-9

Library of Congress Cataloging-in-Publication Data
Discontinuous discourses in modern Russian literature.
Includes index.
1. Russian literature—20th century—History and
criticism.   I. Kelly, Catriona.   II. Makin, Michael.
III. Shepherd, David (David G.)
PG3017.D5   1989   891.7'09'004   88–18157
ISBN 978-0-312-01996-9

Contents

Acknowledgements	vii
Note on Transliteration and Translation	viii
Notes on the Contributors	ix
Introduction	xi

PART I THEORY   1

1. Bakhtin, Benjamin, Sartre: Toward a Typology of the Intellectual Cultural Critic   3
   Dana Polan

2. Dialogism as a Challenge to Literary Criticism   19
   Ken Hirschkop

PART II TEXTUALITY   37

3. Canon Fodder? Problems in the Reading of a Soviet Production Novel   39
   David Shepherd

4. Toward a Poetics of the Absurd: The Prose Writings of Daniil Kharms   60
   Ann Shukman

5. Petrushka and the Pioneers: The Russian Carnival Puppet Theatre after the Revolution   73
   Catriona Kelly

PART III SEXUALITY   113

6. Text and Violence in Tsvetaeva's *Molodets*   115
   Michael Makin

7	Radical Sentimentalism or Sentimental Radicalism? A Feminist Approach to Eighteenth-Century Russian Literature *Joe Andrew*	136
8	Men Who Give Birth: A Feminist Perspective on Russian Literature *Barbara Heldt*	157

Index   169

Acknowledgements

The editors would like to thank the British Academy, the British Council, the Taylor Institution, Oxford, and New College, Oxford, for financial assistance towards the cost of the 1984 conference 'Discontinuous Discourses in Modern Russian Literature'.

Thanks are also due to the editors of *Essays in Poetics* for permission to reprint David Shepherd's 'Canon Fodder? Problems in the Reading of a Soviet Production Novel' (11/1, 1986), and to Indiana University Press for permission to include in Barbara Heldt's 'Men Who Give Birth: A Feminist Perspective on Russian Literature' brief passages from her book *Terrible Perfection: Women and Russian Literature*, published in 1987.

Note on Transliteration and Translation

Transliteration is according to British Standard 2979 (1958), except in quotations, where the original transliteration is retained, and in some familiar forms (e.g. Stravinsky). All translations are the authors' own unless otherwise indicated.

Notes on the Contributors

The editors

Catriona Kelly is Research Fellow in Russian at Christ Church, Oxford. She is a specialist on the Russian theatre, and her major interest is the Russian street puppet show *Petrushka*. She is also active as a translator, and her version of Leonid Borodin's novel *The Third Truth* was published in 1989.

Michael Makin is Assistant Professor of Slavic Languages and Literatures at the University of Michigan and was formerly Research Fellow at New College, Oxford. He specializes in modern Russian poetry, and is writing a book on Marina Tsvetaeva.

David Shepherd is Lecturer in Russian Studies at the University of Manchester. He specializes in Soviet literature and literary theory, and is currently writing a book about Soviet metafiction.

The other contributors

Joe Andrew is Lecturer in Russian Studies at the University of Keele. He is the author of *Writers and Society during the Rise of Russian Realism* and *Russian Writers and Society in the Second Half of the Nineteenth Century*, editor of *The Structural Analysis of Russian Narrative Fiction*, and translator, with C. R. Pike, of *The Formalists, the Futurists and the Marxist Critique*. His latest book is *Women in Russian Literature 1780–1863*. He is editor of *Essays in Poetics*, and organizes the work of the British Neo-Formalist Circle.

Barbara Heldt is Professor of Russian at the University of British Columbia. She is the author of *Koz'ma Prutkov: The Art of Parody* and of *Terrible Perfection: Women and Russian Literature*. She has translated Karolina Pavlova's *A Double Life*, and is currently working on contemporary Russian women authors and on women's autobiography in Russia.

Notes on the Contributors

Ken Hirschkop is a Teaching Fellow in English at the University of Southampton. He is completing a book entitled *Bakhtin and Democracy*, and is co-editor, with David Shepherd, of a forthcoming collection of essays, *Bakhtin and Cultural Theory*. He has written on Bakhtin, discourse theory and the politics of modern culture for *New Left Review*, *Poetics Today*, *News from Nowhere* and *Essays in Poetics*. His current research interests are the development of a politicized theory of discourse and the politics of modern cultural forms in the Soviet Union, England and the United States.

Dana Polan teaches Film and English at the University of Pittsburgh. He is the author of *The Politics of Film and the Avant-Garde* and *Power and Paranoia: History, Narrative, and the American Cinema, 1940–1950*.

Ann Shukman has written and lectured extensively on many aspects of Russian literature and Russian literary theory, including semiotics. She has held teaching appointments at the Universities of Birmingham and Keele. Her current research interests include the ideas of Mikhail Bakhtin.

Introduction

All the chapters in this book, apart from those by Catriona Kelly and Michael Makin, are based on papers read at the conference 'Discontinuous Discourses in Modern Russian Literature', held at Mansfield College, Oxford, in June 1984. The conference was intended to challenge some dominant trends in scholarship, Western and Soviet, on Russian literature and culture: an emphasis on seamless continuity between authorial intention and text; a profound suspicion of the historical, political and ideological as factors in literary production and reception; and a deeply entrenched belief in a 'high' culture whose transcendent aesthetic value is above interrogation. At the same time, we felt that the very significant and radical Russian contribution to recent developments in literary-critical theory deserved more attention within the rather conservative world of Slavic studies, where theory has generally been adopted – if at all – with considerable caution as a means of reinforcing cherished concepts and practices. Hence the title: the queries and comments which it provoked – whether amused, bemused, or outraged – confirmed our hope that such a deliberately unsettling intervention would be timely.

Eighteen papers were delivered at the conference, under the broad headings of 'Bakhtin and the Russian Contribution to Post-Structuralism', 'Feminist Readings of Russian Literature', 'Questions of Poetic Analysis', and 'Problems of Russian Prose Narrative'. It has not been possible to include them all in this volume. Our selection was determined not only by availability of papers and limitations of space, but also by the desire that no single heading be over-represented at the expense of others, and that the items included complement one another in a way appropriate to the slightly altered principles of arrangement adopted for publication. No disrespect is therefore intended to those conference participants whose papers have not been included: Boris Gasparov ('Structural Poetics vs. Semiotics of Literature: The Tartu-Moscow Semiotic School in the Late 1970s'); Sidney Monas ('Verbal Carnival: Bakhtin, Rabelais, *Finnegans Wake* and the Growthesk'); Simonetta Salvestroni ('Bakhtin: Between the Russian Culture of the 1920s and the New Contemporary Ideas'); Efim Etkind ('Kompozitsiya poeticheskogo proizvedeniya i printsipy ego rassmotreniya'); Valentina Polukhina ('Issledovanie metafory v razvitii: I. Brodskii'); Gerry Smith ('Out for the Count: Quantitative Metrics and Literary Interpretation'); Ralph Bogert ('Mandel'shtam's Path from *Stone* to *Sorrow*: Semantic Problems'); Barbara Lönnqvist ('Intertextual Humour in Zamyatin's Short Story "Slovo predostavlyaetsya tovarishchu Churyginu"'); Chris Pike ('Questions of Identity in Soviet Science Fiction'); Nina Perlina ('The Reciprocity of Literary Theory and Artistic Praxis: Mikhail Bakhtin and Konstantin Vaginov in the 1920s'); Michael Nicholson ('The Narrator in *One Day in the Life of Ivan Denisovich*'); and Gareth Williams ('Uneasy Rider: Babel' and His Reader in *Konarmiya*').

The most noteworthy Russian contribution to recent reassessments of established critical practice is undoubtedly the work of Mikhail Bakhtin. Dana Polan and Ken Hirschkop in Part I illustrate Bakhtin's potential for a radical impact on cultural studies well beyond the limits of Slavic studies, and highlight the challenge to seemingly secure critical categories posed by his work, especially his much discussed and appropriated notion of 'dialogism'. Rejecting the widespread tendency to see in Bakhtin's complex, contradictory work little more than a neo-Formalist armoury of descriptive terms with which to defend and fortify the bastions of close textual analysis, Polan and Hirschkop show how Bakhtin can and should be used to mount a vigorous assault on the very foundations of traditional textual criticism.

In Part II David Shepherd shows how the use of Bakhtin for close textual analysis forces the critic to acknowledge that reference to 'the text itself' is not enough. Using the example of 'classic', 'conformist' Soviet works by Marietta Shaginyan, he argues that Bakhtin compels us to consider context – social, political, historical – in order to account not only for the production but also for the varying reception of texts, for their arrangement in hierarchies and canons. Criticism emerges as a *practice* with an all-too-often forgotten history, capable of rendering Shaginyan's apparently straightforward texts deeply problematic. Ann Shukman takes a slightly different view of context, focusing on its importance to the specific act of literary communication. Her application of Bakhtinian theory, supplemented by the ideas of other theorists of communication, to the work of Daniil Kharms confirms the resistance to easy recuperation for which they are renowned. The deconstruction of the apparent opposition between 'easy' and 'difficult' literature, enacted by the juxtaposition of

Shepherd and Shukman, is followed by Catriona Kelly's interrogation of the very notion of 'high' art in her discussion of Soviet appropriations of the pre-Revolutionary carnival puppet theatre. She emphasizes the need to remain sceptical of traditional, allegedly self-evident, criteria of cultural value, and insists that criticism should concern itself with cultural phenomena which are traditionally relegated to the status of objects of purely documentary or ethnographical interest. The history of the Soviet puppet theatre shows how the preservation of original texts, notwithstanding its association with continuity and conservatism, can in some cases be a radical gesture, restoring to some works their potential for disruption and political subversiveness. A radical criticism does not, it becomes clear, always require the negation of canons and traditions.

In Part III Michael Makin takes up two of the main issues raised by Kelly – the opposition of 'high' and 'low' forms as affected by the appropriation of folkloric works by *belles lettres*, and the importance of the physical and sexual. His discussion of Tsvetaeva's *Molodets* shows that, contrary to the usual critical viewpoint, imposition of greater narrative and formal coherence leads to marked disruption of the original folkloric text, accompanied by subversion of sexual convention and stereotype. Radical treatments of female sexuality have been rare in Russian literature and literary criticism, both perceiving women in terms of what they have to offer men, denying them the autonomy of their own desires. (There is, it should be noted, a preponderance of men among Slavists. The fact that two of the male contributors to this volume take a feminist approach may on the one hand suggest that feminism is more than a question of biological gender; but on the other hand some might ask whether the male interest in feminism does not signal a reluctance to leave any mode of critical discourse unexplored and unappropriated, to miss any opportunity of allowing the masculine monologue to continue.) Joe Andrew's treatment of key texts of Russian Sentimentalism argues that their account of women, as it is perceived *now*, is not necessarily a function of their authors' intentions (such scepticism towards this traditional and basic assumption is shared by a number of contributors). Soviet criticism considers the works of Fonvizin, Karamzin, and in particular Radishchev, radical, not to say revolutionary, in their treatment of the Russian people (*narod*), but Andrew shows that in fact this radicalism is severely limited by the exclusion of women other than in their traditional hypostasis. Barbara Heldt's essay on childbirth in Russian literature shows how only those aspects of women's sexuality and bodies conventionally acceptable to men have been included in literature. Her study, as well as giving a provocative account of this question, challenges the whole complacent tradition of the representation (and indeed participation, as this volume unfortunately testifies) of women in both literature and criticism.

As a whole (though not, we hope, one claiming seamless coherence), this collection is intended to highlight some of the most glaring contradictions and absences in traditional criticism. It also aims to question and dispel notions about the exclusiveness and elitism of literary theory, which, in its genuinely radical forms, can help us to reject the conventional aloofness of literary criticism from the interests and problems which people encounter in the conduct of their lives – conflicts in personal and political values, issues of sexuality and gender, and so on. Indeed, this threat to traditional elitism posed by theory-informed criticism helps to explain the widespread suspicion of literary theory against which this volume is directed.

CATRIONA KELLY
MICHAEL MAKIN
DAVID SHEPHERD

Part I
Theory

1
Bakhtin, Benjamin, Sartre: Toward a Typology of the Intellectual Cultural Critic

Dana Polan

To begin, an anecdote ... In a small, but culturally rich, village, an intellectual takes an upper-floor room in an inn that looks out onto the market square. From his window, the intellectual witnesses 'a ballet that ... couldn't even be seen in the Châteaux of Louis II of Bavaria'. The scene here is that of 'la vie quotidienne', the everyday world of the market as energetic activity of economic interaction: 'Towards nine o'clock, when I got up, it was an orgy.... Pieces of money made their entrance on the scene in a syncopated rhythm and, slowly, young women pushed and pressed forward.' Soon, the intellectual decides to change from passive observation to active participation, and join the scene of city-life. But 'scarcely had I descended fully dressed onto the square, than the bustle and freshness of the spectacle had disappeared. I understood that all the gifts of the morning must be received in high places ... Instead of dance and music, there was nothing more than exchange and traffic. Nothing can seem as irrevocably lost as a morning.'[1]

While existing quite adequately as a simple component in a touristic description, this anecdote, written by Walter Benjamin, can seem to have the allegorical density of so many of Benjamin's little tales. Most especially, we might read it as a condensed representation of the complicated place and position of the contemporary radical, or would-be radical, intellectual. A number of recurrent images intersect in the tale: first, the initial position of the intellectual as observer from on-high of the energy of the urban masses; second, the notion of that urban energy as a seductive Voice that calls out beckoningly to the intellectual; third, the desire of the intellectual to move from sheer intellection to involvement; fourth, the sense of social reality as a form whose meaning is not fixed, but depends on one's point-of-view, one's perspective in relation to it (so that the market changes as one approaches it); finally, the intellectual's (self-assuring) declaration that perhaps the long-distance view is the best and perhaps most appropriate one for an intellectual to entertain.

It is these sorts of figures of intellectual practice and its ambivalent relations to the world of quotidian events that I want to explore in this chapter. Specifically, I want to construct a composite image of intellectual practice based on a triangulation of three intellectuals who revolve in ambiguous ways around an interest in materialist perspectives on culture and society: Walter Benjamin, Jean-Paul Sartre (especially in his work from the mid-1950s on), and Mikhail Bakhtin. But what I propose is less an historical account of these figures (or any potential historical interweaving of the three, as when Sartre offhandedly but irrevocably dismisses Bakhtin in an (in)famous interview);[2] rather, I would suggest that critical theory has to move beyond historical and factual reconstruction to an active engagement with the possibilities in the present of the figures of the past.

In particular, ambiguities in the biographical trajectory of intellectual figures – for example, what was the nature of Benjamin's conversion to Marxism? – can lead to a kind of academic empiricism, the endless search for the one fact that will prove the nature of a life unequivocally. Indeed, in the case of Bakhtin, this temptation of empiricism is amplified since biographical uncertainties (the infamous Bakhtin–Voloshinov question) mean not merely that we have to learn how to read Bakhtin's texts but also which texts to read.

For example, important as Michael Holquist's painstaking historical reconstructions of Bakhtin's life may be, they can only be an adjunct to the theoretical task of interpreting Bakhtin, of reading him in the sense that new critical theory has given to the term 'reading': that is, the active writing by the reader of a possible version of the read text. Indeed, the value of Holquist's 'biographical' work – for example, his essay in *boundary 2* on Bakhtin's cultural response to the Russian Revolution – may be less its re-construction of a life than its *construction* of a theoretical position out of that life.[3] For example, Holquist suggests a way of reading Bakhtin's Rabelais book as an allegory of power, a symbolic response to the present encoded in an analysis of the past. But this suggestion by Holquist of a way to read the

Bakhtinian text is one that could never be guided by the facts of Bakhtin's life alone; rather, Holquist writes as a theorist who clearly uses Bakhtin's notion of dialogic writing to read Bakhtin's writing itself and discover there an evaluation of its historical moment.

A montage, like the one I propose, that reads historical figures together has the critical advantage then of facilitating the construction of theory; reading a life against another breaks the critic out of biographical teleology, out of notions of the historical figure as specially endowed thinker, an originary instance out of which an original thought wells up in brilliant and unique intensity. Again, in the case of the three figures, legends of unique greatness and great uniqueness threaten to block any attention other than sheer reverence of the most non-analytic sort. On the one hand, this blockage leads to the kind of paradox evident in Todorov's book on Bakhtin, which declares Bakhtin to be one of the important philosophers of our century but never really argues this assertion and ends up only suggesting Bakhtin's resemblance to figures like Martin Buber.[4] On the other hand, the reaction to reverence can itself become locked into an ideology of reverence; here, one simply argues that the figure under consideration is not the one really worthy of reverent attention. This seems to be the case, for example, in the critical use of Sartre today; through a kind of backlash against earlier elevation of Sartre, Sartre now serves as the Other, the scapegoated figure, for a critical theory that proudly announces its overcoming of the Sartrean problematic: for example, in a recent essay on the Habermas–Gadamer debate, Martin Jay is able to dismiss Sartre in one sentence for his ostensible lack of a theory of language.[5]

Thus, far from engaging in the easy descriptive task of scoring similarities and differences among the three figures, my goal is a *critical* one: to suggest that, in sometimes differing, sometimes parallel ways, the cultural criticism of Benjamin, Sartre and Bakhtin can demonstrate an acceptance of the irreducible complexity of materialist positions and can belie any simple or 'vulgar' approach to the construction of a materialism. In some ways, this grouping may seem a curious one. For example, while Terry Eagleton has well suggested parallels between Benjamin and Bakhtin in his book on Benjamin, Dominick LaCapra, in *A Preface to Sartre*, will argue that it is precisely a Bakhtinian appreciation of the carnivalesque potentiality of language that is lacking in Sartre with his supposed faith in a transparent, totalizing language of pure dialectical reason.[6] I will suggest, however, that it is quite possible to read Sartre along Bakhtinian lines. Moreover, I would argue that each theorist provides a way of reading the others, allowing us to appreciate the gaps or silences of each critical text according to a larger composite model. That three figures in three different situations come back again and again to the same sorts of questions – even if they propose differing answers – can suggest a regularity of concerns for the project of critical theory. Combining aesthetics and politics, and working to synthesize a number of methods in a new critical discourse with a new critical style, the work of these figures poses questions that are perhaps inescapable for any contemporary critical theory.

Most especially, I would suggest that all three figures provide us with necessary elements for a theorization of the ties of modernity and cultural production. The modern experience here is not a reflected essence or content that lies *behind* the artistic or cultural text. Rather, modernity is a force of the textuality itself, influencing cultural production, meaning, and reception. Abstractly, Sartre and Bakhtin construct the bases for a social anthropology, the most fundamental encounters of individuals serving as micro-versions of larger social economies. Sartre's theorization of the look of the Other as situationally influential on self-identity, and Bakhtin's notion of every speech-act (including even the most seemingly interior discourses of the unconscious mind) as necessarily dialogic, both suggest that existence is always already social existence, that the field of the self is the field of the other.

But Benjamin's study of the Look and of social interaction in his *Charles Baudelaire* suggests a way to historicize this anthropology and understand its inflections in varying situations.[7] For Benjamin, the new world of the modern city creates a shock for the nature of perception and forces social relations into new modes; most especially, the shock of the New is received by the aristocrat especially as a threat of disenfranchisement or marginalization that he reacts to with all the aggressiveness of an agonic life–death struggle. Benjamin's city, however, is a dialectical one; even if the aristocrat is progressively forced out of the historical picture, the poet works between aristocracy and proletariat to convert shock into artistic raw material.

Such an understanding of the self–other relationship as a symbolic response to an historically rooted situation allows us to understand Sartrean and Bakhtinian anthropologies as themselves ultimately historical – as responses to worlds in transition. For example, with Benjamin, both Sartre and Bakhtin suggest that one of the effects of the capitalist experience is to obscure the dialogical nature of social relations and to either fetishize it or convert it into an interaction of figures who hide their investments in ideology and evaluation behind fixed masks and the hierarchy of reified roles. Significantly, both Sartre and Bakhtin seem to offer the same set of contrasting alternatives to this function of modernity in contributing to a theatricalization of social relations. On the one hand, both thinkers opt at certain moments for a utopian politics of pure transparency: the imagination of a social mode in which all social subjects would stand visible before all Others in a field of pure reciprocity. But, at the same time, both Sartre and Bakhtin draw back from this utopian myth and suggest that an im-mediate or non-mediated vision of the social totality is impossible. Thus, Sartre's writing claims to approach, while never reaching, moments of transparency; for example, *L'Idiot de la famille* claims that it is possible to know the life of a man and then stops just before the necessary synthesizing volume. Similarly, Bakhtin's carnival is at best a fleeting site of transformed social relations. On the one hand, Bakhtin emphasizes the temporariness of the carnival in the yearly cyclicity of social life. On the other hand, the development of the modern age brings not the intensification of the carnival mode but its progressive degradation and displacement from a collective force to a merely Romantic and subjective attribute.

Moreover, both Sartre and Bakhtin imply that the actual function of an emergent dialogism is not to allow some sort of positive or transparent knowledge of social relations but, quite differently, to parody and disrupt existing relations through a kind of spectacular re-staging of those relations in an alternate mode. That is, what is proposed is not a cognitive grasp of Truth by a social subject who observes sociality from the standpoint of some supposedly objective position. Rather, for Sartre and Bakhtin, the relation of social figures – such as Sartre's Genet or Flaubert, or Bakhtin's carnival participants – to their time is one of an elaborate staging of that time and not some intellective understanding of it.

Likewise, the role of the cultural critic – the figure of Sartre and Bakhtin themselves – is not so much to record passively or transparently the dialogic struggles of the subjects of their study.

Instead, the critic's role is itself dialogic. First, the critic's word is always an answer to other words; for example, Bakhtin works to break Rabelais out of a critical tradition that would read him simply as high-art writer, while Sartre reads Flaubert against a whole Romantic tradition of individual genius.

To be sure, critics always write against the background of the already written, the work of other critics. But here particularly there seems to be a carnivalesque desire on the part of the newer critics themselves to overthrow a received image of literature in a particularly scandalous way. Thus, just as Bakhtin finds in Rabelais a lowering of the high, so too Bakhtin's own book is a deliberate lowering, finding the influences of Rabelais's writing in folk culture and eschewing the heightened approach of a post-Kantian aesthetic for the methods of social and material history. Similarly, Sartre gives us not Flaubert the great artist to be appreciated simply through an impressionistic and belletristic criticism. Here, too, the high is brought low. What had been supposed to be high art is now found to have all-too-ordinary origins – Flaubert's situation as second son in a family lorded over by an analytic Doctor. Ultimately, Flaubert's own proclaimed desire to be a godly figure that soars over the human realm is undone parodically by the key image of *L'Idiot de la famille*: Flaubert's all-too-physical fall to the ground, a fall that Sartre reads as an intended will-to-failure.

Moreover, in all three cases, the cultural critic works to construct a new form of writing, one hopefully more adequate to the complex nature of a new social world in vibrant transition. Yet 'adequacy' of critical style here seems not to mean a style more adequately *reflective* of the social moment. Critical style here is not so much caught up in a quest to capture Truth in a transparent language. Rather, there is an attempt to empower a new approach to reality through a new language – language, then, literally as rhetoric. For this new style of writing, uninterested in the kind of retrospective verification that is the goal of what Timothy Reiss has called the analytico-referential discourses of classical knowledge, if verification is to be had it will have to be pro-spective, a verification through writing's effects.[8] There is first of all an attempt to use language against itself, to re-evaluate the common reference of linguistic units and explode the ideology of dictionary-meaning through a vibrant encounter with history. To take one famous example, Bakhtin's use of the word 'Novel' has all the force of a carnivalesque polemic behind it. As Michael Holquist notes, in Bakhtin's hands the 'Novel' ceases to be the genre which seems to have risen, as Ian Watt would have it, with Defoe, and becomes virtually the form of all dialogically explicit language; the term breaks generic bounds and becomes open-ended, all-encompassing.[9] At the same time, this expansion of the 'Novel' has as a corollary a carnivalesque restriction and debasement of the notion of 'Poetry'. Far from traditional aesthetic notions of poetry as the elevated complexification of referential discourse, Bakhtin deconstructs the standard values of the poetry/prose distinction by finding in the obsessive singularity of the poetic word a monologic reduction of the semantic richness of the dialogue of everyday language. Emphatically, however, this is a deconstruction and not a simple reversal on Bakhtin's part, since his notion of a dialogism underlying all speech-acts – even ones that seek to repress the dialogical imagination – leads back to a new reading of poetry: a reading of the ways in which it reveals sites of dialogism between the crevices of a dominant monologism. Ultimately, Bakhtin would seem to construct a new sort of language, neither simply extra-textually referential nor simply auto-referential. Language here is a blend of style and meaning, of a meaning created through a play of style: as Bakhtin says of a passage from Rabelais, 'The first part is constructed like a chain. The word that ends one sentence starts the next and thus each link is joined to the succeeding one. Such a construction increases the density, the unbroken wholeness of this world made of abundant fat, meat, bowels, and childbirth.'[10]

Significantly, though, this invocation by Bakhtin of a Rabelaisian style sounds not unlike the Bakhtinian style itself in the Rabelais book, a complex montage that chains elements together in an ever-expanding textuality. Indeed, it is possible to imagine that critical theory in general – and certainly in the three figures under consideration – is a kind of vast writing-machine that generates a flow of words irreducible to any attempt to mirror simply a subject of writing. Most immediately, the literary text turns into a site where the nominal subject of the analysis ends up reading or writing the critic, not the other way round. In Bakhtin on Rabelais, or Sartre on Genet, Flaubert, or Freud, or Benjamin on Baudelaire and Paris of the Nineteenth Century, the critic's encounter with his subject leads to a symptomatic breakdown of a referentially adequate, classically austere critical discourse. Sartre and Benjamin suggest two opposed forms of this breakdown. On the one hand, Sartre's writing expands vertiginously, but not so much to better capture its object through an act of massive referentiality as to demonstrate the sheer resistance of words to a referential project: the culmination perhaps of this excess is Sartre's (in)famous stopping of the flow of biographical reconstruction in *L'Idiot de la famille* to declare, 'I admit it; this is all a fable.' Benjamin appears to go in a reverse direction, looking for the smallest fragment – a writing of aphorisms – in which an explosive new shock can burst out. Critical writing here becomes increasingly fragmentary, a montage of bits of experience that are splayed out on the page with no totalizing discourse behind them (so much so that Benjamin even toyed with the idea of making the Arcades book nothing more than a collage of primary quotations).

Beyond Nina Perlina's attempts to use stylistics to resolve the authorship question, or Michael Holquist's and Caryl Emerson's comments on the theoretical implications of translating Bakhtin,[11] Bakhtin's style has not received much theoretical investigation, and yet, as with Sartre or Benjamin, in Bakhtin too we can find a use of language not as positive mastery of a subject but rather as a demonstration of language's textually skewed relationship to an *a priori* field of reference. In the Rabelais book especially, there seems to be an attempt to turn critical language itself into a parodic replaying of the original Rabelaisian text: *Rabelais and His World* is a comically encyclopedic work, run through with digression, incessant repetition, deliberate excess (such as Bakhtin presenting the whole history of a literary form to back up the smallest of points about the Rabelaisian text), sudden turns and twists, and deconstructive interminglings of high and low (as when Bakhtin uses a highly austere philological language to trace the genealogy of various vulgarities). *Rabelais and His World* seems to work between the Sartrean and Benjaminian options for a new critical style: the book is simultaneously an elongated argument, and the condensation of critical argument around a few key images and themes that are given a virtually auratic privilege in the text.

But to suggest such a slippage between style and subject in the writing of the critical theorist is not to imply the failure of critical theory. Rather, it is to suggest that the success of the writing may be elsewhere than in any attempt at referentiality. The writing here suggests that the best way to invoke the nature of modernity is not to *refer* to modernity but to make writing itself modern, to allow it to take on the forms of a world in transition. Hence, for example, the emphasis on movement and process in the work of critical theorists. What Edward Said, in *The World, the Text, and the Critic*, calls 'travelling theory' – the notion that theory is situationally dependent and changes as situations change – is here a travelling not so much of the topics of criticism as of the discursive shape of the critical writing itself.[12] Thus, for example, the work most considered to be the mark of Benjamin's *transition* to Materialism – his text, 'One-Way Street' – plays out a notion of transition in its very structure: a series of aphorisms that approximate the geography of a street and move the reader on a journey through new forms of signification. Similarly, just as movement is a primary *theme* of *Rabelais and His World* – condensed in discussions of Rabelais's journeys through France; of the new voyages of discovery in Rabelais's age; of the movement of the crowd in the market and the carnival – this movement of modernity informs the writing of the book itself. Thus, while Gary Saul Morson is no doubt justified, in his influential essay on Bakhtin, 'The Heresiarch of *Meta*', to claim that 'Baxtin's model implicitly constitutes a retrospective justification of Russian literature',[13] the Rabelais book at least suggests a Bakhtin who is interested in building an international, and not national, criticism. The book travels across national boundaries and, as well, across temporal limits, finding Rabelais to be ultimately no more than the paradigmatic textualization of forces that are at work everywhere and in every age.

More generally, we might suggest that one of the major accomplishments of contemporary critical theory has been to stake out the interconnections of power and space, and to suggest that temporal movement can perhaps provide one with a different position in space and perhaps a different relation to power. Travel becomes necessary as a way of allowing a shifting of one's emplacement in the order of things – for example, against Morson's suggestion that Bakhtin seeks to 'celebrate the Russian tradition, whose greatest works, after all, are novels'.[14]

Bakhtin as much seems to indicate that any celebration of a tradition, even a counter-tradition, ends up spatializing knowledge in a reified array. For Bakhtin, tradition itself should be studied dialogically, any single strand transformed by a montagist juxtaposition of any one tradition with another. Thus, in the way that

Alvin Gouldner argues in *The Dialectic of Ideology and Technology* that we can only know the nature of an ideological practice of a culture by knowing the ideological practice of another culture, we find Bakhtin declaring in *Rabelais and His World* that

> The Italianization of the French language and the struggle against it are a new and important document in the history of linguistic interaction. We have here two national idioms, and their interorientation not only lends a new element to the awareness of language as a peculiar whole with its own limits and perspectives but also leads to the consciousness of concrete historic space.[15]

We might go so far as to suggest that writing in the case of critics like Bakhtin or Benjamin or Sartre takes on a form that is perspectivalist or cubist, here again becoming part of a particularly modern conception of the relativity of knowledge in space and time. In this respect, Bakhtin's comparison of the dialogical situation to a sculpture that one has to move around to appreciate fully, is strikingly close to Benjamin's famous invocations of the breakdown of aura in the age of mechanical reproduction, a breakdown that Benjamin specifically links to a movement through space. Indeed, Bakhtin's Rabelais book is readable as a contribution to the history of the demythification of aura, as the challenge to Latin of vernacular languages and printed texts challenges the vertical hierarchy of dominant power. Even Sartre's image, in *Critique de la raison dialectique*, of the intellectual in an upper-floor room who looks out of a window and attempts to totalize the experience of two workers separated by a wall, becomes in this respect a negative confirmation of the force of perspective: the intellectual's totalization here can only always be a totalization in externality, blocked from anything more than a long view of working-class life.

Hence the interest for the critical theorists of scandalously marginal or decentred figures, figures who are simultaneously inside and outside the dominant system: for example, Bakhtin's Rabelais who is both priest and subverter of medieval religion; Benjamin's Baudelaire who works to hold flowers and evil together in a single image and who is simultaneously thought of by his contemporaries as a subversive and a police spy; Sartre's Flaubert who sets out to make a literature of Nothingness and finds himself celebrated by Napoleon III through what Sartre calls an 'objective programmation' by which the artist's subjective neuroses come to match the 'objective neuroses' of his age. To be sure, some of this interest in the eccentric figures of cultural history derives from the intellectual's admiration for things exotic or *outré*; this often seems especially to be the case with Sartre, whose protestations that he is not at all attracted to Genet or Flaubert frequently appear to be the result of a psychological disavowal. None the less, there is something more profound in this intellectual appreciation of the scandalous figure: the very attempt to sum up an age (Rabelais's, Flaubert's, Baudelaire's) in a figure who seems in a skewed relation to that age enables a perspectival or dialogic reading of the age. In Benjamin's book, for example, the nineteenth century is not only an age of industrial rationalization – the enclosing of workers within the regime of repetitive tasks; rather, the century *is* that, but encompasses *also* the gambler who resembles the worker in the repetition of gestures, *and* the poet who ventures through all the experiences of life and tries to hold them all together in the fragile space of a poem. Adorno criticized such a montagist writing as Benjamin's, arguing that Benjamin was engaging in the worst of vulgar materialism by somehow suggesting that all experiences, no matter how diverse, were referrable back to an originary economic force.[16] But what Benjamin is proposing appears to be a notion of the cultural field as a dialogic totality for which no totalizing discourse is appropriate; the social field is a multiplicity, not a unity.

Hence a drive in the critical theorists for a new vocabulary of polysemy, the construction of a new language of greater rather than lesser complexity, the fabrication of words that hover between meanings, like Derrida's series of dialogic words: differance, position, erasure. These new words refer to ambiguous situations but they also refer ambiguously: words like Sartre's *practico-inerte* or Bakhtin's *heteroglossia*. Indeed, as Michael Holquist notes in the case of Bakhtin:

> It is the need to confront this multiplicity [of meanings in the speech-act] in a principled way that impels Bakhtin to coin some of his more outré terms.... He does so as well to highlight his contention that language is never – except for certain linguists – what linguists say it is. There is no such thing as a 'general language', a language that is spoken by a general voice, that may be divorced from a specific saying.[17]

Bakhtin's concentration on what Holquist calls here a 'specific saying' is an essential one, for it is necessary to emphasize that dialogism is not the breakdown of meaning *per se* but rather its expansion from the monological position of single meanings. This is an important distinction since there is all too evidently the temptation to somehow immediately assume that the most dialogic form of language would be that of a society's most avant-garde forms – forms of abstraction, deliberate non-sense, aesthetic rarefaction.

At the present moment, this temptation to turn cultural critics into apologists of or for an avant-garde seems especially prevalent in the critical use of Bakhtin (although Richard Wolin's *Walter Benjamin: An Aesthetics of Redemption* or Dominick LaCapra's *Madame Bovary on Trial* evince a similar desire to read Benjamin and Sartre respectively as apologists for pure art).[18] In the case of Bakhtin, much of his current success, I would argue, comes from a reading that applies him to a high-art canon and is able to do so by treating him in virtually formalist terms as a thinker of the complexity of pure *aesthetic* form. Bakhtin here is made to participate in an ideology of 'High Art', not so different from New Criticism. Is it so accidental that most of the proclamations of Bakhtin's importance have come almost exclusively from departments of literature (and from defenders of tradition, such as Wayne Booth)? Is it accidental that, despite the amount of research conducted to resolve the Voloshinov–Bakhtin authorship questions, there has been little attempt to read the literary critical work along with the philosophic and materialist investigations? The partial use of Bakhtin to enhance descriptions of literary complexity in works of high art allows literary criticism to continue doing what it has always done while appearing to do something more.

Yet, the prime importance for me of the three figures I have presented is that they offer a way to begin a critical examination of mass and popular culture. Their theorization and practice refuse to see such culture as inherently monological, the formulaic repetition of uninteresting themes – the kind of attitude that is presented with all the matter-of-factness of an ostensibly obvious common sense in a recent book of theory, J. M. Bernstein's *The Philosophy of the Novel*:

> Autonomous literature represents the culmination of a social process by which realism's ambivalent critical and collusive

relation to our practical ideology was broken in two, one half of which preserves its critical impetus by creating a world apart, while the other half, the world of popular fiction, which inundates itself in the raw facts of power, money, success, middle-class sexual fantasies, airports, and automobiles, has lost all ability to write against our time.[19]

Against this, Benjamin emphasized the simultaneous progressive and regressive potentials of popular culture, and the fact that culture's effect (whether positive or negative) depends on the productive situation in which it operates and the way it uses the techniques of existing forms and emergent forms. Similarly, Sartre suggests that popular culture may be one of the few arenas in which the utopian impulse for dialogic interaction defies the staid order of a patriarchal bourgeoisie: in *Les Mots*, Sartre's first visit to the cinema is a glorious discovery of a world of reciprocity that Sartre's reading and writing somehow seeks to return to. Moreover, the recent publication of Sartre's scenario for John Huston's life of Freud suggests that a role of the oppositional cultural producer might be to try to carnivalize forms of dominant ideology from within; against Huston's wishes for a screenplay that would have all the teleology of a classic narrative of epistemological growth, Sartre writes a virtual anti-narrative, filled with gaps, reversals, and a disturbing multiplication of narrative strands.

Finally, Bakhtin suggests that popular culture can work against the stases of dominant hierarchical culture; and, indeed, recent theorizations of punk rock – as in Dick Hebdige's *Sub-Cultures* – or of the contemporary horror film – as in Robin Wood's anthology, *The American Nightmare: Essays on the Contemporary Horror Film* – suggest that many popular forms take a far from affirmative stance toward the proprieties of middle-class ideology. To take an example (although one that is perhaps already a little too canonic), Hitchcock's film, *The Birds*, uses the bird attacks precisely as a kind of *textual* upsetting of the proprieties of middle-class existence. Much of the film chronicles the crushing banality of a couple in the process of formation. At moments, the deadness and insipid stereotypicality of the couple make the film resemble an Antonioni film on alienation. But it is precisely at the height of such moments that the birds attack, breaking up order and doing so in a complex arrangement of point-of-view shots that frequently put the spectator in the position of the birds against the banal humans.

Further possible links between Bakhtin and mass culture are discernible in the way that Bakhtin reverses the usual hierarchy and has modern high culture descending from folk culture as its monologizing degradation: much of today's popular culture works to create a new composite form in which high and mass work together and interchange forms. Indeed, as Peter Wollen argues in *Readings and Writings: Semiotic Counter-Strategies*, it is perhaps most appropriate to see popular and avant-garde culture alike as oppositional sub-cultures, both potentially taking a carnivalesque attitude toward dominant ideological practice.[20] For example, as Wollen points out, Roland Barthes's *S/Z* can seem to bear an uncanny resemblance to black rap music; both forms begin with a primary text that ultimately serves as little more than a pre-text for the contemporary figure's voice to play in and around. This is not to automatically valorize alternate popular culture, however. Or at least, it is not to valorize it in traditional aesthetic terms – analysing, for example, this or that work of popular culture along elevating canonic lines, as Bakhtin is now being used to analyse figures from a high-art tradition. Here, it is necessary to note that Bakhtin's interest in popular culture is not in any supposed abstraction or elevation of this culture from earthly concerns; neither escapism nor transcendental spiritualism, popular culture is a form through which quotidian desires are channelled and processed. And yet, against the critiques of Bakhtin as naively logocentric in his ostensible faith in a Voice of the people, I would argue that Bakhtin's evocation of folk culture is not a form of nostalgia for the innocent simplicity of a folk culture that would somehow grasp the truth of social life. Popular culture, as Bakhtin invokes it and as it operates today, is a complex form that is accessible to logocentrism and monologism only at the cost of critical reduction. Before we can say that formal complexity or carnivalesque play are positive values of a culture, whether popular or avant-garde, we would need to theorize the varying social spaces in which such complexity and play take place. Indeed, as Dominick LaCapra argues in *Rethinking Intellectual History*, an historical study like Le Roy Ladurie's *Carnival de Romans* can potentially do nothing so much as suggest the dangers of carnival for popular struggle; through the reversals of the carnival, dominant power was able to pinpoint the danger points of its hold on society and so emerge from the carnivalesque strengthened.[21]

The case of Bakhtin especially implies that we need to think of the lineage of critical theory not as a tradition of fixed bodies of knowledge to be unambiguously applied in scientifically controlled ways. The theories of the past change as our culture changes. What I have tried to suggest here is a way of thinking out the history of intellectual practice that would merge the two senses of history as event and writing – history, then, as our particular and hopefully open way of writing the past for our present.

NOTES AND REFERENCES

1. Walter Benjamin, 'Weimar', trans. Jean Lacoste, in *Sens unique*, Paris, 1978, pp. 299–300.
2. Jean-Paul Sartre, 'Sur "L'Idiot de la famille"', in *Situations X*, Paris, 1976, pp. 106, 109–10.
3. See Michael Holquist, 'Bakhtin and Rabelais: Theory as Praxis', *boundary 2*, 11/1–2, 1982/83, pp. 5–19. See also, Katerina Clark and Michael Holquist, *Mikhail Bakhtin*, Cambridge, Mass., 1984, for expanded discussion of the relation of Bakhtin's writing to its time.
4. See Tzvetan Todorov, *Mikhail Bakhtine: le principe dialogique*, Paris, 1981.
5. See Martin Jay, 'Should Intellectual History Take a Linguistic Turn: Reflections on the Habermas–Gadamer Debate', in *Modern European Intellectual History: Reappraisals and New Perspectives*, ed. Steven Kaplan and Dominick LaCapra, Ithaca, 1983, p. 83.
6. See Terry Eagleton, *Walter Benjamin, or Towards a Revolutionary Criticism*, London, New York, 1981, and LaCapra, *A Preface to Sartre*, Ithaca, 1978.
7. Benjamin, *Charles Baudelaire: A Lyric Poet in the Era of High Capitalism*, trans. Harry Zohn, London, 1973.
8. See Timothy Reiss, *The Discourse of Modernism*, Ithaca, 1982. For a recent defence of materialism as a pro-spective rhetoric, see Frank Lentricchia, *Criticism and Social Change*, Chicago, 1983.
9. See Holquist's Preface to Mikhail Bakhtin, *The Dialogic Imagination*, Austin, Texas, 1981, pp. xv–xxiv.
10. Bakhtin, *Rabelais and His World*, trans. Hélène Iswolsky, Cambridge, Mass., 1968, p. 222.
11. See Nina Perlina, 'Bakhtin–Medvedev–Voloshinov: An Apple of Discourse', *University of Ottawa Quarterly*, 53/1, 1983, pp. 35–47, and Holquist's and Emerson's Introduction to *The Dialogic Imagination*.
    Since the original writing of this essay, Caryl Emerson has examined the complications of Bakhtin's style in her Editor's Preface to Bakhtin's *Problems of Dostoevsky's Poetics*, Minneapolis, Manchester, 1984.
12. See Edward Said, *The World, the Text, and the Critic*, Cambridge, Mass., 1983.

13. Gary Saul Morson, 'The Heresiarch of *Meta*', *PTL: A Journal for Descriptive Poetics and Theory of Literature*, 3, 1978, pp. 423–4.
14. Ibid, p. 424.
15. Alvin Gouldner, *The Dialectic of Ideology and Technology: The Origins, Grammar and Future of Ideology*, New York, 1976; Bakhtin, *Rabelais*, p. 470.
16. See Adorno's interchange with Benjamin in *Aesthetics and Politics: Debates Between Bloch, Lukacs, Brecht, Benjamin, Adorno*, London, New York, 1977, pp. 101–41.
17. Holquist, Preface to Bakhtin, *The Dialogic Imagination*, p. xxi.
18. See Richard Wolin, *Walter Benjamin: An Aesthetics of Redemption*, New York, 1982; and LaCapra, *A Preface*.
19. J. M. Bernstèin, *The Philosophy of the Novel: Lukacs, Modernism, and the Dialectics of Form*, Minneapolis, 1984, pp. 250–1.
20. See Peter Wollen, *Readings and Writings: Semiotic Counter-Strategies*, London, New York, 1982.
21. See LaCapra, *Rethinking Intellectual History: Texts, Contexts, Language*, Ithaca, 1983, pp. 295–6.

2
Dialogism as a Challenge to Literary Criticism

Ken Hirschkop

Dialogism has become the focus of a lot of recent literary discussion. Of the many new concepts which owe their introduction into literary studies to Bakhtin, it seems destined to be both the most popular and the most protean and controversial. Within Bakhtin's writings alone there are many different definitions and formulations of dialogism, different not only in the sense of alternative but also contradictory. The range of possible definitions has only been increased by the critical assimilation of the last few years. It is tempting to assume that the relation between the elusiveness of this concept and its current popularity is direct, but part of the appeal must also lie in the clear way in which this concept connects literature to larger social questions at a time when this connection is being closely examined. For dialogism is not used by literary criticism today as only another analytical tool for the formal analysis of texts: it is also treated as the symbol, or index, of a social ideal. The dialogism of texts is simply the concentrated form of a dialogism in social life generally. In a familiar gesture, we find that the analysis of literature is supposed to lead us to the recognition of a hidden aspect of our social life – in this instance, the fact that we exist only in dialogue (whatever that is held to mean). In Bakhtin studies, this connection is pointed to with especial bluntness or crudeness, most obviously by endless reminders, in critical articles and conference papers, that the critic speaking or writing knows he or she is engaged in dialogue.

The question which remains to be settled is what one means by dialogue, both as social ideal and formal quality of texts. The entropic character of Bakhtin's writing and criticism of it certainly casts a fuzzy penumbra around dialogism, but a rough critical consensus seems to be emerging which is shaped by a general imperative to fit Bakhtin to the project that literary criticism sets itself – the formal analysis of particular texts, conceived of as discrete objects. The very nature of literary criticism prescribes a certain shape for Bakhtin interpretation, and it is this interpretation that I would like to describe and contest in what follows. For Bakhtin, at certain moments, offers us not new analytical tools for literary criticism but a conceptualization of culture which would break with the present practice of literary criticism altogether and which suggests a map of our social life very unlike that outlined by Anglo-American Bakhtin criticism today.

Inevitably the interpretation I shall offer privileges some texts and formulations of Bakhtin over others. In particular, I shall concentrate on the essay 'Discourse in the Novel', because it is there that dialogism is formulated in the ways I think most useful. This is a methodological necessity in all criticism, but it is particularly true for Bakhtin: there is no unified meaning behind these texts and any act of interpretation must perforce endorse certain statements and reject others.[1]

Not only selection is involved. In many cases contradictions and elisions can only be dealt with by pushing Bakhtin's ideas to logically necessary conclusions which they avoid. Thus it is fairer to describe this process as managing the contradictions of Bakhtin rather than finding his meaning. This is especially necessary because so many of his innovations involve investing old concepts with new significance – as with style, genre, intention, novel – so that in the texts they hover mid-way between old and new senses or else switch back and forth, even within a sentence (the best example being, in 'Discourse in the Novel': 'the style of a novel is its combination of styles').[2] When what is at stake is a critique of the traditional terms in which we think of language and literature, it is obviously important not to confuse the received meanings of these words with the new ones which are sometimes only subtly suggested. This is precisely the failing of so much work on Bakhtin today. As a result, the problems which Bakhtin confronted are not solved but merely camouflaged by a new battery of terms. Dispensing, for the moment, with the political overtones of the word, it would be fair to question much of what we have been offered recently because it is simply too conservative. Blunting the more theoretically radical implications of Bakhtin's texts, much recent Bakhtin criticism misses the possible solutions to the theoretical problems which Bakhtin discusses in his work.

In 'Discourse in the Novel' the most essential theoretical problem addressed is the inadequacy of the Saussurean conceptualization of the linguistic process of discourse, and the categories of analysis which derive from this conceptualization. Saussure divides the whole of speech, or what we would call discourse, into *langue*, a system of linguistic forms which make speech possible, and *parole*, the actual historical act of speech. In this division, discourse is split up into internal and external elements and, just as importantly, the inside and outside of discourse are characterized in particular ways. *Langue* is structured and systematic but also, significantly, social and synchronic; the social-structural and a-historical are thereby necessarily related in opposition to *parole*, which is the individual, historical and non-systematic aspect of discourse. The significance of this group of paired oppositions is that it defines the way we think of historical change or activity in language: it must be something asystematic with its explanation in things individual rather than social. A social or structural explanation of the historical act of speech or of the creative aspect of *language* is impossible under the terms of this scheme, because, as Bakhtin puts it:

> It is precisely the individuality of the speaking subject that is acknowledged as that style-forming factor which turns a language and linguistic phenomenon into a stylistic unity.[3]

For Bakhtin this problem presented itself as an inability to account for style, the consistent patterns of linguistic usage. Because Saussurean linguistics defines discourse as the usage by an individual subject of a general, socially existing system of usable linguistic forms, the motivating force behind actual language use (its purposiveness or intentionality) can only be described in individualist terms. Style, a particular pattern of usage, is therefore only comprehensible as the incarnation of an individual will in language.

There is an important corollary to this in the categories which underlie our approach to literary criticism. When the text is formalized as an object which means 'by itself', then that which endows it with meaning is located outside of the textual process, usually in the form of an authorial intention, ideology or social spirit which precedes the text and its structured nature. For us, literary conventions and techniques are a kind of *langue*, but their creation and interpretation are *parole*. In literary criticism, cultural practices are divided into inert formal works and the active forces which endow them with meaning, from the outside. In 'Discourse in the Novel' Bakhtin attempts to deconstruct this opposition of inside and outside, form and subject, by his emphasis on a 'stylistics of genre', those 'fundamentally social paths of the life of discourse'.[4] The suggestion that the 'life of discourse', its actual historical performance, is a matter of social analysis, challenges the Saussurean assumption that linguistic performance is a question of *parole*, that is, individual use. A stylistics of genre would recast our entire approach to the analysis of discourse by mixing up those binary oppositions which gathered around the poles of *langue* and *parole*. The historical nature of discourse, no longer thought of as *parole*, would be amenable to social and structural analysis. The linguistic forms of *langue* would no longer be endowed with meaning by virtue of their place within a static synchronic system of language, but would acquire meaning and, to that extent, actual formal definition historically. Taken seriously, such a stylistics of genre would force us to substantially revise our approach to literary analysis. We could no longer assume that the meaning of a text was embedded within it, because the text would only acquire significance as a particular historical utterance. This historical meaning would in turn not be something individual and self-sufficient, like an authorial vision or intention, but would be the way in which a text entered into a socially defined configuration of utterances. Thus the differential nature of meaning described by Saussure is historicized when the text's meaning is considered in its dialogical aspect – for example, as a response to earlier utterances and a provocation of later ones.[5] The analysis of style would, by this route, become the analysis of historical relationships between utterances and of the regular patterns of these relationships which are called genres.

The theoretical critique of Saussure offered by Bakhtin proposes to replace the analysis of style as a phenomenon of *parole* – an analysis which necessarily explains style in individualist terms – with one which explains it as a dialogical phenomenon and therefore as something social and historical. The justification for this critique, however, is not only theoretical, for the recognition of the necessity of a social analysis of style goes hand in hand with a recognition of the essentially social nature of our lives: the complete interdependence of individuals. Saussurean linguistics is, from this perspective, not only wrong, it is also politically and morally pernicious, encouraging a private individualism. Its formalist tack, far from being a mere theoretical error, serves a centralizing and repressive bloc which, however wrongheaded its theoretical precepts, wields a tremendous power in the cultural arena. As such it is a political opponent. This is evident in the tone of 'Discourse in the Novel': it is not only a theoretical treatise but also a call to battle, recounting a history of struggle between popular and official culture in which the former is seen as the very incarnation of the sociality of language. Dialogism is, in this sense, not a theoretical analysis of discourse but a specific form of discourse itself in which the essentially dialogical nature of all discourse is made manifest or conscious. This tradition of 'novelistic' discourse is, implicitly, what has made Bakhtin's recognition of dialogism possible. Conversely, the formalist linguistics culminating in Saussure has consistently marginalized this novelistic tradition by consigning it to the realm of the vulgar, the rhetorical, or the popular. In 'Discourse in the Novel' this official strategy is described as a politically motivated misreading of culture, not a mere disinterested error. The theoretical struggle between Bakhtin's dialogical theory of discourse and the monological theory of Saussure parallels the larger cultural struggle between the novelistic–popular and poetic–official.

Dialogism, then, is a concept operating on two levels. As a theory of discourse it is superior to its monological opposite, Saussure, simply because it is truer. But as a specific discursive practice it is preferable on the basis of criteria which are more political or moral in nature. The latter claim is dependent on the former; novelistic discourse is superior because in it the truly dialogical nature of discourse, its essential sociality, is both recognized and exploited. By contrast, in Bakhtin's theoretical scheme, the poetic is a discourse which is at once social – because all discourse is by nature dialogical – and yet anti-social by virtue of its attempted imposition of an individualistic form on discourse. But the attack on the poetic and Saussure is cast in very strange terms. Rather than being seen as social forces to be politically opposed on moral grounds, they are, for Bakhtin, objectionable precisely because they are anti-social. The critique of Saussure is thus reduced to a theoretical one: the politico-cultural centralization in which linguistics participates is explicable only as a theoretical error, a misrecognition of the nature of discourse.

To comprehend what is at issue here it is necessary to examine

Bakhtin's social critique as it is presented in 'Discourse in the Novel'. The opposition between popular and official is not, as one would expect, described as an opposition between social forces, but as an opposition between a vital and developing society and a ruling force which represses and centralizes it. Contradiction, plurality, historical development – these are the essence of social life, and thus a unifying and centralizing ruling group serves a function which is literally anti-social. The significance of this can be clarified by comparison with the Marxist conceptualization of a ruling class. In Marxist theory, the bourgeoisie serves a definite social function: it is simultaneously progressive by virtue of socializing the means of production and repressive by aiming to maintain private property. It is not opposed to history or social development *per se*, but struggles for a particular course of development. Bakhtin forgets the revolutionizing role of the ruling class and sees in it a purely repressive force. Its social function is disregarded, and one can only guess that this is because he recognizes only the *political* dominance of a social group, severing this from the larger socio-economic aims which that political practice serves. Political rule thus appears as an end in itself with no intrinsic social purpose. The only reasonable explanation for this anti-social ruling force is that a group from society has forgotten its social nature and has adopted a role for itself which is best described as 'pretentious'.

This curious theoretical state of affairs is reproduced in the opposition of the novelistic and poetic. Like the ruling social group the poetic is both obviously and necessarily social – a discursive form *in* social life – and relentlessly anti-social in its goals and practice. It can only be accounted for as a discursive practice which has mysteriously forgotten or repressed its dialogical nature. The poetic utterance is, like any other of course, a response to past discourse and an anticipation of future discourse. It has significance only by virtue of its relations to other utterances. In all these respects it is dialogical; it just pretends that this is not the case. Consciousness of this essential dialogism is therefore what distinguishes the novelistic from the poetic utterance; these are the only terms by which they can be differentiated.

This ambiguity in the term 'dialogism' – both essence of discourse and 'conscious' form of it – affects the entire conceptual structure of Bakhtin's argument and causes enormous interpretive difficulties. While any description of the origins of this position is contestable, a fair estimate would be that it is the consequence of political opposition to a ruling social group combined with the tactical belief that positive social change can only come about by enforcing a recognition of our essential human sociality on our potential or real oppressors. The appeal is made to a true social condition (the dialogical nature of language and being) which we need only become conscious of. The centrality of consciousness in this politics makes Bakhtinian theory easily assimilable into a literary criticism which, throughout its diverse twentieth-century forms, appears as formalist but is always ultimately subjectivist. The characteristic method of literary analysis is to analyse textual effects as if they were the result of 'the words on the page', and not of intertextuality, critical practice or institutional constraints, and then to trace the coherence of these effects back to a subject, whether this be the vision of an author, some form of *Zeitgeist*, or a structure or a quality of subjective experience. This is necessarily the endpoint of any formalist analysis because something must endow these lifeless forms – words – with meaning. If the difference between dialogism and monologism is a difference of consciousness then that fits neatly into the received tasks of literary analysis. It can then be assumed that texts are intrinsically (i.e. as a formal quality) dialogical or monological, depending only on what is written, and not, for example, on how they are read. This having been decided, dialogism or monologism can then be explained as a direct consequence of a certain attitude of the text's author or as the direct translation of a political intention. The latter takes the form of the contention that to be monological is simply to be assertive or 'absolutist'. By contrast, dialogism is 'open-mindedness'. This of course reduces categories of social analysis to the subjective intentions of speakers. Style, in Bakhtin's terms, is explained as a unity of language traceable to the unity of a subject.

The belief that what separates dialogism from monologism is consciousness also has important implications for the way the opposition of Bakhtinian dialogical theory and Saussurean monological theory is construed. If monologism is only discourse which misunderstands itself, then Saussure is to be faulted only with having made an understandable theoretical error. Formalist linguistics is no longer a politically dangerous practice but simply a theoretically inadequate one. And, perhaps, it is only inadequate and not entirely wrong about discourse. When Saussure is construed as merely inadequate theory, rather than as a theoretical force which actually shapes a practice of discourse (the poetic), then Bakhtin is turned into a theorist of *parole*; indeed, the matter is often put in this way. Dialogical analysis seizes that concrete level of discourse which escapes Saussure and his followers, who are castigated for merely being too abstract.

Although Bakhtin, as theorist of *parole*, is presented as making a revolutionary break with Saussure, the thrust of his critique is in fact evaded. Bakhtin opposes centralizing theories of language (of which Saussure is the modern culmination) not because they are in error but because their social and political effects are so morally undesirable. That the objectionable social practice of the poetic is explained as ultimately rooted in a simple misperception or error on the part of a ruling official stratum, is a consequence of Bakhtin's politics, which must be taken to task for such naïveté. If this explanation is accepted at face value, then Saussurean linguistics and Bakhtinian theory are opposed only as competing theories of the same object rather than as ideologies justifying different discursive practices. Bakhtin's focus on style as that which Saussurean linguistics cannot explain ceases to signal the beginning of a deconstruction of the central categories of this linguistics. If style is assumed to be *parole*, then a Bakhtin who simply theorizes *parole* without threatening the definition of it does not change the essentials of our analysis of style. For what defines the monological perspective of language is not the *exclusion* of concrete utterances, contextual factors, stylistic and pragmatic aspects of language. It is, rather, the assumption that all those are intelligible as *parole*, i.e. by reference to something outside of and preceding discourse, usually the individual subject. The distinction between abstract linguistic form and concrete actual utterance is the one decreed by Saussure's initial gesture of dividing discourse into *langue* and *parole*. To interpret the distinction between a monological and a dialogical account of language as equivalent to that between abstract linguistic relations and concrete interpersonal ones, is really to change nothing, leaving the terms of the monological division of form and subject intact. Much Bakhtin criticism has done just that, following uncritically in Bakhtin's footsteps. Michel Pêcheux claims that the history of recent semantics is characterized by its attempt to integrate the extra-linguistic *residue* which determines meaning (context, subjective intentions, style) into the systematicity of linguistics. It is difficult to see the recent heroization of Bakhtin as the theorist of concrete utterance as anything other than an awkward attempt to do the same, this time under the sign of interpersonal context. A more critical approach must start by asking the question: what is monologism, if not a form of discourse? Why do we assume that it is not in the nature of language that it can be both monological and dialogical? Far from questioning the theoretical point that language is inherently dialogical, this in fact broadens and strengthens the claim. If dialogicity is the fact that an utterance's meaning or effects are determined by its orientation among other utterances then surely it is evident that monologism is a *particular* form of orientation, a precise strategy for manoeuvering within a discursive universe. What distinguishes monologism from dialogism as a discursive practice is not the absence or presence of different socio-ideological languages but the *kind* of relation established between the languages. Monological discourse is characterized by a hierarchical relation between languages, dialogical discourse by a contradictory relation. Monologism – poetic discourse – is, then, a form of that essential dialogism implied in Bakhtin's theory, not a mysterious denial of it. The poetic and novelistic confront each other as different forms of discourse whose difference has to be explained in terms other than mystification or self-consciousness. The novelistic utterance, historicizing and unfinished as it is, is no more natural to language than the oppressive strategies of the poetic. Language is equally at home in the service of oppression or subversion, communication or obfuscation. This points us to a possible way of characterizing the distinction between novelistic and poetic: it is a question of the effects of *power* that each form produces. Poetic discourse produces or reproduces a relation of submission to an authoritative language, whereas the novelistic subverts this authority. The difference is, one could say, a 'performative' one.

The difference can be elucidated by a consideration of what Bakhtin describes as the central category of the centralizing forces of language: unified language (*edinyi yazyk*). Like all the categories associated with the poetic and monological, unified language leads a double life. This is summed up in Bakhtin's description of it as 'not actually existing but, in its essence, always projected'.[6] It opposes actual heteroglossia and 'at the same time is real as a force overcoming this heteroglossia'.[7] Like poetic discourse it both mystifies and yet has real effects which must be accounted for. This category 'crystallizes in the real albeit relative unity of a ruling conversational (everyday) and literary language, a "correct language"'.[8] This should be carefully distinguished from what unified language presents itself as theoretically: an empirical description of a national language, a catalogue of its lexical forms and syntactic and grammatical rules. Unified language, as a system of linguistic norms, is by its very nature prescriptive rather than descriptive. It exists as a political objective of a ruling social group rather than as an empirical description of the rules and forms of actual speech. It is not therefore an abstract unity, a *langue*, within which the stratification of heteroglossia can be found. Any project of linguistic formalization, at no matter how general or abstract a level, necessarily proceeds not by accounting for the actual variety of speech but by setting up a prescriptive unified language valorized as correct or proper, thereby defining all speech which defies its rules as incorrect. This is a theoretical and not a historical fact, because discourse cannot be explained by formal rules. The monologizing project of formalization is therefore doomed in one sense, although it has real effects. The institution of a standard form of English might serve as an example of this process. A correct form of a national language is established by the definition of rules for correct usage; all speech which varies from this discursive practice is considered incorrect, uneducated, or a 'regional dialect'.

Although only a small percentage of a national population may actually speak this correct language, its institution may affect the entire populace. The correct ruling language exerts a normative pressure on actual heteroglossia, which is marginalized, placed in an inferior relation to this ruling language, because heteroglossia violates the norm. The force of this marginalization cannot be overestimated. One need only think of the way non-standard forms of English are perceived to appreciate the real pressure unified language is able to exert. It is crucial to understand the nature of this pressure in order to grasp the process of linguistic centralization. Unified language does not centralize by persuading a heteroglottic populace to speak an élite literary dialect. Instead, unified languages have been developed in, and have themselves supported, specific social institutions responsible for political and cultural centralization. These 'correct' or 'standard' languages unify not by permeating a populace but by virtue of their location in key institutions. The true political nature of unified language is clear if one considers that what has always defined a language as national has not been whether it was spoken by the citizenry at large but its political and administrative stretch. The constitution of a national language is dependent on its institutional location and not some existent homogeneity of speech. This is as true, in Bakhtin's terms, for a national language which comes into being through a process of standardization which excludes heteroglossia as it is for the more obvious situation of Latin in the Medieval period, which culturally centralized empires and affected all discourse although it was only used by a small élite. To centralize through the establishment of a unified language is therefore to fix and marginalize the actual discourse of a society in relation to a normative *langue*. It is this kind of repression of heteroglossia which is the goal of unified language, and not the actual permeation of its practice into a population.

To describe this unification is to reach beyond the terms of linguistics, which cannot account for the force of unified language. Although it affects the discourse of an entire population it does not affect it at the linguistic level. The effects are more properly political or ideological: a certain form of popular 'linguistic' consciousness is organized in which the correct-standard language carries authority, thus ensuring the ideological subjection of the people. The real purpose of unified language is not communication within the people but domination over them. Its specificity as discourse cannot be analysed within the formal categories of linguistics.

Yet this immediately draws attention to one of the most difficult characteristics of Bakhtin's writing: the formal categories are 'overloaded'. The effects which discursive forms produce cannot be explained in linguistic terms, as can be seen from the above. But the social practices which produce these effects are described within a strictly formal terminology. Forms therefore take on a 'subjective' life. It is, for instance, the novel which criticizes, subverts, judges, and unified language which represses. The discursive practice which Bakhtin calls novelistic is a complex system of audience, linguistic forms, social conventions, subject positions and so forth, but this does not seem to be recognized in the decision to call this practice 'novelistic'. Doubtless this ambiguity arises from the complexity of Bakhtin's attempted deconstruction of the outside/inside dichotomy in linguistics. In redefining discourse he is mixing the subjective intentions and force which previously preceded or motivated language with the forms of language itself, which are no longer seen as brute, lifeless, and manipulable material. Language does indeed have a power of its own, defining its subjects rather than remaining their instrument, and the recognition of this is evidenced by this curious overloading of categories.

In the case of unified language, it is necessary to acknowledge that as a specific discursive practice it involves not only certain words and grammatical practices but also a set of cultural institutions whose purpose it is to establish these forms as *norms*. Grammars, educational institutions, dictionaries, universities, Royal Societies: these are what constitute a particular linguistic form as correct and standard. This is not denied by Bakhtin. Curiously, when discussing the existence of a specific literary language in the historical section of the essay, he does refer to these institutions and their role in constituting a literary language.[9] But in general this institutional level is elided in Bakhtin's account, so that formal categories of discourse are endowed with a theoretically unexplained political charge. This too can be understood as a consequence of Bakhtin's implicit belief that political oppressors were stricken by some form of mystified consciousness. Lacking any adequate social theory, the social function and therefore the material determinants – precisely those cultural institutions – of this false consciousness remain out of sight.

The reverse side of this problem is that spontaneously deconstructive force wielded by the novel. As the self-criticism of discourse, the novel demystifies any poetic discourse by its mere presence. The essence of discourse having been made manifest in the novel, it is impossible for the poetic to pretend to be anything other than the essentially dialogical thing it is: in Bakhtin's terms, it is 'novelized'. This seems problematic, for novels have simply not had this kind of devastating discursive effect; but it focuses attention on what is required for a novel to be 'merely present'. Just as the authority of the poetic is constructed by certain social institutions, the subversive power of the novel can only be constituted by an intervention at the institutional level; the production of a novelistic effect is not a simple act of writing or a consequence of an individual will or attitude. The elision of this institutional level is perhaps more graphically displayed in Bakhtin's literary history, in which discursive practices of the most diverse sorts are homogenized under the rubric of the novel. The institutional differences between an ancient work, a chivalric romance, and a nineteenth-century novel are smoothed over in the interests of a continuously subversive literary tradition, a tradition which is textual. The production of novels, despite Bakhtin's specification of its precise socio-historical conditions, requires only the lifting of an unnatural poetic repression. Demanding only consciousness of one's actual cultural situation, novel-writing is the most natural act in the world. Ever since that fundamental liberation of linguistic consciousness which marks the beginning of history for Bakhtin, novel-writing has been blocked only by the occasional imposition of an alien political or religious authority.

The disjunction between the hypothetical naturalness of novelistic prose and the extraordinary power of its word indicates that something is missing in this account. The power of novelistic discourse is predicated upon the belief that it is only language made self-aware, and that therefore a quality of consciousness is all that is required for its production. However, if the novelistic and the poetic are two forms of dialogism rather than its manifestation and its repression respectively, then the labour of novelistic demystification will involve something more substantial than revealing a dialogic essence which was there all along. The misunderstanding of the poetic in Bakhtin has its converse error in an overestimation of novelistic power: no linguistic pattern can liberate consciousness from the effects of monologizing cultural institutions. Novelistic and poetic discourse are represented in 'Discourse in the Novel' by texts, but they are in reality more than texts. Mere linguistic patterns, according to the grounding assumptions of dialogical theory, have no style of their own, but are made effective by a series of contextual factors. Novels and poetry are more properly seen as complete social practices: organizations of readerships, patterns of authorship, forms of reproduction (printing, public performance, etc.), appropriate subjects and themes, as well as formal paradigms and stylistic usages in the narrow sense. Perhaps most significantly, they are also institutions of criticism. All of these factors participate in making texts novelistic or poetic.

The theoretical point at issue is the deconstruction of inside and outside referred to above. In traditional stylistics the external facts of authors, readers, contexts, criticism and social life were expressed in the internal linguistic patterns of a discourse; every stylistic unity was simply a linguistic transposition of a unity outside of language. Not only does this perspective transform the signifiers of *langue* into lifeless forms, it also implies that the intentions and contexts which animate those forms are somehow endowed with a pre-linguistic meaning. But a 'stylistics of genre' such as Bakhtin envisaged recognizes that in a discursive practice, whether poetic or novelistic, authors and readers do not exist outside of language but have their very identities constituted for them in discourse. Their unity is a discursive fact, not something pre-existent. The true unities are genres, those social forms of discourse in which inside and outside, linguistic texts and non-linguistic contexts, are mixed. In this exchange the context or outside loses some of its power to invest linguistic form with meaning, but only because linguistic form itself – the structural reality of *langue* (grammar, lexis, syntax) – has the power to determine the consciousness of subjects who use it and the meaning of the contexts which surround it. The gain in this reconceptualization is that discourse has force and effectiveness in its own right and not merely as the reflection of some determining outside. The effects are various; they were earlier described as political/ideological. What distinguishes the style of the novel from the style of poetry is this difference of political effect: poetry establishes the power and authority of a particular language in its relation to heteroglossia, whereas the novel subverts this in its relativization of linguistic consciousness. In neither case can the effect be reduced to the communication of a meaning; discourse has no single function assigned to it. It can intimidate, confuse and obfuscate as well as embolden, clarify and communicate. It is *dialogical* because these effects are all types of relations; the concrete form and content of these relations is what distinguishes the genres of discourse.

When the novel is defined as the auto-criticism of discourse this effectivity is denied it. In so much Bakhtin criticism, the novel represents the dialogical reality of language for us, but in so doing it ceases to be a material force within reality. To the extent that the novel is conceived of as the reflection, even in intensified form, of a dialogic reality outside of it, it is dematerialized as discourse. Its effect – the relativization of linguistic consciousness – is the result of a realistic depiction of a discursive world (heteroglossia) external to it. By the logic of this argument the novel itself plays no part in the construction of that reality as we see it. But the novel not only reflects discursive reality, it is also a force within it and thus cannot encompass that reality within itself. The relativizing effects of the novel depend on its opposition to another genre, the poetic. Thus, not only is all discourse dialogical (relational) but the significance of genres themselves is dialogical in nature. As a self-identical form of discourse the novel means nothing; it is only when it is placed in relation to the poetic that it acquires meaning.

This bears on that moment in Bakhtin interpretation which is most clearly political in its intent. There is a common sense that Bakhtin has uncovered a novelistic form of discourse that reveals for us the relativity of all statements and all claims to truth. This relativism is explicitly rejected by Bakhtin (in *Problems of Dostoevsky's Poetics*), but it is also a rejection of the principle of dialogism in so far as it is the result of a failure to situate the novel dialogically in relation to the poetic.[10] Relativism has a specific political meaning when it opposes a ruling discourse which presents itself as timeless, natural and self-evident. The discursive strategy of the novel is shaped by its cultural opponent and it is therefore a mistake to confuse the relativization which is the novelistic effect with a theoretical truth about discourse as such. This conflation is made possible by the continual inability to theorize the poetic as anything other than something which distorts or mystifies the dialogism of discourse. When it is accepted that both the novelistic and the poetic are different kinds of dialogism then any adequate theoretical description of discourse will have to account for the possibility of both genres. As the poetic seeks to establish its language as eternal, sacred and natural, the novelistic must subvert it by exposing its discourse as historical, prosaic and social: if there is a truth about discourse it must somehow embrace both possibilities. This possible theory is, of course, the 'stylistics of genre'; those theories which exchange it for an endorsement of the novel as the revelation of truth about discourse end up trapped in the categories it proposed to transcend. The relativist position asserts that all discourse is historical, but it takes the form of this historicity from the division of *langue* and *parole* decreed by Saussure. These categories maintain that order and structure exist only synchronically and that history therefore is completely random, unstructured mutability. It was not Saussure's claim that discourse is static and ahistorical but that the historical dimension had nothing to do with the structural dimension. Any genuine transformation of this Saussurean paradigm must aim for a historicization of structure and a structuration of history. The relativism which sees every attempt at systematization as a denial of history only repeats the Saussurean problematic.

History can only be brought from the outside of language to the inside if discourse is rethought in institutional, or as Bakhtin would say, generic terms:

> Discourse lives outside of itself in its living orientation towards an object; if we completely disengage ourselves from this impulse then all that remains for us is the denuded corpse of discourse from which we can learn nothing about either the social situation or the life destiny of a given discourse.[11]

The social functions discourse performs, and the practical effects it initiates, should be the object of our inquiry, and this entails a prior recognition that the purpose of discourse is not always communication. It is only when language is abstracted from the discursive practices in which it is found that it becomes a formal structure with predefined effects. An analysis of discourse which proposes to be social must be prepared to accept something larger than formal structures – texts – as its object. To understand how and why texts are able to signify, they must be inserted into the social institutions which make them effective. The obvious political point needs to be emphasized: as critics, we are part of these institutions, and one expects that an examination of the kind of discourse produced by virtue of our activities will go hand in hand with an assessment as to whether we consider its effects desirable.

The reintegration of style and language outlined here suggests that distinctions between genres – the distinctions which are important – are distinctions between forms of ideological practice. Discourse is not simply the encodement of ideas or intentions or even world-views; its functions are various. It can be dialogical or monological, novelistic or poetic, and its effects can be mystification, subjection, instruction or exhortation. Because it has effects which cannot be described as simply meanings, it is something performative in nature. Because these effects are social and political, discourse is ideological. The justification for any particular discursive practice must be sought in a judgment about its social effects and not in a spurious appeal to an unvarying essence of discourse. This of course requires some reference to larger social and political values, but here we should not shy away from Bakhtin's example. In 'Discourse in the Novel' Bakhtin analyses discourse, but also pleads with us to intervene on the side of the popular, the novelistic and the subversive, pointing out that the formalist analysis of texts is not a socially neutral operation but a discursive practice which aims to centralize, monologize and oppress. This is the true challenge Bakhtin poses for us.

NOTES AND REFERENCES

1. This is exactly what Michael Holquist and Katerina Clark do not do in their recent *Mikhail Bakhtin*, Cambridge, Mass., 1984. Rather than choose among the many formulations, they try to find their ultimate unity in a master philosophical theme. I think the result is, inevitably, a certain conceptual fuzziness.
2. M. M. Bakhtin, 'Slovo v romane', in *Voprosy literatury i estetiki*, Moscow, 1975, p. 76.
3. Ibid, p. 77.
4. Ibid, p. 73.
5. A point made by Julia Kristeva in *Desire in Language*, Oxford, 1980, p. 65, where she shows how Bakhtin makes the diachronic synchronic.
6. Bakhtin, p. 83.
7. Ibid, p. 84.
8. Ibid.
9. Ibid, pp. 193–4.
10. Bakhtin, *Problemy poetiki Dostoevskogo* (4th edn), Moscow, 1979, p. 81.
11. Bakhtin, 'Slovo', p. 105.

Part II
Textuality

3
Canon Fodder? Problems in the Reading of a Soviet Production Novel

David Shepherd

I

For such a staunch supporter of the Soviet Union's literary and political institutions, Marietta Shaginyan (1888–1982) has received comparatively little attention from its literary critics – and predictably less from those elsewhere. To British and American Slavists she is probably best known as the author of *Mess-Mend, or A Yankee in Petrograd* (1924), recently analysed as an example of 'Red Pinkertonism',[1] and the 'production' novel *Hydrocentral* (1930–31). The designation 'production' or 'Five-Year Plan' novel seems enough to identify *Hydrocentral*'s place in Soviet literature, to tell us why it was written – in response to official calls for literature to reflect and promote the policy of industrialization – and how it should be read. Hence in surveys of Soviet literature such as Ronald Hingley's *Russian Writers and Soviet Society, 1917–1978* the novel is simply grouped with others of the same category, and this grouping provides the necessary commentary. Hingley mentions Shaginyan as one of a number of writers who produced novels about the first Five-Year Plan, including Leonid Leonov. He goes on to qualify the place of Leonov's *The River Sot* and *Skutarevskii* among classic production novels – *Hydrocentral*, Valentin Kataev's *Forward, Time!*, Mikhail Sholokov's *Virgin Soil Upturned* and Il'ya Erenburg's *The Second Day* – by referring to Leonov's 'great originality and subtlety', his 'ingeniously oblique approach that enabled him to work within the censorship while yet continuing to present a world all his own, and to project a markedly individual literary personality'.[2] But there is no such qualification of the place of *Hydrocentral*; the unspoken assumption seems to be that there would be no grounds to question its place in the canon.

Soviet surveys of Soviet literature are just as eloquently laconic on the subject. The *Short Literary Encyclopaedia* calls *Hydrocentral* 'one of the best examples of the Soviet production novel'.[3] Histories of Soviet literature published in 1974 and 1975 place the novel alongside works by Leonov, Kataev, Erenburg and Fedor Gladkov which all exemplify the type of production novel anticipated by Gladkov's 1925 novel *Cement*.[4] Indeed, as early as 1932, in V. Kirpotin's speech to the First Plenary Meeting of the Organizational Committee of the Union of Soviet Writers, *Hydrocentral* was among the works of Soviet literature singled out as models worthy of emulation.[5]

Why, then, take the trouble to write about a novel whose subject-matter seems to obviate detailed commentary, whose 'conformity' with the demands made of mainstream Soviet literature is so overwhelmingly taken for granted? The main reason is to challenge the adequacy of such an evaluation of *Hydrocentral* – not on the dubious traditional grounds of aesthetic value hitherto undiscovered and so forth, but because the novel reveals something about how and why not only it, but other texts as well, are hierarchized, placed in relation to one another, how they come to find (or to be given) their place in a literary canon.

II

Such a re-evaluation of *Hydrocentral* is best begun by a brief examination of the novel *Kik*, published two years earlier in 1929 in the journal *Zvezda*.[6] *Kik* has received even more cursory treatment from critics than *Hydrocentral*, but is an important work directly and explicitly concerned with some of the questions raised more obliquely in the later novel. Its frame of historical reference seems precise, but is actually deliberately confused and confusing: the action takes place apparently five years after the end of the Civil War, but immediately following an abortive attempt by White elements to usurp power in Karachai in the Caucasus. Reconsolidation of Soviet power involves, among other things, the establishment as a 'mass-circulation printed organ' (2, p. 6) of a local paper, the *Amanaus Pravda*, hitherto only a wall newspaper. The paper announces the arrival of one comrade L'vov, a Bolshevik who has played a large part in clearing the area of Whites, and his sudden disappearance during a bison hunt. The same edition carries, apparently at the instigation of the local cinema, an advertisement for a forthcoming film, *The Deed is Done*. When it becomes clear that the cinema knows nothing about either the film or the advertisement, the GPU begins to suspect that the title may in fact be a codeword in an anti-Soviet, pro-White plot, which accounts for L'vov's disappearance. Four people, all more or less members of the intelligentsia, are detained under suspicion of being involved in the plot. During their week or so in captivity they indulge, naturally, in a little mutual denunciation, and, less naturally but more importantly, write their 'literary' accounts of what might have happened to L'vov, basing these on information about local events printed in the *Amanaus Pravda*. Their efforts form the bulk of the text of *Kik*: a narrative poem, 'The Horn of Diana'; a detective story, 'Thirteen-Thirteen'; a melodrama in verse, 'The Witch and the Communist' (the acronym of the Russian title, 'Koldun'ya i kommunist', provides the title of the work as a whole); and a film scenario, 'The Earth and the Eye'. In the concluding section of the work a detailed critical analysis of these versions of L'vov's disappearance is given by none other than L'vov himself who, it turns out, had actually been in hiding while the White plot was foiled.

Obviously a work consisting almost entirely of generically diverse literary accounts of the same event can legitimately be read as more than incidentally concerned with questions of writing, the nature of literature, its role in representing contemporary *realia*.[7] In a preface to *Kik* written in 1956 for her *Collected Works*, Shaginyan claimed that the work was produced in reaction to the tendency among writers to confine themselves to only one genre, in contrast with great writers, such as Turgenev, who were at home in a variety of genres. The task she set herself was 'to pass a test of competence in all literary genres'.[8] However, although an impressive variety of genres is represented in *Kik*, it is difficult to read it as simply a concentrated demonstration of Turgenevian versatility. More significantly, it is concerned with the adequacy of the genres used as a means of representing contemporary reality. Bound up with this is the *manner* in which the various accounts of L'vov's disappearance are represented. To use the terminology of Mikhail Bakhtin's essay 'Discourse in the Novel', the discourse of each account is 'another's word' within the discourse of *Kik* as a whole; and, as Bakhtin says:

> Another's speech, introduced into a specific context, however precisely it may be conveyed, is always subject to certain semantic changes. The context enclosing another's word creates a dialogizing background whose influence may be very great.[9]

The immediate context in this case is the juxtaposition of the four different hypothetical versions of L'vov's disappearance, which places them in an implicit dialogic relationship *vis-à-vis* one another as they stake their contending claims to represent what might have happened. The juxtaposition makes clear the provisionality of each account – not only the possible disparity between it and what it claims to represent, but also the possibility of viewing things in a different perspective. Perhaps it would be better to use the Russian word *uslovnost'*, since this carries the sense not only of 'provisionality', but also of 'conventionality' – another important feature of all the versions of L'vov's appearance. They are all more or less explicit stylizations of familiar genres – in the case of 'The Horn of Diana', of the Byronic poem about the romantic loner seeking to escape from an inimical world. The poem (written by a poet El' who, to emphasize the 'literarity' of the whole thing, is before his arrest taking a cure for the writer's disease, consumption, in the local sanatorium) presents L'vov as a disillusioned, solitary figure, who uses the opportunity of a bison hunt in the wild countryside of romantic tradition to escape from the oppressive reality of life under Soviet power. After his escape, the hero experiences predictable problems of adjustment, but finally settles down to a contented life in a Turkish coastal village until, in the epilogue, the appearance of a Communist ship puts him to flight once more. This stylized representation of an immediately recognizable, dated type of literary discourse is further enriched by its own self-conscious interest in its relation to its subject-matter. It frequently foregrounds the disparity between what such poems traditionally represent and the material offered by Soviet reality. For instance, the second Canto (*Pesn' vtoraya*) begins with an address to Diana the huntress, pointing out that she has traditionally been an object of poets' attention, and follows this with a mock-idyllic picture of the hunt:

> The muses' favourites, while yet in the baptismal font,
> As they stepped onto life's threshold,
> Sang, virgin Diana, of you and of
> Your horn's urgent call!
> Before whose eyes, in a blaze of resounding glory,
> As a fairy-tale of old, did there not arise,
> Rushing through the oak-woods,
> The carnival of your visions?
> Intoxicated by the scent of their prey,
> In the pale dawn,
> The hounds would paw the air,
> Thrust their nuzzles into the wind, strain to escape
> From the huntsmen, trembling, to scatter
> On all sides, like spray ...
> And for so long afterwards we
> Dreamed of their sensual yelping.
> Shall I ever forget the bitter taste of shot,
> The soaring of the broken wing ..?
> That age's memory is engraved
> Upon an ancient snuffbox. (2, p. 29)

Opposed to this is the new world, where the call of the duck to the drake on the river is replaced by the cursing of the foreman as man harnesses natural waterways in service of the new God, electricity:

> Where once the duck upon the water quacked
> Its urgent call to the drake –
> Rises the grey skeleton of a workmen's hut.
> A pump growls, a saw squeals,
> Men haul stones and planks,
> A wave breaks against a sluice-gate,
> An extinguished cigarette butt clenched
> Between his teeth, a foreman curses ...
> (Well, this is no place for a prim young lady):
> 'To the left, damn you ...' (2, p. 30)

A text whose provisionality as representation is already foregrounded by its context itself takes up the theme of the problematic nature of representation, the relation between discourse and its object. We might see in this an ironic reversal of the way in which, for example, Pushkin's 'romantic' poems, such as *The Prisoner of the Caucasus*, implicitly and explicitly question the adequacy of romantic cliché as a way of dealing with the world; here, on the contrary, the cliché is defended against upstart reality. The poem never allows itself to lose sight of its problematic relationship to the things it claims to portray; tongue in cheek, it constantly addresses its own fictionality, its own *uslovnost'* and that of its antecedents.

It would be possible to look at the other accounts of L'vov's disappearance in terms of their concern with the same problems; but this brief analysis of 'The Horn of Diana' should give some indication of the complex intertextual relations of *Kik* with literary antecedents, its intense obsession with possible ways of giving fictional accounts of the world.

The discourses represented in *Kik* are not, furthermore, exclusively 'literary': there are also excerpts from the *Amanaus Pravda*, letters to and from various characters about the White plot, records of conversations between the detainees, and so on. The use of different typefaces for different documents and, in later editions, the reproduction of the layout of a newspaper, with advertisements, headlines, columns of various sizes, often surrounded by the ends and beginnings of adjacent columns – all this provides graphic textual illustration of the overt concern of *Kik* with the representation of types of discourse, with the 'images of language' Bakhtin has shown to be the product of novelistic discourse.[10]

The few Soviet critics who have bothered to comment on *Kik* in any detail have tended to propose less involved readings of the work's significance for the theme of writing, and to view the represented discourses in a perspective which excludes the dialogic relation of those discourses to the theme of representation. Shaginyan's most devoted critic, Lyudmila Skorino, in her 1981 study *Marietta Shaginyan the Artist: Life and Works*, does not acknowledge the problematic nature of the proliferation of discourses; for her, the four versions are equally and unselfconsciously inadequate to their task: 'The futility of these attempts – to embody events artistically without understanding their essence – is exposed satirically by Marietta Shaginyan'.[11]

The principal instrument of the 'satire', for Skorino as for earlier critics, is comrade L'vov and his analysis of the four literary texts. Without at first revealing his identity, he returns the manuscripts to their authors. He points out the shortcomings of their portrayals of L'vov, their anachronistic use of literary convention – in particular the absurdity of the poet El"s recourse to Byronic models in 'The Horn of Diana'. Turning to their selection of material, he again asserts that it leaves much to be desired. They should have paid more attention to the conversion of a disused nunnery into a textile factory, and the reasons for having a textile rather than a tobacco-processing factory in the area; they should have shown greater knowledge of local sheep-rearing, should have dealt more seriously with agriculture, with electrification. Anticipating their objection that '"economic problems" are not the subject of paeans and portraits', L'vov forcefully contends that all this is nevertheless appropriate material for literature: 'Does not our transitional economy offer many fascinating conflicts? Is not the struggle between the plan and anarchy capable of inspiring the writer?' (3, pp. 45, 46).[12]

This brief summary of L'vov's lengthy disquisition should give some idea of why Soviet critics have endowed it with such significance. It clearly reproduces much of what was being urged upon Soviet writers at the start of the first Five-Year Plan, and adumbrates the emergence of the prescriptive official aesthetics of Socialist Realism a few years later. Some early critics, however, were less than wholehearted in welcoming L'vov's criticisms as a solution to the problems raised in *Kik*. A. Selivanovskii, writing in 1929, suggested that L'vov is not quite a Marxist, and that his speech does not answer all the questions posed by the use of different genres in the work. However, like M. Gel'fand, he feels that L'vov and the work as a whole are moving in the right direction.[13]

This unease of early critics with the openly heterogeneous, discontinuous texture of *Kik* gives way in later accounts of the novel to a virtually unqualified acceptance of L'vov's speech as an imposition of reassuring continuity, uniformity, an all-encompassing solution. This is certainly how Shaginyan reads it. In her 1956 preface, she says that *Kik*'s

> hidden content became clear as the novel developed, and in the end I set it out as the experience I myself had gained of this work – in the words of my hero L'vov in his critical speech. What then is the principal content of *Kik*? It is theoretical, and is an essay in Soviet aesthetics, a kind of aesthetic manifesto of the first ten years of our creative work.[14]

This view underlies Skorino's conclusions about the work; so great is her confidence in L'vov as a spokesman for the new realistic aesthetics that she feels able to say of his speech 'it is as though life itself passes sentence on literature', that L'vov demonstrates how old forms 'have come into contradiction with the real movement of life and do not reflect the new laws of human existence'.[15]

This way of looking at L'vov is supported by the familiar, reassuring gesture of demonstrating how *Kik* slots neatly into place in the inexorable development of the author's *oeuvre* and points forward to *Hydrocentral*. Again, Shaginyan has made this point: 'in [*Hydrocentral*] I began to overcome the element of conventionality [*to uslovnoe*] which was characteristic of my manner of writing in *Kik* and earlier'; and 'After *Kik* I simply found it tiresome to return to conventional [*uslovnye*] works like [*Mess-Mend*], they became tedious to write, and I took great pleasure in my enormous and intensive labour on *Hydrocentral*.'[16] The same notion of a writer's progression to better things is prominent in recent Soviet histories. The 1974 history speaks of the 'newness' of 1930s prose, whose causes are to be sought 'in the new character of the collectivism of Soviet people and in the scarcely changing nature of socialist production'; this newness is particularly evident when writers' works from the 1930s are compared with their efforts in the previous decade – *Hydrocentral* with *Kik*, Leonov's *The River Sot* and *The Road to Ocean* with *The Thief*, Gladkov's *Energy* with *Cement*.[17]

But does L'vov's criticism really answer all the questions raised? And is the progression to *Hydrocentral* really so straightforward and inevitable? To answer these questions we must first turn to *Hydrocentral*.

III

What is the significance of the production novel of which *Hydrocentral* is 'one of the best examples'? Perhaps the most exhaustive and stimulating answer to this question is to be found in Katerina Clark's recent study *The Soviet Novel. History as Ritual*. Clark argues persuasively that 'the novel is *the* privileged genre of Socialist Realism', that 'the Socialist Realist novel forms a tradition that rests on canonical exemplars', serves 'as the official repository of state myths'.[18] The production novel ('the novel about how the plan was fulfilled or the project was constructed') is for Clark 'the most common type of Stalinist novel *by far*', the basis of the 'Master Plot' which she sees as the yardstick of canonical status.[19] She does a thorough job of establishing the sources of the Soviet novelistic canon and identifying its 'core group' of texts. This group, consisting of, among others, Gor'kii's *Mother* and *The Life of Klim Samgin*, and Gladkov's *Cement*, does not include *Hydrocentral*.[20] But on the occasions when she mentions the novel, Clark makes it quite clear that she shares Soviet views of its conformity with the canon. She refers to it as 'M. Shaginyan's Five-Year Plan classic', and does not disagree with Kirpotin's classification of it as a model work in 1932.[21]

So even a critic as heroically dedicated to scrupulous dissection of Soviet 'classics' as Clark sees no reason to do other than acquiesce in the canonical status customarily granted to *Hydrocentral*. And it is true that *Hydrocentral* contains many of the functions of Clark's 'Master Plot' (an exemplary model of the production novel along the lines of Propp's typology of the folktale). The novel is set in a 'small, fairly closed world' – that of the Dzorages hydro-electric dam construction project on the river Dzoraget in Armenia. (Shaginyan, in eager response to official calls for writers and their work to be actively engaged in the economic life of the country, spent a good deal of her time observing the development of this very real project after its inception in 1927.) In the early stages, 'Setting up the Task', it soon becomes clear that 'all is not good in the microcosm': the files relating to the project are in total disarray; there is a bad case of pilfering of building materials which necessitates a public trial for the culprit. (These are 'prosaic' obstacles to the fulfilment of the plan.) There is a 'Climax', in which 'Fulfilment of the Task is Threatened': a directive arrives from the 'centre' (Moscow) halting the whole project pending a review of its viability; remaining prospects for its advancement are damaged by a violent spring flood which destroys a newly built wooden bridge providing the only link between the two sides of the river (a *'Dramatic/heroic (mythic)'* obstacle); an extraordinary commission comes along to sort things out; a meeting is held at which the general unrest and disorder at the project, and the shoddy construction of the fated bridge, are attributed to the bureaucratism (*sluzhbizm*) of one of the bosses; the project is finally declared viable, and in the 'Finale (or Celebration of Incorporation)' there is a speech by a new chief engineer from Moscow, who explains to an attentive, newly politically conscious audience (including some schoolchildren on an outing conveniently at hand as symbols of the future) the reasons for electrification and the importance of a national electricity grid for the unity of the Soviet Union.

This rather skeletal outline of the plot presents *Hydrocentral* in terms of some of the principal functions of Clark's Master Plot.[22] But perhaps more significant are those functions *not* represented in the novel. Clark does make it clear that the order and number of functions in any given novel may vary, but the hiatuses are often particularly gaping in the case of *Hydrocentral*. Perhaps the most conspicuous absence is the very hallmark of the genre – 'how the plan was fulfilled or the project was constructed'. All that actually gets built is a drainage tunnel and the notorious wooden bridge which promptly gives in to the inadequately anticipated challenge of the elements. And, though some sparks do fly, not a watt of electricity is produced.

Another important absence in this account of the novel is the hero, around whom Clark's Master Plot centres: in the 'typical' production novel it is the hero who 'sees that all is not good in the microcosm', 'concocts a scheme for righting the wrong', overcomes bureaucratic opposition to his plan, 'mobilizes "the people" and inspires them to follow his plan'; he sees it through via a series of more or less major upheavals in his professional, political and personal circumstances (the 'Transition', 'Climax' and 'Finale'). There is no such supremely active and dominant hero in Shaginyan's novel, and some standard functions of the hero which are to be found in the work are not always allotted to the same character.

That is not to say, however, that the novel lacks a hero of any sort. The undisputed candidate for the position is one Arno Arev'yan, a tall and lanky man of mixed Armenian and German descent whose red hair earns him the name 'Ryzhii' ('Redhead'). He wears spectacles with broken lenses, a woman's jacket, and a variety of somewhat bizarre footwear. Armed with a doctorate from a German university, but no Party membership card and no particular profession, he first takes on the job of 'archivist' and sorts out the files of the Dzorages project, then becomes a foreman with a team of surveyors. He develops in the course of all this an attachment to a Party activist, Mardzhik Malkhazyan, and after a touchingly gauche scene in which they obliquely declare their love for each other, abruptly all but vanishes from the novel with some of the most important action still to come. Overall, although he possesses the asceticism and lithe athleticism of the standard Soviet hero, Ryzhii cuts rather a curious, unorthodox figure.

Not surprisingly, Soviet critics have had something to say about the presence of such a character. Most have *not* followed the line taken by E. Dan'ko in an early review of the novel in *Na literaturnom postu* that 'in *Hydrocentral* there are no human heroes. The hero of the novel is the business of construction.'[23] Instead they have berated Ryzhii precisely for his inadequacy to the role of 'human hero' which is thrust upon him by Shaginyan. In 1933 Shaginyan explained that she had introduced Ryzhii as a 'wandering figure' to unite the disparate thematic elements of the novel, making him the 'bearer of the plot'.[24] To maintain interest in Ryzhii, elements of the detective story were introduced. Early on in the novel he tells another character that he had once worked as a hairdresser, but does not have time to explain the exact circumstances. This unexplained feature of his biography recurs at various stages as a motif suggesting his rootless, enigmatic quality, even giving various characters reason to believe that it is a cover for a politically suspect past (at one stage Ryzhii is summoned by the police, but only to have possessions that had been stolen in a mugging returned to him). It is this very emphatic *uslovnost'* of Ryzhii which has caused critics most discomfort. I. Grinberg, in a 1937 article on the heroes of Five-Year Plan novels, refers to him disparagingly as a 'thoroughly enigmatic and conventional [*uslovnyi*] character'.[25] A. Margaryan, in a 1956 monograph on Shaginyan, denies that Ryzhii has any unifying role in the plot, and criticizes the detective-story elements, characterizing them as 'a purely literary, conventional plot, which complicates the structure of the work, detracts from its clarity and balance'.[26] And the 1974 *History* says that this 'literarification' of the plot 'proved to be the work's weakest point'.[27] In spite of such reservations, however, most critics see Ryzhii as more than a structural element; for many, he is, in the words of A. Glagolev, reviewing the novel in 1931, the 'ideological centre' of the novel, the bearer of the greater part of its ideological content.[28] This view has persisted in subsequent criticism. In 1950, E. Kolpakova, discussing several novels of the first Five-Year Plan period, wrote with some disquiet that 'the non-Party philosopher Arev'yan turns out to be more intelligent and [politically] conscious than all the Communists', while Margaryan takes up a point made by several others, including Shaginyan, that Ryzhii is the mouthpiece of the author, expresses her definitive views on the issues raised in the novel.[29]

This final assertion is, as we shall see, reductive in the extreme, but there is little doubt that, difficult though it may be to see this bizarre figure as a spokesman for truth and ideological rectitude, Ryzhii does articulate some of the novel's discourse on ideological matters. In the construction-site club he ponders the impending trial of the suspected thief and the evening of entertainment which is to follow it, and wonders about the ideological role and relevance of the master of ceremonies (*konferans'e*) at such events in the new Soviet context.[30] He discusses with a visiting German writer the superiority of planned economic production over the vicissitudes and ideological vacuity of the Western free-market system (2, 1930, pp. 105–6). But this 'ideological centre' of the novel turns out to be as unpredictable and eccentric in this function as he is in relation to other standard functions of the conventional production-novel hero. The culmination of the novel is the speech about the importance of electrification made not, as might be expected, by Ryzhii, but by the engineer from Moscow. Ryzhii is now just a 'strange' figure noticed among his audience by the speaker (4, 1931, p. 58).

Ryzhii's eccentricity, then, goes further than his appearance and background, and extends to his relationship to key 'canonical' features of the novel, which is thrown correspondingly 'off-centre'. He is a force for discontinuity rather than continuity. More interesting, however, than the presence of these anomalies is the fact that, even for those critics who express deep disquiet about Ryzhii and his role in the novel, the anomalies make little or no difference to their appraisal of its canonical status: this remains apparently unimpeachable. The purpose of pointing this out is not to lambast critics for logical inconsistency, but to highlight a particular type of critical paradox which urgently requires closer scrutiny. Such scrutiny is best conducted in the light of a detailed examination of one or two typical instances in Ryzhii's role as ideological centre, and of the specific character of his 'ideological' discourse.

I have already mentioned Ryzhii's encounter with a German

writer, whom he meets as he travels by train to take up his appointment as archivist. The writer concedes that the Soviet Union has begun to produce material goods, 'things' (*veshchi*), on a large scale; however, he sees in this not the new economic principle he had been led to expect, but an unsuccessful attempt to emulate the advanced industrial nations of Western Europe – unsuccessful because the socialization of industry has simply led to a proliferation of 'owners' (*khozyaeva*) which stifles enterprise. Ryzhii, after explaining the reasons for some of the temporary shortcomings of the Soviet economy, goes on to prove his assertion that 'what we are making are not things':

'We are making *planned* things, dear Herr. The difference? The differrence is enormous, colossal. Every factory, every construction project, every works you will be visiting in our country is manufacturing, processing or building a thing plus the new society, plus a trade union, plus the [ideological] armouring of young people, plus club work, plus the works meeting, plus control, plus inventory, plus the Plan. The thing plus the Plan – that comes from above, the thing plus control – that comes from below. You think we have dozens of owners, but you are mistaken, – we have dozens of factors, not owners.... That is the new principle you have looked for and failed to find – an economy without a private property owner.'

(2, 1930, pp. 105–6).

Ryzhii's language here is immediately recognizable as the clichéd rhetoric of Soviet industrialization, the sort of thing to which Soviet critics might gratefully point as proof of the genuine Soviet quality of a text, while their Western counterparts are more likely to throw up their arms in despair at the incursion of such 'unaesthetic' material into literature. The importance of this passage for the undeniable ideological, political function of *Hydrocentral* as production novel is underscored by slight modifications made to it in the edition published in 1949. This edition, according to the accompanying biographical note, represents a reworking of about three-quarters of the whole novel. I have been unable to establish any single overriding reason for such an extensive revision, but most of the changes are easy to understand in the light of the particularly restrictive conditions prevailing in the literary world in the late 1940s. References to squalor, sexuality, and the specific racial characteristics of Armenians are assiduously expunged. Positive and negative characters become even more polarized. And more markedly 'official' concepts enter the production rhetoric. So, when Ryzhii in 1949 says his piece about 'dozens of factor, not owners', he adds 'and the unified thought of the Party' a gesture towards the role of the Party as a unifying force which throughout is a far more prominent motif in this version than in the first.[31]

Ryzhii also emerges as a more committed spokesman for the Party – of which, however, he is not yet a member – in the revised version of his love scene with the Party activist Mardzhik. He gropes towards his oblique declaration of his feelings through a discussion of the problems at the project, and finally pours out his heart in a new passage:

'I have understood the line of the Party in this chaos of events and moods,... and want to tell you...'
He suddenly blushed like a young boy, he was unable to finish what he was saying. It had become impossible for him to remain outside the Party, he was drawn towards the Party.
(p. 326)

It is not only in Ryzhii's speech that pointedly 'official' language receives greater prominence in 1949. A soldier is introduced into the train encounter with the German writer, and his thoughts provide a new, retrospective gloss on the writer's views of the problems in the Soviet economy: the soldier detects in these a knowledge of recent 'rightist deviation', of 'Bukharin's harmful theory of the integration of the kulak into socialism', of sabotage in the Donbass and kulak resistance (p. 82). There are countless other instances of such embellishment of the text with 'ideologically sound' new concepts, perhaps none more obvious or less surprising than the appearance of two epigraphs; the first is from Lenin, and the second from the Great Leader himself: 'Does not our work proceed under the sign of self-criticism from below? Is it not a fact that self-criticism makes the Party masses and the proletarian masses in general more active?' (p. 5). Lenin and Stalin are both referred to and quoted throughout the novel with far greater frequency. (Stalin has of course subsequently slunk off the pages of the novel.)

Overall, then, the revised version of the novel contains a far higher proportion of sound official concepts and rhetoric, has become, it might seem, even more conformist than the first version. Or has it? The examples of official discourse I have cited might be classed as what Bakhtin in 'Discourse in the Novel' calls 'authoritarian discourse' (*avtoritarnoe slovo*), discourse which:

> demands from us recognition and assimilation, it is forced upon us regardless of the degree to which it is inherently convincing for us; we find it already associated with authority.... it allows no play with the context framing it, no play with its boundaries.... It has become inextricably bound up with authority – political power, an institution, an individual, – it stands and falls together with that authority.[32]

But, says Bakhtin, authoritarian discourse has a negligible role in the novel because its refusal to be represented is at odds with the representation of discourse which characterizes, or more precisely defines, the novel. And when it is introduced into the novelistic context its resonance is altered, it 'loses its authority, it simply becomes an object, a *relic*, a thing'.[33] Represented, it becomes part of the novel's complex mass of conflicting 'images of language', its limits are exposed, its provisionality foregrounded by its context. The voice of authority becomes a voice among others which by their mere presence can place a question mark against that authority.

The provisionality of the 'official' discourse in *Hydrocentral* is not difficult to establish. In the first place, the text is by no means stylistically monolithic – its various styles constitute a 'dialogizing background' of ideologically heterogeneous, competing voices. Ryzhii, although references to his hairdresser past have been removed, remains in the 1949 version a strikingly enigmatic, unorthodox character; there is still a tension between his eccentricity and his status as spokesman for unity, for centrality, which undermines the authority of his words. Similarly, the reference to Bukharin's theories, kulak resistance and so on are *quoted* discourse – the thoughts of the soldier in the train, which are given as indirect free speech, that 'hybridizing' form of discourse which Bakhtin sees as so fundamental to the dialogically self-critical character of novelistic discourse.[34] And the hieratic words of Lenin and Stalin usually occur at one remove, *quoted* in the thoughts and recollections of particular characters,[35] or as typographically distinct epigraphs at the beginning of a text in which the role of quotation and the representation of language as provisional is ultimately as important as it is in *Kik*. To give the authority of final word in the dialogue to Ryzhii's talk of Plan and Party, or to the references to Stalin's speeches, is to bring to these particular quoted discourses an authority possible only if their embeddedness in a context of conflicting voices and contending viewpoints is repressed or unnoticed.

The same can be said of L'vov's speech at the end of *Kik*: the *uslovnost'* of his discourse, like that of the four fictional versions of his disappearance, is revealed by the 'dialogizing background' of the text. So the notion of the progress from the self-interrogation of *Kik* to the self-assurance of *Hydrocentral* does not hold up under examination. And a more detailed analysis of *Hydrocentral* than I have been able to offer here might reveal that the revisions of 1949 contribute in the final reckoning not to the text's conformity, but to its subversiveness, by exposing the historical specificity of a discourse whose 'authority' depends on its being able to present itself as transhistorical. Stalin gets his 'self-criticism from below', but it is not quite of the type he expected.

Clearly this assertion of the apparently spontaneous, subversive capacity of the text of *Hydrocentral* to deconstruct any discourse which falls within its scope is at best problematical, and at worst demonstrates cavalier disregard for history. The 1949 edition was acceptable then in the Soviet Union, and is now – without the references to Stalin, but with most of the official rhetoric still intact. To explain this apparent paradox we need to highlight something implicit in Bakhtin's treatment of authoritarian discourse: authority does not inhere in that discourse, but derives from the function ascribed to it in a given context, a context, however, which will usually insist on the inherence of the authority, disregarding the dialogic constitution of the discourse. And this context involves not only the *writing* of what is acceptable at a given historical moment, but also the *reading* of a text as acceptable.

This is what accounts for the apparently contradictory attitudes of Soviet critics towards *Hydrocentral*, and in particular towards Ryzhii; it also accounts for their attitudes towards *Kik*. Critics such as Selivanovskii and Gel'fand who in 1929 expressed reservations about *Kik*'s ideological soundness were working in the context of developing official poetics, and indeed contributing towards its development. Critics like Skorino, writing after the secure instalment of Socialist Realism, are able to read the text without such reservation because their context gives greater authority to L'vov's closing speech, to the aesthetic positions he propounds in it. Their context also allows them to see the 'natural' progression from *Kik* to *Hydrocentral* spoken of by Shaginyan and therefore reinforced by the traditional privileging of the author's view of her own work. Recent critics of *Hydrocentral* may point out flaws and inconsistencies in the novel, but are obliged by their context to invest in the official discourse represented in the novel an allegedly inherent authority which guarantees the text's place within the myth-bearing Soviet literary canon. So Ryzhii, though eccentric, can seemingly paradoxically remain at the 'ideological centre' of things because the implications of his eccentricity for the authority of his discourse can be not noticed. Another consideration, particularly important for the survey works which mention the novel, is the importance of not reading the novel in any way which might undermine carefully constructed Soviet notions of an organically developing body of Soviet literature with living links to the equally organic pre-Revolutionary tradition. The relationship of such profoundly conservative critical concepts to the nationalistic, conservative political context of the Soviet Union requires further elaboration. But as long as such concepts hold sway in the Soviet Union, as long as the context determines that all this is what the critic shall seek and find, the canonical status of *Kik* and *Hydrocentral* is secure.

IV

Katerina Clark, as I have already said, has done an admirable job in establishing the nature of the functions given to 'classical' Soviet novels. But her concern with demonstrating how particular texts conform to a particular model, rather than confronting the difficult moments where the text refuses to lie on the Procrustean bed of the Master Plot, suggests an over-eager acquiesence in the concept of totally inherent function, inherent conformity, with little or no regard for the production of these categories by the context in which the texts are read. This is confirmed when we examine the opposition Clark draws up between the functions of the novel in the Soviet Union and in the West. In her introduction,

Clark tells us that the novels of writers such as Melville, Flaubert and Dickens 'perform a fairly homogeneous aesthetic function in the literary systems of America, France and England'.[36] The distinctive, exceptional character of Soviet literature is played down when she deals with post-Stalinist prose concerned with matters – 'death, divorce, neglect and human frailty' – whose natural, pre-ordained centrality to 'literature' she sees no reason to question.[37] And in her conclusion she says, 'instead of doing what we have come to think of as the work of literature, Socialist Realism performs an essentially mythological task'.[38] The implication throughout is that Socialist Realism is an aberration, a deviation from the 'natural' state of literary affairs, that it is exceptional in having a political, ideological function rather than being about a generalized 'humanity'. But surely what the Bakhtinian premisses on which Clark bases so much of her argument make clear is that 'what we have come to think of as the work of literature', the assumptions which make *us* value a text as 'literature', are also produced by specific political and cultural contexts, are also 'ideological'. Is it really any longer possible to use the word 'literature' as though it were a directly-signifying, supra-ideological, authoritative definition of a particular text and particular hierarchies of texts?

It is because I think this question must still be asked, particularly in the field of Russian and Soviet literary studies, that I am not trying to claim for Shaginyan the uniqueness, 'markedly individual literary personality' and ability to dodge the censorship which Ronald Hingley claims for Leonov. I am not suggesting that, now that we have discovered the 'real' Shaginyan, we remove *Kik* and *Hydrocentral* from an otherwise unaltered Soviet canon and ceremoniously install them in some alternative canon of 'true literature'. What I do want to suggest is that from the approach taken in this essay even to texts as seemingly uninteresting as those of Shaginyan we can learn how important it is to remain aware of reading and criticism as productive activities. Criticism does not simply find, recognize and elucidate, but constitutes and produces in specific contexts the hierarchical arrangements of texts which form canons, Soviet or Western. The canons themselves do not form naturally or organically, they have no inherent, transhistorical stability; and we can question not only the place of individual works within a given canon, but also the very premisses upon which that canon rests.

In this sense, as Ken Hirschkop makes clear, even the most openly 'subversive' text does not 'spontaneously deconstruct' the discourses of authority; this function too requires the reader and his context.[39]

Of course, given that our contexts change, so too must our readings, which are therefore *necessarily provisional*; on the other hand it would be fecklessly irresponsible to suggest that the range of meanings we may give to a text is at any moment infinite, that any reading is so shot through with an awareness of its own provisionality that it is wholly without stability and validity. Jonathan Culler in *On Deconstruction* writes, 'meaning is context-bound, but context is boundless'.[40] But this boundlessness, however, seductive the degree of semantic *jouissance* it appears to offer the hedonistic deconstructionist, is purely theoretical, is in practice limited at any given moment: not all readings of a text are available at all times; the range of possible contexts is limited by historical, social and political factors; and our contexts may well demand of us that we recognize our readings to be also *provisionally necessary*. In Stalin's Soviet Union, such recognition was essential for the professional and physical survival of writer and critic alike. In the Western academy the need is less pressing. However, I do recognize my own specifically Bakhtinian and polemical context in asserting the provisional necessity of reading *Hydrocentral* as a 'production novel' in the sense that we can learn from it about the production of literary meaning and value, and of literary canons; that its theme is the generation not of electricity but of discursive eccentricity; that it tells us less about the tasks of construction than about those of deconstruction.

NOTES AND REFERENCES

1. R. Russell, 'Red Pinkertonism: An Aspect of Soviet Literature of the 1920s', *Slavonic and East European Review*, 60/3, 1982, pp. 394–400.
2. Ronald Hingley, *Russian Writers and Soviet Society, 1917–1978*, London, 1979, p. 76. See also Gleb Struve, *Russian Literature Under Lenin and Stalin, 1917–1953*, London, 1972, p. 249.
3. *Kratkaya literaturnaya entsiklopediya*, vol. 8, Moscow, 1975, col. 576.
4. *Istoriya russkoi sovetskoi literatury* (2nd edn), ed. P. S. Vykhodtsev, Moscow, 1974, pp. 272–4; *Istoriya russkoi sovetskoi literatury (1917–1940)*, ed. A. I. Metchenko and S. M. Petrov, Moscow, 1975, p. 335.

5. See Katerina Clark, *The Soviet Novel: History as Ritual*, Chicago, London, 1981, p. 263.
6. Marietta Shaginyan, 'K. i K. Roman', *Zvezda*, 2 and 3, 1929. In later editions the novel is entitled *Kik*, with the subtitle *Roman-kompleks*. I shall use the later form of the title, but refer to the original *Zvezda* publication, indicating issue and page number in the text.
7. Such questions were, of course, the subject of much theoretical debate in the late 1920s, but they also frequently became a theme of works of literature. M. Gel'fand, writing in 1929, cities *Kik* and two other works published in the same year, Konstantin Vaginov's *Trudy i dni Svistonova* and Mikhail Prishvin's *Zhuravlinaya rodina*, as examples of an 'increased interest in self' on the part of contemporary writers. He also mentions works by Il'ya Sel'vinskii, Konstantin Fedin, Boris Lavrenev, Veniamin Kaverin, Osip Mandel'shtam and Nikolai Aseev ('Zhurnal'noe obozrenie', *Pechat' i revolyutsiya*, 8, 1929, pp. 67–72). For a similar view, see A. Selivanovskii, 'Mezhdu prosvetitel'stvom i marksizmom', *Oktyabr'*, 8, 1929, p. 170. For a more recent discussion of the topic with greater historical scope, but touching on some of the texts mentioned by Gel'fand, see D. Segal, 'Literatura kak okhrannaya gramota', *Slavica Hierosolymitana*, 5–6, 1981, pp. 151–244.
8. Shaginyan, *Sobranie sochinenii v shesti tomakh*, vol. 2, Moscow, 1956, p. 412.
9. M. M. Bakhtin, 'Slovo v romane', in *Voprosy literatury i estetiki*, Moscow, 1975, p. 152.
10. Ibid, p. 177.
11. Lyudmila Skorino, *Marietta Shaginyan khudozhnik. Zhizn' i tvorchestvo* (2nd rev. edn), Moscow, 1981, p. 192.
12. The reference here to 'plan' underscores the markedly anachronistic character of *Kik*'s narrative, its combination of historical events taken from various points in the 1920s. The following passage, in which L'vov opposed the 'music' of the Plan to the 'sounds having no definite pitch' which Blok mistook for the music of the Revolution (3, pp. 46–7) was, however, omitted from later editions.
13. Selivanovskii, p. 173; Gel'fand, p. 70.
14. Shaginyan, *Sobranie sochinenii*, vol. 2, p. 413.
15. Skorino, pp. 193, 194.
16. Shaginyan, 'O sotsialisticheskom realizme' (Address to the Organizational Committee of the Union of Soviet Writers in 1934), in *Ob iskusstve i literature. 1933–1957. Stat'i i rechi*, Moscow, 1958, p. 158; *Sobranie sochinenii*, vol. 2, p. 414.
17. *Istoriya*, 1974, p. 272.
18. Clark, pp. xiii, xii.
19. Ibid, p. 256.
20. Ibid, p. 4.
21. Ibid, pp. 101 (where she erroneously gives the date of the novel as 1932) and 263.
22. Ibid, pp. 255–60.
23. E. Dan'ko, 'O Gidrotsentrali', *Na literaturnom postu*, 26, 1931, p. 47.
24. Shaginyan, *Kak ya rabotala nad 'Gidrotsentral'yu'. (Moi tvorcheskii opyt – rabochemu avtoru)*, Moscow, 1933, pp. 32, 33.

25. I. Grinberg, 'Lyudi, perestraivayushchie mir', *Literaturnyi sovremennik*, 11, 1937, p. 178.
26. A. Margaryan, *Marietta Shaginyan. Tvorcheskii put'*, Erevan, 1956, p. 83.
27. *Istoriya*, 1974, p. 274.
28. A. Glagolev, '*Gidrotsentral'* M. Shaginyan', *Novyi mir*, 9, 1931, p. 158.
29. E. Kolpakova, 'Romany o sotsialisticheskom stroitel'stve perioda pervoi pyatiletki', *Doklady i soobshcheniya* (Filologicheskii institut. Leningradskii gosudarstvennyi universitet im. A. A. Zhdanova), 2, 1950, p. 25; Margaryan, p. 27. Cf. Shaginyan, *Kak ya rabotala*, p. 31.
30. Shaginyan, 'Gidrotsentral'', *Novi mir*, 3, 1930, p. 67. The novel was serialized in *Novyi mir* in 1930 (1–7, 10) and 1931 (2–4). Subsequent references to this edition, indicating issue, year and page, will be in the text.
31. Shaginyan, *Gidrotsentral'*. *Peremena* (Biblioteka izbrannykh proizvedenii sovetskoi literatury, 1917–1947), Moscow, 1949, p. 81. Subsequent page references to this edition will be in parentheses in the text.

    Many of the alterations made in this edition are typical of the kind of revision that was widespread in post-war Soviet literature: see Maurice Friedberg, 'New Editions of Soviet Belles-Lettres: A Study in Politics and Palimpsests', *American Slavic and East European Review*, 13/1, 1954, pp. 72–88.
32. Bakhtin, pp. 155–6.
33. Ibid, p. 156.
34. See ibid, pp. 113–21.
35. See, for example, the recollections of Lenin by Kosarenko, the head of supplies at the construction site, in the 1949 edition, pp. 266–7.
36. Clark, p. xi.
37. Ibid, p. 239.
38. Ibid, p. 252.
39. See Ken Hirschkop's contribution to this volume, p. 30, and especially his discussion of the institutional nature of context, pp. 27–35. On this last point, see also my 'The Authority of Meanings and the Meanings of Authority: Some Problems in the Theory of Reading', *Poetics Today*, 7/1, 1986, pp. 129–45.
40. Jonathan Culler, *On Deconstruction: Theory and Criticism After Structuralism*, London, 1983, p. 123.

4
Toward a Poetics of the Absurd: The Prose Writings of Daniil Kharms

Ann Shukman

Daniil Ivanovich Yuvachev, who adopted the pen name of Daniil Kharms, was born in Petersburg in 1905 and died in a Leningrad prison in 1942. He was a leading member of the group of writers who called themselves the *Oberiu* group, and like many off-beat writers of the 1920s and early 1930s found employment as a children's writer in Samuil Marshak's 'academy', the publishing house, *Detgiz*. He was arrested and exiled briefly in 1931, but returned to Leningrad to continue a hand-to-mouth existence, often on the verge of starvation, until he was arrested again in December 1941.[1]

Most of his short prose writings date from these last years of his life. These spare narratives, or evocations of situations – some not more than a few lines long – are experiments in minimalist writing, in alogicality. A few details of everyday existence are chosen and juxtaposed, or repeated until they become ridiculous. Violence is described in the style and language of a child's tale, or disjointed and unexplained events taken from recognizable everyday life are so presented as to evoke a feeling of shock and horror. Events either have no cause or consequence or are provided with causes or consequences that defy normal common-sense perceptions of reality. Kharms's prose writings have justifiably been described as 'literature of the absurd': they share with, for instance, the plays of Ionesco the same defiance of accepted norms of logic, causality, and communication.[2]

This chapter attempts to analyse the nature of this 'absurdity' in terms of convention-breaking, using as conventional norms three different models of communication: those by Jakobson (1960),[3] by Voloshinov/Bakhtin (1926/1930)[4] and by Revzin and Revzina (1975).[5]

I

According to Roman Jakobson's well-known six-point communications schema, for an act of communication to take place there must be present six factors: an addresser, an addressee, a message, a 'context' (i.e. a referent, something outside the message to which the message refers), a physical contact (print on paper, radio waves, telephone cable, etc.), and a code (i.e. a shared language). In the case of a work of literature, the addressee is the unspecified readership, often potential rather than actual, perhaps 'posterity'.

A small number of Kharms's prose pieces actually deal with the problem of the disappearing 'context'. The philosophical problem posed is: how to write about something which, it turns out in the course of the writing, is not there. What then is the status of the words, the discourse, being used? This question is posed at the very start of the eleven-line piece 'The Red-Haired Man' (1939)[6]: 'There was once a red-haired man who had no eyes or ears. He had no hair either so that he was called red-haired conventionally.' First problem: how can a man be called red-haired if he has no hair to be red? Second problem: how can the man himself be said to exist if his physical features are eliminated? The piece proceeds to describe the man apophatically, in terms of the attributes he does not possess: he has no mouth, no nose, no hands, no feet, no stomach, no back, no spine, no innards ... 'He had nothing!' So, the piece concludes, as it's hard to make out what we are talking about, 'we'd better not talk about him any more'. Although the 'him' of this last sentence grammatically refers back to the 'red-haired man' of the first line, semantically 'he' has ceased to exist. The stream of words has continued, making sense grammatically and syntactically, but increasingly detached from any reality in any possible world. The only reality left is 'our' discourse, which itself is unreal since who 'we' are is not explained. The result is that the conventionally named 'red-haired man', the topic of the piece, is reduced to a mere few words on a sheet of paper.

The same problem is returned to in the piece entitled 'On Phenomena and Existences No. 2'.[7] Here one Nikolai Ivanovich is seated at table before a bottle of vodka. The same apophatic process takes place: feature after feature of the phenomena are said not to exist until the conclusion is reached:

What are we saying? Didn't we say that both inside and outside Nikolai Ivanovich nothing exists? And since nothing exists either inside or outside then it means the bottle doesn't exist. Isn't that so? But then remark what follows: if we say that nothing exists either inside or outside the question arises – inside and outside what? Surely something at least must exist? Well, perhaps it doesn't. Then why say 'inside' and 'outside'? No, we've obviously reached a dead-end. And we don't know what to say ourselves. Goodbye.

As with the 'red-haired man', the referent, the topic of discourse, the phenomena of the 'real' world, is verbally dismantled, until the only 'reality' left is that of the speaking voice and an implied listener to whom the speaker bids 'goodbye'. Kharms has, as it were, created in these stories a solipsistic universe where the speaker is in control over the world, able even to destroy it *by language* and defiant of the normal rule of communication that discourse must be *about* something. Kharms wrote of the power of the artist in a self-revelatory letter to Klavdiya Vasil'evna Pugacheva dated October 1933: 'My concern now is to create correct order ... I am the creator of the world and that is the main thing in me.'[8]

II

The language theory of the Bakhtin circle in the 1920s was based not so much on the mechanics of communication as on the problem of the transfer of meaning in communication between two people. The basic unit of communication is the utterance, and the meaning of an utterance is always determined by context (using the word now in the sense of circumstances, not in Jakobson's sense as referent). Part of the context of any verbal communication is the common knowledge and common *evaluation* which the interlocutors bring to the given situation and which has a formative part to play in their dialogue. So instead of Jakobson's six-point schema, Bakhtin/Voloshinov isolated eight factors which are present in any act of communication: the speaker or author, the listener or reader, the actual utterance itself, the topic (or theme of the conversation, which may be another person), the situation (time and space), the language used, the common knowledge of the topic or situation which is implied or assumed, and the common evaluation of the circumstances which is implied or assumed. The Bakhtin school even went so far as to assert that the most important factor in the act of communication is what is *un*spoken, this assumed shared knowledge and evaluation. In this sense 'every utterance is like an enthymeme',[9] that is, a logical syllogism in which one stage in the reasoning is left out. (The enthymeme 'Socrates is a man – Socrates is mortal', for example, omits the intermediary stage 'all men are mortal'.) But the unspoken factor that exists according to the Bakhtin school in every communicatory act or situation, and especially in literature, is not necessarily a logical one: far more frequently it is an evaluationary one. It may imply disagreement as well as agreement. But the point is that values are somehow involved.

So we might argue, then, that some of the effectiveness of Kharms's pieces is the result of his playing on the implied social and cultural values of his potential readership. Several of Kharms's stories, for instance, deal with the experiences of the weak – the blind, the dispossessed, the starving. Nothing in the writing overtly makes any appeal to the readers' sympathies or compassion, but the force of these stories comes from the readers' realization that the events so baldly and factually described are events which from the point of view of the values of common humanity are profoundly shocking. The very absence of explicit authorial evaluation faces the reader with a void at the point where the expectation was for a shared reaction.

Take the case of Abram Dem'yanovich Pantopasov, the hero of 'A Story',[10] who one day goes blind. 'Blind and disabled Abram Dem'yanovich was chucked out of his job and given a miserable pension of 36 roubles a month.' This money is nowhere near enough to live on and so he is forced to forage in dustbins and garbage tips. How to sift through the garbage when he cannot see, is a problem, and how to locate the dustbins in strange yards is another. 'It was fine if the yardman was kind, but others would yell at him so loud he lost all appetite.' Alone, rejected, and starving, it seems Abram Dem'yanovich was condemned to the miserable existence of a social outcast. But this story ends happily: miraculously Abram Dem'yanovich regains his sight. His return to 'normality' brings with it re-acceptance into society. All doors are now open to him, he is feted. 'And,' the story concludes,

'Abram Dem'yanovich became a great man.' In a scant forty lines Kharms has created a miniature, biting, social satire, dependent for its effect on the assumed moral standard that it is society's duty to care for the disabled and not to ignore them.

In 'A Dream'[11] the emaciated Kalugin is treated as garbage. 'The hygiene commission inspecting the apartments and seeing Kalugin found him to be unhygienic and no use for anything and ordered the housing agency to throw Kalugin out with the refuse. They folded Kalugin in half and threw him out like the rubbish.' Absurd? Yes, of course. But also a bitter reversal of humanistic values.

Similar too is Kharms's frequent estranged treatment of death and killing. The doctor in 'A Thorough Investigation' kills his patients in order to investigate thoroughly all aspects of death.[12] In 'Mashkin killed Koshkin'[13] the point of the story is not the killing, but the deadpan, rhythmic, blow-by-blow account of the fight. In 'What They Sell in the Shops Nowadays',[14] Tikakeev kills Koratygin with a cucumber, but, again, the point of the story is not the killing, but the size of the cucumber, and the concluding words are: 'What big cucumbers they sell nowadays in the shops.' Absurdity is achieved through a reversal of the 'normal' values which would treat death as a tragedy, and a major event in comparison with the size of a vegetable! In 'The Cashier',[15] the reversal of values is epitomized by the fact that the police take away a living woman from the shop instead of the dead Masha who is left propped up in the cash desk.

Alice Stone Nakhimovsky has commented about another piece, 'Rehabilitation', that it 'works off the contrast between the reader's internalized values regarding the sacredness of human life, and the character's blissful indifference towards them',[16] a comment which could be applied as well to the stories we have considered above. 'Rehabilitation' itself,[17] one of Kharms's most horrendous pieces, is the confession of a murderer and rapist who mutilates his victims and defecates on them. It is told by the murderer himself, self-satisfied and indifferent to the enormity of his crimes, in thirty lines of what must be some of the most shocking prose ever written in Russian.

The play on assumed values is not concerned only with such major issues as society's attitude to its weaker members, or attitude to death and dying. There are a series of stories which work on the reader's assumed standards of hygiene, cleanliness, and decency. In 'The Flop',[18] all the actors on stage are sick, one after the other. In 'Fedya Davidovich',[19] the hero steals a lump of butter from his wife, hides it in his mouth, and takes it along the corridor to sell to a sinister corpse-like man in the neighbouring apartment for a rouble fifty. In 'The Start to a Very Nice Summer's Day',[20] the little boy eats something disgusting out of the spittoon while the peasant Kharitonov undoes his flies and shouts indecent words to the women. These jars to the reader's sensibility are particularly telling in that they occur in what purports to be a literary text, which in the Russian tradition shunned mention of the seamier aspects of physical life. But Kharms's intention surely was to shock, and by shocking to affirm the opposite: the purity and order which it is the task of art to reflect. If we take seriously his remarks in the same letter to Pugacheva which was quoted above, where he says that 'the purity of order' (*chistota poryadka*) is what art is all about, and in this art reflects the true world, then the muckiness and disorder depicted or evoked in Kharms's stories are a device to jolt the reader into a recognition of how out of kilter the actual world is.

Kharms's technique is rarely to put in an evaluative epithet or comment; indeed authorial intervention is minimal in all these writings. The style is that of telegraphic reportage: short sentences built round nouns and verbs of action, few adjectives, few dependent clauses or phrases. It is for the reader to supply reaction, comment and evaluation on the basis of the cultural values which these stories depend on for their effectiveness, by negating and reversing them.

III

In 1971 the theoretical linguist Isaak Revzin and his wife Ol'ga Revzina published an analysis of Ionesco's plays in the Tartu journal, *Works on Sign Systems*. The absurdness of these plays the authors put down to their infringement of certain presuppositions which lie behind every normal act of communication. Developing Jakobson's communications schema, they added to the basic six points the following eight axioms which they claim are normally operative in the act of communication: 1. That the context ('reality') is constructed in such a way that some if not all events can be explained causally (this they call the axiom of determinism). 2. That between addresser and addressee there is some common memory, some measure of information that they share (the axiom of common memory). 3. That addresser and addressee will to some extent share the same prognosis of the future, what will happen next (the axiom of the same prognosis). 4. That the addresser will be informing the addressee of something new (the axiom of informativeness). 5. That addresser and addressee have in mind the same reality, i.e. that the topic of their discourse remains the same (the axiom of identity). 6. That there is some correspondence between the text and reality, some measure of truth (the axiom of truthfulness). 7. That the text will describe reality with some degree of reduction because of the shared memory and shared prognosis of the communicators (the axiom of incomplete description). 8. That the text is coherent (the axiom of the semantic coherence of the text).[21]

The Revzins' analysis of Ionesco's *The Bald Prima Donna* and *The Lesson* demonstrates how Ionesco builds up the effect of absurdity by systematically breaking these eight axioms. Some, but not all, of the axioms are broken by Kharms in his short prose pieces to achieve a similar sense of the absurd, notably axioms 1, 2, 4, 5 and 8. But, by contrast, axioms 6 and 7 are strictly adhered to, so that for Kharms the 'absurd' is for the most part firmly fixed in a recognizably real world. Axiom 1 (the assumption of causal explanation in the world) is frequently broken. Kharms's world is a place where things occur at random, without rhyme or reason, where the sequence of cause and effect is ignored. 'What Happened on the Street'[22] begins with an accident: a man jumps off a tram and falls under a car. 'The traffic stopped and a policeman began to investigate how the accident occurred. The driver went on explaining something for a long time, pointing to the back wheels of the car.' But no explanation is forthcoming. The victim of the accident is not mentioned again, while various people – 'some chap or other', 'some lady or other' – look on or come and go, or even fall off the bollard they are sitting on. Then, 'At this time, some chap carrying a chair fell flat down under a tram. The policeman came up again, the crowd gathered again and the traffic stopped.' Again some irrelevant detail and the story ends: 'Well then, after that everything again became fine and even Ivan Semenovich [who has not been mentioned before!] popped into the canteen.'

Axiom 2 (shared memory) is explicitly broken in the story 'Sonnet'.[23] The 'I' narrator finds he has 'suddenly forgotten' which comes first, seven or eight. He can count up to six and cannot continue. But it turns out the neighbours also have forgotten which comes next, seven or eight. They ask the cashier in the food store on the corner of Znamenskaya and Basseinaya streets. She says: 'It seems to me that seven comes after eight if and when eight comes after seven.' Delighted at this response they go to the park to count the trees, but only get into an argument – until they are distracted by a child falling off a bench and breaking his jaws. And that is the end of the story. There are other stories involving the loss of shared memory: for instance where the hero is not recognized by his closest neighbours, often after a misfortune has befallen him. The neighbours 'have forgotten' who he is. This happens to the carpenter Kushakov in the story of that name,[24] and it happens to Kalugin in 'A Dream'.

Axiom 4 (a text must provide new information). Kharms experiments with texts with minimal or pointless information. For instance, 'The Encounter': 'Well once a man was going to work and on the way he met another man who had bought a Polish breadstick and was going his own way home. That's really all.'[25] (And that *is* all!) The 'Anecdotes from Pushkin's Life' provide other examples.[26] Of the seven four-, five-, or six-line 'anecdotes', one goes as follows: 'Pushkin loved to throw stones. Whenever he saw stones he would start to throw them. Sometimes he'd get so carried away that he'd stand there all red, waving his arms, throwing the stones, it was just terrible!' Is this minimal information or anti-information, one wonders. In any case the axiom of informativeness is defied.

Axiom 5 (the identity of the topic of discourse) is broken in the stories discussed in section I (the red-haired man who didn't exist, etc.). It is also broken in such stories as 'What Happened on the Street', where what is announced as the topic of the story – the man falling under the car – is simply ignored and forgotten as the story proceeds to tell about other, extraneous, people and events.

Axiom 6 (correlation between the text and reality). One of the fascinations of Kharms's writings is the close bond he establishes between the text and the physical reality the text describes. His world is full of objects from everyday urban life – bread and trams, parks and flats, rubbish-bins and bollards – and the activities described are the activities of everyday existence – shopping, eating, scratching, quarrelling. Street names are specified, and many of the pieces have a recognizably urban setting, though a few are set in the country, or even have no setting at all. This grounding in a real world inevitably makes one read the stories as a commentary on the actuality of the time, a time out of joint, a time of craziness and unpredictability. So axiom 6 is adhered to, and so too is axiom 7.

Indeed, with his minimalist texts Kharms takes the axiom that the text is smaller than the reality it describes to the extreme. In the Revzins' categories, axiom 7 depends on the common memory and common prognosis of the interlocutors (in literature: author and readers): in other words, the text does not need to specify every item of reality, because a large part of it can be implied and left to the assumed knowledge and experience of the readers. In the case of Kharms this assumed knowledge is played on by the recognizability of common everyday actions and situations. The factor of the shared prognosis is lacking and his pieces have no thrust to the future.

Kharms's reductionism is one of the most striking features of his prose writings. Of the prose pieces available to us so far, the vast majority are no longer than one page (a notable exception is the thirty-six-page story, 'The Old Woman'[27]), yet the reality evoked is for the most part not a fantasy one, but grounded in a world familiar to the reader, though made strange by the breaking of the other axioms.

Axiom 8 presupposes the coherence of the text. All of Kharms's pieces have grammatical and syntactical coherence, but some, such as 'What Happened on the Street', discussed above, lack normal semantic or narrative coherence. Another example is 'Symphony No. 2',[28] where the narrator starts to write about Anton Mikhailovich, then switches to Il'ya Pavlovich, then to Anna Ignat'evna, then about himself and his various lady friends, without saying anything substantial or significant about any of these characters.

An important and curious story in this respect is 'Connection', dated 1937 and addressed to 'the philosopher'.[29] In twenty numbered brief paragraphs a series of bizarre incidents are recounted which, unbeknown to the participants, link them to each other, mostly through objects which are lost, found, or bartered. The story ends with a concert at which the performer is the violinist whose hat had been knocked off by hooligans at the start of the story. In the audience is the son of one of the hooligans. This is how the story ends:

> 18. After the concert they went home in the same tram. But in the tram that followed theirs the driver was the very same conductor who long ago had sold the violinist's overcoat at the second-hand shop.
> 19. And now they were travelling through the town late at night: in front, the violinist and the hooligan's son, and behind them the driver, the former conductor.
> 20. They travelled and they never knew what connection there was between them and they would never find out until death itself.

Could it be that what seems like lack of coherence in life, or in narrative, is just the superficial appearance that conceals a deeper connection between all people and things? The question is raised but left open.

In his introduction to the Kharms pieces published in *Russkaya mysl'*, I. F. Petrovichev says of Kharms's world:

> The world seems like a disordered heap of different elements – sometimes without any connection between them, and sometimes connected to each other in ways that man is totally unable to understand ... This break between the different elements of reality is the profound cause of human sufferings. And the search for God is the search for fundamental order.[30]

But in spite of the potential metaphysical overtones of his writings, in spite of the horror, the violence, the dislocation and the sleaziness that characterize his verbal universe, Kharms makes us laugh. And the span of that laughter reaches from what Petrovichev has called 'the terrible, tragic laughter ... which is echoing through all of world literature of our time'[31] to a child's delighted laughter at the absurdity of nonsense word-games.

Kharms's techniques of norm-breaking are skilfully used at some times for sheer play with the conventions of communication, at others to work on the readers' susceptibilities, at others again to construct so inconsequential a narrative as to make the reader raise the question of whether reality itself is not similarly a-causal and ultimately inexplicable. The cumulative effect of reading Kharms's pieces is profoundly disturbing, not least because of not knowing from line to line whether to expect nonsense or tragic absurdity. The force of Kharms's pieces is achieved by the fact that each broken convention is accompanied by a reinforcement of one or more of the other conventions: so that the reader while being lurched out of normality on one level is gripped tight by the normality of another level – which may be the recognizable Leningrad setting, or simply the conventional grammatical and syntactical coherence of the text, or the expectation of being told something new and interesting. There is a degree in convention-breaking beyond which a writer cannot go: to break all communicatory conventions would result in a text comprising totally meaningless word- or sound-strings. To adhere strictly to them all will produce works of reportage and not literature. Poetry makes play with our knowledge of language, the novel and short story with our knowledge of the world. Kharms works on both, sometimes separately and sometimes together, to produce a literature of the absurd that strikes at our buried assumptions and forces questions about the very status of reality, reader and text.

NOTES AND REFERENCES

1. Alice Stone Nakhimovsky, *Laughter in the Void: An Introduction to the Writings of Daniil Kharms and Alexander Vvedenskii* (*Wiener Slawistischer Almanach*, Sonderband 5), Vienna, 1982, chapter 1. See also Il'ya Levin, 'Mir umyshlennyi i mir sozdannyi', *Kontinent*, 24, 1980, pp. 271–5, and the summary chronology of Kharms's life in *Russkaya mysl'*, 3550, 3 January 1985.
2. The most important collection of Kharms's prose writings is still Daniil Kharms, *Izbrannoe* (Colloquium slavicum, band 5), edited and introduced by George Gibian, Würzburg, 1974. Other prose writings have appeared in: *Neue russische Literatur*, Salzburg, 2–3, 1979–80, pp. 135–42 (publication by Gleb Urman); *Vremya i my*, Tel Aviv, 53, 1980, pp. 182–91; *Kontinent*, 24, 1980, pp. 271–95 (publication by Il'ya Levin); *Soviet Union/Union Soviétique*, Arizona State University, 7, 1980, pp. 228–37 (publication by Il'ya Levin) (reprinted in *Russica-81: Literaturnyi sbornik*, New York, 1982, pp. 353–60); *Poiski i razmyshleniya*, Paris, 2, 1982, pp. 36–8; *Russkaya mysl'*, 3550, 3 January 1985 (publication by I. F. Petrovichev). In addition, Nakhimovsky gives English versions of several unpublished stories in the text of her study. We

may expect more to appear eventually: the collected work of Kharms scheduled for publication by K-Presse, Bremen, is to be in ten volumes, of which four volumes of poetry have so far appeared. The project came to a halt after the arrest in the Soviet Union of one of its editors, Mikhail Meilakh, now released.

Among notable works of Kharms criticism, besides those mentioned above, are: A. Flaker, 'O rasskazakh Daniila Kharmsa', *Československá rusistika*, 14, 1969, pp. 78–84; A. Aleksandrov and M. Meilakh, 'Tvorchestvo Daniila Kharmsa', *Materialy XXII nauchnoi studencheskoi konferentsii*, Tartu, 1967, pp. 101–4; R. Milner-Gulland, '"Kovarnye stikhi": Notes on Daniil Kharms and Aleksandr Vvedensky', *Essays in Poetics*, 9/1, 1984, pp. 16–37. See also the bibliography in Nakhimovsky, pp. 184–9.

The extensive study of Kharms by Jean-Philippe Jaccard came to the author's notice too late for its conclusions to be taken into account in this study: see Jean-Philippe Jaccard, 'De la réalité au texte. L'absurde chez Daniil Harms', *Cahiers du Monde Russe et Soviétique*, 26/3–4, 1985, pp. 269–312, and 'Daniil Harms. Bibliographie', ibid, pp. 493–522.
3. Roman Jakobson, 'Closing Statement: Linguistics and Poetics', in *Style in Language*, ed. T. Sebeok, Cambridge, Mass., 1960, p. 353.
4. V. N. Voloshinov (M. M. Bakhtin), 'Discourse in Life and Discourse in Poetry' ('Slovo v zhizni i slovo v poezii'), trans. John Richmond, in *Bakhtin School Papers* (*Russian Poetics in Translation*, 10), ed. Ann Shukman, Oxford, 1983, pp. 5–30, especially 10–13; V. N. Voloshinov (M. M. Bakhtin), 'The Construction of the Utterance' ('Konstruktsiya vyskazyvaniya'), trans. Noel Owen, ibid, pp. 114–38, especially 123–6.
5. O. G. Revzina and I. I. Revzin, 'Semioticheskii eksperiment na stsene (Narushenie postulata normal'nogo obshcheniya kak dramaticheskii priem)', *Trudy po znakovym sistemam*, Tartu, 5, 1971, pp. 232–54, especially 242.
6. The piece is entitled 'Golubaya tetrad' No. 10'. Text in Kharms, *Izbrannoe*, p. 47. Nakhimovsky notes that the comment 'against Kant' is written next to the text in the Blue Notebook (p. 84).
7. 'O yavleniyakh i sushchestvovaniyakh No. 2', *Kontinent*, 24, 1980, pp. 280–1.
8. Text in *Russkaya mysl'*, 3550, 3 January 1985.
9. Voloshinov (Bakhtin), 'Discourse in Life', p. 12.
10. 'Istoriya', *Izbrannoe*, pp. 77–8.
11. 'Son', ibid, pp. 54–5.
12. 'Vsestoronnee issledovanie', *Kontinent*, 24, 1980, pp. 291–3.
13. 'Mashkin ubil Koshkina', *Izbrannoe*, p. 102.
14. 'Chto teper' prodayut v magazinakh', ibid, pp. 100–1.
15. 'Kassirsha', ibid, pp. 79–82.
16. Nakhimovsky, p. 75.
17. 'Reabilitatsiya', *Russica-81*, p. 360. English in Nakhimovsky, pp. 75–6.
18. 'Neudachnyi spektakl'', *Izbrannoe*, p. 95.
19. 'Fedya Davidovich', ibid, pp. 74–6.
20. 'Nachalo ochen' khoroshego letnego dnya (Simfoniya)', ibid, pp. 96–7.

21. Revzina and Revzin, pp. 242–3.
22. 'Proisshestvie na ulitse', *Izbrannoe*, pp. 65–6.
23. 'Sonet', ibid, pp. 49–50.
24. 'Stolyar Kushakov', ibid, pp. 63–4.
25. 'Vstrecha', ibid, p. 94.
26. 'Anekdoty iz zhizni Pushkina', ibid, pp. 110–11.
27. 'Starukha', ibid, pp. 129–65.
28. 'Simfoniya No. 2', ibid, pp. 98–9.
29. 'Svyaz'', ibid, pp. 123–5.
30. *Russkaya mysl'*, 3550, 3 January 1985.
31. Ibid.

5

Petrushka and the Pioneers: The Russian Carnival Puppet Theatre after the Revolution

Catriona Kelly

The focus of Mikhail Bakhtin's study of Rabelais is the European tradition of the carnival, especially the subversive and taboo-breaking comic genres performed on the market-place: clowning, short plays, comic songs and so on. Bakhtin's book is wide-ranging. He discusses the origins of carnival in Greek and Roman religious rites, and its later manifestations in other European countries. But there is only one reference in his book to the native Russian tradition of the carnival – a dismissal of its importance:

> The clearest, most classical carnival forms were preserved in Italy, especially in Rome. The next most typical carnivals were those of Paris. Next came Nuremburg, which adopted a more or less classical form at a somewhat later period. In Russia this process did not develop at all; the various aspects of folk merriment of a national or local character (shrove days, Christmas, fairs) remained unchanged. They offered none of the traits typical of Western European amusements. Peter the Great, as we know, tried to bring to Russia the later European style of the 'feast of fools' (for example, the election of the All-Clowns' Pope) and the pranks of the April fool, but these customs did not take root, and did not mix with local traditions.[1]

Bakhtin's division of the Russian 'fair' from the Western European 'carnival' is misleading. The 'feast of fools' was certainly not popular in Russia. But many other popular amusements at the *narodnye gulyan'ya* (funfairs or carnivals) and *yarmarki* (trade fairs) had originated at the Western carnival. The traditional Western 'quarrel of feast-day and Lenten foods' was Russified as a mock battle between the followers of *Shirokaya Maslyanitsa* (Abundant Shrove) and the adherents of the Lenten foods *Red'ka* (Radish) and *Khren* (Horseradish), who tried to prevent her triumphal entry to start the Russian carnival.[2] All the most important carnival amusements in Europe – roundabouts, roller-coasters, harlequinades, puppet-shows, performing animals, Big Wheels, swings, stalls with fairings and gingerbread – were found in Russia too. These were at least as popular as the carnival amusements which were of local origin, such as the dancing bears and the mumming shows.[3] There were incidental differences between the Russian and the Western forms of the various attractions. The appearance of some of the rides was different, as a result of the much greater cold in Russia during the traditional carnival season (Christmas, Shrovetide, Easter and Whitsun, which began in Russia on the seventh *Thursday* after Easter, *Semik*). The patrons had to be protected from extremes of temperature, so the Russian Big Top, or *balagan*, was made of wood, and roundabouts were enclosed by wooden shells. The Russian roller-coaster was known as a *ledyanaya gora* (ice hill); it was covered by a layer of ice and people slid down it on toboggans or special sledges, not mats or carts. The literary genres, such as the puppet shows and the peep shows, naturally incorporated topical and satirical material of purely local interest.[4]

The Russian fair of the eighteenth and nineteenth centuries was in fact a harmonious (or more often cacophonous, but always exciting and entertaining) combination of Western and native traditions; superficially it resembled the Western carnival. Moreover, there is plenty of evidence that the 'carnival spirit' in a general sense – unabated hedonism, licentiousness and emphasis on the physical – always characterized Russian popular amusements. The German traveller Adam Olearius was disgusted by the debauchery he witnessed as a visitor to Muscovy in 1636:

> [The Muscovites] are wholly given up to all licentiousness, even to sins against Nature, not only with Men, but also with Beasts, he who can tell most stories of that kind, and set them out in most gestures, is accompted the bravest Man. Their Fidlers put them into songs, and their Mountebanks make publick representations of them, and stick not to show their Breeches, and sometimes all they have to their Spectators. Those who lead

> Bears about, Juglers and Puppet-players, who erect a stage in a moment, by the means of a coverlet, which, being ty'd about their wast, is brought over their heads, and within it show their Puppets, representing their brutalities and sodomies, make sport to the Children, who are thereby induc'd to quit all sentiments of shame and honesty ... There's no place in the World where drunkenness is more common than in Muscovy. All, of all conditions, Ecclesiasticks and Laicks, Men and Women, Old and Young, will drink strong-water at any time, before, at, and after their meals.[5]

The *narodnye gulyan'ya* and *yarmarki* were beginning to decline at the end of the century. The fairs were no longer so important for trade; there was now more diversity of popular entertainment; new forms had grown up, such as the circus acts and *feerii* (pageants) held in the suburbs of St Petersburg. There were also political reasons: the authorities, nervous of the unrest which might result from such large gatherings, moved them from their original central sites to sites on the periphery. But most Russians born before the Revolution had attended fairs and carnivals, and retained strong impressions of them. Benois's recollections in his memoirs are typical:

> There were larger numbers of paralytic drunks in evidence here than elsewhere in Europe, and they were louder, more riotous, and sometimes more frightening. By nightfall the squares where these amusements took place had been entirely taken over by drunken peasants and workmen; the mass drunkenness had a demonic ruffianly grandeur which is well conveyed by the fourth scene of Stravinsky's *Petrouchka*.[6]

Bronislava Nijinska, who was born in the early 1890s, had vivid memories of the Nizhnii Novgorod fair, which she had visited as a small child.[7]

The Revolution, the famines of the early 1920s and the Civil War hastened the decline of the Russian carnivals, but did not kill them off completely. Nina Simonovich-Efimova, a well-known Soviet puppeteer, recorded that in 1925 the back streets off the Novinskii Boulevard in Moscow were still home to a thriving community of street showmen, as they had been since the 1850s.[8] In 1919 she and her husband helped revive the old Moscow *gulyan'ya* at Sokol'niki; the event was repeated in 1923.[9] Vsevolodskii-Gerngross records that dancing bears still performed in Leningrad and in many other places well into the 1920s, though their appearances were spasmodic.[10]

Bakhtin was born in Orel in 1895; at this stage the traditional *yarmarki* and *narodnye gulyan'ya* were still widely held in the provinces. It is unlikely, therefore, that he had never been to a carnival himself and that he was ignorant of the traditions of street entertainment in Russia. Why, then, did he ignore the Russian carnival?

Bakhtin frequently voiced admiration for popular culture, but it is significant that in his book on Rabelais his enthusiasm is directed at mass entertainment belonging to an epoch which was historically and geographically remote (France in the Middle Ages). It is quite possible that he found contemporary forms of street entertainment less congenial. The Russian pre-revolutionary left-wing intelligentsia was uneasy about the popular appeal of the entertainments offered at the *narodnye gulyan'ya*, which they considered jejune and unfunny as well as insufficiently improving and educational. Simonovich-Efimova described the street puppet-show, *Petrushka*, as an entertainment by hooligans for hooligans.[11] Lev Shcheglov was scathing about the level of entertainments provided in the *balagany* at a fair which he visited in Yaroslavl' in 1895.[12]

The *Narodnyi teatr* or Popular Theatre movement originating in the 1860s rose directly from the dis-satisfaction of members of the intelligentsia with the popular entertainments then on offer. The organizers of such theatres were aware of the immense popularity of the mobile street theatres, and of their vast influence on an illiterate population denied access to other forms of theatre. In 1884 the biggest Russian popular illustrated periodical, *Niva*, had 78 000 subscribers; in the 1870s any performance given in one of the large *balagany* might be seen by up to 60 000 spectators over the ten-day Shrovetide season, and there were five such *balagany* on the Admiralty Square in St Petersburg alone.[13] The sponsors of the *Narodnyi teatr* hoped to channel this huge audience for their own purposes; their aim was to propagate high culture among the masses, not to perpetuate popular culture. The aims of the movement were summed up by A. N. Kremlev, who presented a project for an *obshchestvennyi teatr*, public theatre, to the *Gorodskaya duma* of St Petersburg in 1896:

The public or popular theatre must not pander to all: it must be *accessible* to all.[14]

The aims of the *Narodnyi teatr* movement were not realized at first; none of the theatres founded had the popularity of the *balagany* or of the *feerii* and other music hall and circus acts shown in parks and gardens in and around St Petersburg. After the Revolution, however, things were different. The attitudes of the progressive intelligentsia now dominated official policy; the street theatrical tradition presented considerable problems. Its popularity could not be denied, but it had unseemly commercial elements and was unduly committed to entertainment, not education. Lunacharskii's article on the circus reflects the distaste which many Bolsheviks felt for popular literary modes:

> No communist ought ever to wave a hand in contempt at any genuinely popular phenomenon, understandable as it is when so-called refined intellects, confronted by popular songs (*chastushki* and *zhestokie romansy*), pulp novels and lurid adventure films, wrinkle their noses as if there was a bad smell.... Naturally there are many undesirable elements in all these forms of art, elements, moreover, which do not contribute to the enjoyment of the masses, but which are merely a routine and unnecessary addition.
> What I have said above is partly applicable to the circus too. As I have already said, its great popularity should be enough in itself to necessitate serious discussion and to introduce enquiries about how to purify and perhaps adapt the circus, whilst at the same time preserving its essential qualities.[15]

The necessary changes in the character of popular entertainment were not to be allowed to happen of themselves; they were to be directed from above. The *narodnye gulyan'ya* were to be purged of undesirable elements and fitted for communist reality:

> It cannot be expected that, if left to themselves, the masses will come up with anything more than noisy merry-making and thronging crowds of people dressed up in their holiday best.
> Like everything else with a capacity to inspire elevated aesthetic enjoyment, a genuine holiday must be organized....
> A festival organized without the help (but also without the hin-

drance) of Dionysus would perhaps be rather greyer than before, but it would certainly also be infinitely more decent.[16]

One of the first acts of the new cultural administration was to turn the *Narodnyi dom* (People's Palace) in St Petersburg, which until then had been a sort of music hall, into a theatre for the performance of realist drama.[17] And by the end of the 1930s the process of organization and adaptation had gone so far that most types of popular entertainment bore little resemblance to those on offer before the Revolution. The old community of itinerant entertainers had disappeared; fairgrounds were now permanent and mechanized, and were usually integrated into leisure complexes ('parks of culture and rest'); the circus and puppet theatre had been centralized and 'professionalized' under organizers who often (at least in the case of the puppet theatre) had little sympathy with the traditional street theatre. At the end of the 1920s puppeteers still performed quite regularly in city courtyards; by 1940 they had disappeared altogether.[18]

The complete absence of traditional forms of carnival entertainment in the Soviet Union stands out against the situation in other countries. In Britain, for example, the *Punch and Judy* tradition is still very much alive: over twenty showmen work the beach sites, many more give performances at fairs, children's parties, and so on; recently the surviving showmen's families (where the current performer may be the fourth generation to show) have been joined by enthusiastic converts, such as the Major Mustard group, who have initiated a revival.[19] In the late 1960s there were over two hundred fairs a week during the season, some of which were still steam-operated.[20] In China the recent establishment of heavily-subsidized state puppet theatres has not yet killed off street puppet shows.[21]

Bakhtin started work on his study of Rabelais in 1934. His remarks on the character of the Russian carnival are not incidental; they must be placed in the context of the manipulation of popular-cultural forms which had been going on since the Revolution. Krystyna Pomorska remarks in her foreword to the English-language edition of *Rabelais and His World*: 'The official prohibition of certain kinds of laughter, irony and satire was imposed upon the writers of Russia after the Revolution.'[22] In fact the prohibition was not immediate; it had two phases. Immediately after the Revolution, the entertainments of the Russian carnival were seized on, since they seemed ideal for the purposes of agitation and propaganda. In the May Day carnivals in Petersburg in 1918 and 1919 circus acts and puppet shows were revived, and new, Socialist elements were added; there were processsions of decorated agit-vans and even agit-trams; the squares were embellished, not now with the traditional fir-branches, but with red banners and caricatures; vast Enemy of the People dolls were incinerated on public bonfires.[23] During and after the Civil War, popular-theatrical forms were adopted by travelling troupes of actors who worked to keep up morale among the soldiery during the war, and after it to propagate literacy and hygiene. Some of these groups used live actors, and based their work on the traditional folk theatre repertoire for live actors, and on the conventions used in the folk theatre. The largest and most important group was the *Sinyaya bluza* (Blue Blouse) movement; its acts mixed circus acts and acrobatics with literary forms, such as *raeshnik* (comic doggerel) and *igrishche* (a comic sketch or short scene). The actors' habit of indicating the function of characters by pinning key details to the outside of their uniform blue blouses was probably derived from the folk tradition; plays of the folk repertoire, such as *Tsar' Maksimilian*, were often performed by soldiers who would pin foil stars and other emblems to their army-issue greatcoats.[24]

Many of the mobile agitprop groups preferred puppets, above all glove puppets, to live actors. The canvas booths, puppets and other equipment used for shows were portable, they could be easily stored, rapidly dismantled and reassembled; an adequate show could be put on by only one operator, using two puppets simultaneously, and perhaps also a musician to provide accompaniment. A puppet theatre was also ideally suited to performances on the back of floats, from the back of vans or even the window of a bus or train.

Throughout the 1920s, active puppet collectives travelled round European Russia staging shows which were based on the adventures of the glove puppet hero of the Russian fairground, Petrushka. The most important groups were the 'Red Petrushka' collective, begun in 1927 under S. Malinovskaya, the 'Red Army Petrushka Group' begun in 1928, the 'Special Automobile and Chemical Factory Petrushka', which played in factory clubs, and the 'Sanitary Petrushka', which 'carried out idiosyncratic and extremely useful educational work in schools, clubs and pioneer camps'.[25]

From the first years of Soviet power, the puppet theatre had a central place in official theatre policy. In 1918 the TEO (*Teatral'nyi otdel*, or Theatrical Dept.) of the *Narkompros* (People's Commissariat of Education) organized a Puppet Theatre Studio in Moscow.[26] After the Civil War the puppet theatres became an integral part of the agitprop campaign in Soviet villages; puppet groups were founded by *Glavpolitprosvet* (Political Education Directive) in many places. The expansion of the agitprop puppet theatre was encouraged by the publication of texts of original plays in the journals *Ranenyi krasnoarmeets* (*The Wounded Red Army Soldier*) and *Doloi negramotnost'* (*Away with Illiteracy*), as well as in separate editions. Numerous manuals and technical articles were produced which advised club organizers in villages how to manufacture their own puppets and booths.[27] For the less enterprising *kul'torg* (culture administrator), sets of puppets were available from central clubs.[28] Many of the new Petrushka plays became popular; Nina Smirnova states that in one Soviet town audience reactions to performances of the puppet group were so strong that people would bring their complaints to Petrushka and ask him to settle them.[29]

The second phase of carnival prohibition began in the late 1920s and gained momentum in the 1930s. The politically committed and socially critical agitprop theatre was defused; one by one, the groups were disbanded. *Sinyaya bluza* was forced to close down in 1932.[30] The various 'Red Petrushka' groups lasted only slightly longer. 'Red Petrushka' itself 'ended its existence, according to the natural order of things' in the mid-1930s.[31] Petrushka's subversive character did not suit the new atmosphere of the 1930s, as the famous Soviet puppeteer Sergei Obraztsov makes clear:

Before the Revolution Petrushka would hit people whom it was not only forbidden to hit, but whom one might not even criticize. He embodied, so to speak, the dream of the common people which could not possibly be realized in Tsarist times. He restored the spirit of justice missing from the world around.

With the coming of Soviet power, though, justice was established, and Soviet law began to do battle with anti-social elements – embezzlers, swindlers, idlers. The services of anarchic boot-boys were no longer required. The more the legal system gained in strength, the more senseless and even harmful Petrushka's arbitrary quarrelsomeness began to seem; it perverted all conceptions of law, of human moral norms, and of right social behaviour. And so the attempt to revive Petrushka the positive–negative hero could not succeed.

The reasons for these failures are obvious. In the modern theatre it is quite in order to perform a classic pre-revolutionary comedy, but it would be quite wrong to use the hero of such a play as the hero of a modern work.[32]

In 1931, the Central State Puppet Theatre was set up in Moscow; the artistic director was Sergei Obraztsov. Since then the Soviet puppet theatre has followed two main lines: productions catering for children, mostly *skazki* (folk tales) or original plays with a cast list of small furry creatures; and productions catering for adults, with performances of Russian and foreign classics adapted for the puppet theatre, and original plays, such as Obraztsov's *The Extraordinary Concert*. Any social criticism is directed at the capitalist West or at pre-revolutionary Russia. Artistic standards are high, but there is no element of riotousness and little to disturb the audience, whether adult or child.

The object of the second part of this chapter is to study the interim period of the prohibition of carnival literature, using as material a selection of agitprop puppet plays dating from the mid-1920s, which will be compared with the carnival Petrushka on which they were based. I intend to show how carnival elements were deliberately written out of the new *Petrushka* plays, and how the new versions distort the original. I will conclude with a study of a little-known updated version of the *Petrushka* text (in which the hero is called 'Van'ka', as was traditional in the South), which was produced by a group of itinerant puppeteers working in the time-honoured manner in the 1920s, and in which linguistic innovations and new characterizations are successfully combined with the traditional orally transmitted text.

The street puppet theatre has been used as a focus for the following reasons. It is, firstly, one of the oldest types of street theatre in Russia. The earliest documentary evidence of its existence is a sketch by Olearius (1636), which illustrates a scene in which a puppet wallops a horse with a broom.[33] Secondly, the Petrushka text was widely known; it was shown at every Russian carnival in the nineteenth and early twentieth century. Until the lifting of theatrical censorship at the end of the 1860s, it was the only substantial *razgovornyi zhanr* (spoken genre) allowed at fairs. The types of humour and in particular linguistic comedy found in

Petrushka are typical of the carnival; none of the other genres offers anything not found in it. *Petrushka* was more widely and more directly imitated than other types of carnival text; the *raeshniki* (comic doggerel verses) published in such collections as *Krasnoarmeiskii fol'klor* (*Red Army Folklore*) bear little resemblance to fairground comedy – a typical title is 'Stalin is Our Golden Sun'.[34] *Petrushka* can safely be used to represent the other fairground genres, which will be referred to for comparative purposes only.

A string puppet, or marionette, version of Petrushka existed.[35] But the more popular version by far was a glove puppet, with a wooden or papier-mâché head and hands and a cloth body. The face of the puppet had a hook nose, small black eyes and a demonic grin showing large teeth. He was usually hunch-backed; sometimes he even had two humps. He was almost always dressed in a pointed dunce's cap, and red, or red-and-white striped, smock and trousers. Petrushka's externals are virtually identical to those of Pulcinella, Hanswurst, Kasparek, Polichinelle, Punch and other European glove-puppet heroes; in character he also resembles them, being a liar, a cheat, a satyromaniac, a coward and a multiple murderer.[36]

The centre of attention in *Petrushka* is the character of the hero. The play normally takes the following course. The musician, the puppeteer's partner who plays the barrel organ throughout the play, announces the imminent arrival of Petrushka. Eventually, when the audience's demands are vociferous enough, Petrushka appears and introduces himself to the public with a series of demonic squeals and cackles (his voice, like that of Punch, is produced by the puppeteer using a special metal and tape *govorok*, or swazzle). Then follow several confrontational scenes – the number varied from three to twelve or more – with other characters whom Petrushka accosts, insults, and then batters to death with his *dubinka* (club). In most versions his fiancée, Pigas'ya, Parashka, Malan'ya, or Akul'ka, also appears and they dance; occasionally they also fight, though the long physical battles of Punch and Judy are unknown in Russia.[37] Finally Petrushka is dragged off to Hell by a vast dog (*Sobaka-barbos*) and the performance ends. Individual puppeteers varied the scheme by using different characters (the most popular were the Gypsy, the Arab, the Soldier and the Policeman, but around ten others were also used).[38] The puppeteer might also vary formulae of language and action with topical references and improvised jokes, according to the mood of the audience.

Scholarly interest in *Petrushka* began around the turn of this century, at much the same time as the fairground tradition began to decline. It was customary then, particularly amongst Symbolists, to see him as a mythical archetype:

> The place and time of Petrushka's birth are shrouded in the mists of antiquity ... Was Columbina not perhaps that doll belonging to the goddess Parvathi whom the god Shiva so loved that he brought her to life? And did not that legendary Columbina perhaps have her own Petrushka?[39]

Benois's reworking of the character was inspired by his view of its symbolism:

> If Petrushka was the embodiment of human spirituality and suffering – that is, of the poetic principle – if his lady, Columbina the ballerina, emerged as a personification of *das Ewig-Weibliche* – then the 'luxurious' Harlequin-Arab became the embodiment of the thoughtlessly captivating, the powerfully courageous and the unjustly triumphant.[40]

Soviet scholars are less interested in the religious symbolism of the *Petrushka* text than in its social meaning: it is commonly seen as a profound criticism of Tsarist reality. Berkov classes it as a 'satire', and sees it as an example of the 'socially critical, satirical direction in the Russian popular theatre'.[41] The most fulsome tribute to the satirical power of Petrushka was made by Gor'kii, who placed the puppet on a level with Faust:

> Besides the tragic future of Faust, another figure was created which is also known to all nations: in Italy – Puncinello [sic], in England – Punch, in Turkey – Karapet, here in Russia – Petrushka. Petrushka is the indefatigable hero of the folk puppet theatre, he defeats everyone and everything: the police, priests, even death and the devil, whilst himself remaining immortal. He is the crude and naive image in which working people embodied themselves and their belief that in the end they themselves would have victory over everyone and everything.[42]

In support of the argument that *Petrushka* is a bitingly satirical text, reference is often made to vicious censorship of the play under the Tsars. Smirnova talks of 'merciless hounding' of the puppeteers by the Tsarist authorities; Krupryanskaya mentions assaults by the church as well as the government.[43] Nineteenth-century documentation indicates that the authorities were indeed often disturbed by the puppet shows. Archbishop Ierimii, visiting Arzamas in 1853, was disgusted by a puppet play being performed outside the cathedral:

> There was a puppet comedy going on right next to the cathedral, which was of a length which offended against all standards of good taste, and of a content which offended against the decency demanded by the virtue of children and young girls.[44]

Another important trend in Soviet criticism of the puppet theatre is analysis of its formal characteristics. P. G. Bogatyrev has written several detailed surveys of comic devices in the puppet theatre, and has shown that the principle of 'oxymoron' (loosely used to mean an opposition with an absurd or comic effect) is central to *Petrushka* as to the Czech puppet theatre and the Russian live folk theatre. Anna Nekrylova's article on *Petrushka* develops this line with particular reference to the Russian puppet theatre, analysing examples such as Petrushka's description of the horse: 'She must be young, you know; there's not a tooth in her head.' She also shows how the comic effect of such descriptions is intensified by alternate use of rhymed doggerel and prose.[45]

The work done by Soviet scholars on *Petrushka* has identified elements which overlap with Bakhtinian notions of the carnival. Petrushka's subversive spirit and his lack of respect for authority reflect the suspension of social rank and feeling of equality which characterized the carnival: 'In the world of the carnival all hierarchies are cancelled. All castes and ages are equal.'[46]

The linguistic comedy discussed by Bogatyrev and Nekrylova, with its mockery of inarticulacy, and oxymoronic structure, is typical of the carnival texts which Bakhtin analyses.[47] But no attempt has yet been made to analyse *Petrushka* as a carnival text; other elements in it which are also typical of carnival literature, such as the stress on eating, have been ignored; others which it is impossible to ignore (obscenity and violence) have provoked embarrassment, been hurried over, and have been dismissed as peripheral. 'The Petrushka showmen are accomplished masters in portraying what is commonly known as indecency', Simonovich-Efimova writes.[48] The same reticence has been shown in the handling of other carnival genres: Berkov writes in his anthology of folk drama that he has deliberately chosen a version of *Tsar' Maksimilian* which is free from obscenity: 'The present text is less littered than others with indecent expressions, which are never met with in the older versions of *Tsar' Maksimilian*.'[49]

Simonovich-Efimova also finds the violence of *Petrushka* perturbing:

> Petrushka kills the Doctor with blows of his stick. The Musician assures him that now he'll be sent to gaol. But Petrushka slings the Doctor over his shoulder and shouts: 'Who'll buy my potatoes? my fine potatoes?' Then Petrushka kills the Policeman with a well-aimed blow on the forehead, then he kills the Musician by banging him several times on the nape of the neck.
> Of course, all this is scenically impressive and even classically simple (I'm not joking), but I cannot force my hand or my tongue to perform this sort of thing in front of children.[50]

These scruples are understandable. Senseless violence to living human beings is not funny; it is safe to assume that few modern Europeans would find a 'comic' spectacle that was offered at the Moscow carnival in the early eighteenth century, in which a clown thief was beaten with birch twigs by each member of the audience of two hundred until the blood ran as a punishment for his mock crime, in the least humorous.[51] But in *Petrushka* the violence is clearly of carnival character. He is only a puppet, not a real actor, and the wooden heads of his opponents make the blows sound much more vicious than they are. His character is well known to the audience, and so his actions are neither unexpected nor shocking. He also anticipates his actions with a variety of innuendoes, all of them crude, comic and transparent, offering to 'pay' the Doctor and Gypsy in roubles, to 'teach the Arab a Russian dance', and so on. The motivation for his fights is irrational, the objects of his aggression unpleasant, and the fights have no vestige of realism. The violence is double-edged, as is the violence of the Rabelaisian mock battles described by Bakhtin: it is disturbing, but finally frivolous.

The belief that the violence and obscenity of *Petrushka* are peripheral to the text has led to only one variant's being published in full in the Soviet Union, though over twenty are held in archives. It appears in Berkov's anthology of folk drama, and is a version recorded in 1902 by a schoolteacher.[52] This version was made by a skilled puppeteer; it is lively and rich in verbal comedy, but lacks the obscenity which most commentators see as characteristic of street theatre. Petrushka's violence is also not so unbridled in this version: he murders only twice (the German and the Soldier); the other characters (the Doctor, the Gypsy) escape with threats and beatings. But Petrushka's attitude is as triumphantly immoral as ever:

> Muzykant, kaprala provodil i kontsy skhoronil. Teper' ya chelovek svobodnyi. Kha-kha-kha! Vot tak Petrushka! Nevestu dobyl, nemtsa ubil, loshad' kupil i podletsa kaprala provodil!
>
> [So, Musician, I've put paid to the Corporal and been to his funeral! Now I'm a free man. Ha-ha-ha! That's my Petrushka! Found a nice wife, ended the German's life, bought a fine mare and seen the Corporal to his bier!]
>
> (*RND*, p. 122)

In other ways this variant of *Petrushka* gives a strong impression of the carnival nature of the traditional glove puppet theatre. There is much emphasis on distorted physicality, an emphasis which Bakhtin had seen as central to the carnival tradition:

> The artistic logic of the grotesque image ignores the closed, smooth and impenetrable surface of the body and retains only its excrescences (sprouts, buds) and orifices, only that which leads beyond the body's limited space or into the body's depths.[53]

The bodies of Petrushka and other puppets exaggerate these 'excrescences and orifices'. All the puppets, especially Petrushka, have huge noses and gaping mouths, in which over-sized teeth are visible. The cheek bones are given unnatural prominence. Petrushka also normally has a hump on his back, or two humps, and is the only puppet to have legs. Since he cannot stand on his legs, they are read by the audience as additional protuberances, which, like his club, signify the phallus.

With glove puppets, distortion of the physique has a dimension absent from the theatre where marionettes or rod puppets are used. Glove puppets are not only grotesque caricatures of the human form in themselves: they also distort the appearance of the puppeteer's hand, on which they sit like vast growths. In the puppet performance certain parts of the human body (fingers, palm) are metamorphosed into others (arms and hands, torso, head).[54]

The *Petrushka* text is also abundantly physical. In the first scene of several variants, Petrushka's fiancée appears. He fulsomely praises her appearance; the Musician expresses scepticism. Both emphasize her mouth and nose:

Muzykant: Khorosha-to khorosha. . . . da kurnosa.
Petrushka: Ai vresh', muzykant! Da ty posmotri, chto za glazki, chto za rotik! Ruchki!! Gubki!! Sheika!!

[Musician: Well, she's pretty enough. . . . but snub-nosed.
Petrushka: Musician, you're lying! Just have a look at her button eyes! her rosebud mouth! What hands!! Lips!! What a neck!!]

(*RND*, p. 116)

Many versions did not stop here. Eremin records that Petrushka's description of what he wants for a dowry often included 'quite unmentionable objects'.[55] The puppeteers would sometimes give *Petrushka* an ending called *Petrushkina svat'ba* (Petrushka's Wedding), in which Petrushka first expanded at length on the physical charms of his fiancée, and then, in the final scene, anticipated his wedding night.[56]

Then follows a scene in which Petrushka buys a horse. It too is grotesquely distorted; indeed, dismembered:

Tsygan: Loshad' khot' kuda! bez grivy, bez khvosta . . .
Petrushka: Chto khvost i griva? odno ukrashen'e. A golova est'?
Tsygan: Tol'ko i est', chto golova odna. . . . Da i ee eshche net . . . konovalu v pochinku otdana. [. . .]
Petrushka: Kha-kha-kha! Vot tak loshad'! Kak raz po mne i po budushchei zhene. Damy truslivy, a loshad' bez golovy, znachit smirnaya budet.

[Gypsy: The highest class of horse! No tail and mane, of course!
Petrushka: So what, no tail and mane? that's only decoration anyway! It's got a head, I suppose?
Gypsy: A head's about all it *has* got – or actually, at the moment, not! It's at the vet's repair shop.
Petrushka: Ha-ha-ha! That's my horse! Just right for me and my bride! The ladies are so timid, and if the horse has no head, it'll be all the quieter for that.]
                                                      (RND, p. 116)

The excrescences of the body can be discarded at any time in Petrushka's world. In a variant of the text quoted by Nekrylova, Petrushka is asked by the Policeman where his hump is, to which he replies, 'At home on the stove'.[57]

Then follows a farcical scene in which Petrushka is first kicked by the horse, then thrown by it when he manages to mount. A doctor is called and examines Petrushka, asking him where the pain is; Petrushka refuses to specify, but it is clearly somewhere in the middle of his body, and the scene which results has considerable possibilities for *double entendre*:

Doktor: Nu govori, gde bolit, pokazhi!
Petrushka: Vot tut.
Doktor: Tut?
Petrushka: Ponizhe.
Doktor: Tut?
Petrushka: Povyshe.
Doktor: Tut?
Petrushka: Ponizhe.
Doktor: Tut?
Petrushka: Povyshe.
Doktor: To ponizhe, to povyshe! Vstan', vstan', da pokazhi!
             [*Beret ego za ukho*]

Doctor: Well then, tell me where it hurts, show me!
Petrushka: Just here.
Doctor: Here?
Petrushka: Lower.
Doctor: Here?
Petrushka: Higher.

Doctor:	Here?
Petrushka:	Lower.
Doctor:	One minute lower, one minute higher! Get up, idiot, and show me yourself! [*Takes him by the ear*]

(*RND*, pp. 117–18)

The scenes which follow are also rich in physical farce. Petrushka kills the German, and crams him into a coffin which is too small; he displays extreme incompetence when instructed in military matters by the Soldier. In these scenes the carnival element is emphasized by mock fighting (Petrushka gets whacked himself before taking revenge) and by abuse. 'Skotina!' ('Animal!') yells the soldier in Berkov's version, though the abuse level is lower here than elsewhere. In some variants Petrushka even called down physical distortion on himself:

Ya Petrushka 'Ratatui',
Chert menya goroyu vzdui!

[I'm Petrushka-Ratatille!
Devil blow me up as big as a hill!][58]

The end of *Petrushka* is rich in carnival comedy. Petrushka first of all sings a song in which he refers to a dog 'with a curly tail' rushing around a vegetable garden:

V ogorode sobaka gulyala,
Zagnula kryuchkom khvostik
I ubezhala...
Nachnem pesenku snachala...

[A dog was walking in the cabbage patch,
It curled its tail into an *o*
And made a dash...
Let's sing this song once more straight through]

(*RND*, p. 22)

An enormous dog with heavily emphasized jaws then appears and drags Petrushka off. The connection with the carnival world was even clearer in variants where the backdrop to the final scene was a painting of a vast pair of jaws; and in which Petrushka was seized by the nose and dragged off screaming, 'Barbos, barbos, pusti moi nos!' ('Barbos, Barbos, let go my nose!').[59]

The text of *Petrushka* continually refers to eating and drinking, archetypally carnival activities, as Bakhtin states:

> Eating and drinking are the most significant manifestations of the grotesque body.[60]

Petrushka himself commonly had the surname *Uksusov* or *Samovarov*, both of which are taken from food words (*uksus* means vinegar). In the South of Russia he was known as Van'ka-Ratatui. The second part of the name is often held to derive from the alarm cry 'Ru-tu-tui!', but Elizabeth Warner has ingeniously suggested another origin: the French *ratatouille*, courgette and aubergine stew.[61] As with his counterparts Hanswurst, Jack Pudding and Jan Pickelhering, Petrushka's name reveals his interest in consumption.

In his opening speech, Petrushka boasts of his capacity as a drinker: 'Bez mery vino p'yu' ('I drink wine without measure'). Later he sings a drinking song:

> Chizhik-pyzhik, gde ty byl?
> Za goroyu vodku pil.
> Vypil ryumku, vypil dve:
> Zashumelo v golove.
>
> [Little birdy, where've you been?
> Drinking vodka on the green.
> I had one glass, I had two,
> Head began to ache right through.]
>
> (*RND*, p. 119)

In this version Petrushka's obsession with eating and drinking does not go beyond talking about it. Other versions were more explicit. Nekrylova cites a scene appearing in several variants where Petrushka boozes with his friend from back home, Filimoshka; and another in which Petrushka visits what he takes to be an eating-house run by a Jew and is offered a variety of inedible substances:

Petrushka: Chto u tebya est', chtoby pokushat'?

Evrei:	Vus u menya est' vse, chto zavgodno.
Petrushka:	Nu, a zharkoe est'?
Evrei:	Vus zharkoe – zharkoe net.
Petrushka:	Govori skorei, chto u tebya est'?
Evrei:	U menya est' kerosin, degot', mylo, svechi, melkie gvozdi, sol', bebul'naya bumaga...

[Petrushka:	What've you got to eat then?
Jew:	[*In a Jewish accent*] Anything you like, shir.
Petrushka:	Well, got any roast meat then?
Jew:	No shir, shorry shir.
Petrushka:	What have you got then, no mucking about?
Jew:	I've got kerosene, tar, soap, candles, tin tacks, salt, sandpaper...][62]

Eremin lists variants in which Petrushka was engaged as a cook and showed his complete inability to even prepare tea properly – 'Chai gotov, da samovar-to ubezhal!' ('The tea's ready, but the samovar's run out the door!') – and a scene in which Petrushka offers hospitality to his aunt Alen'ka and refuses to pay the bill. Ukrainian versions of *Petrushka* also commonly included a scene in which the hero was upbraided by his wife for excessive drinking.[63] In some versions Petrushka demanded his dowry in food and drink: '44 tysyachi i polkvarty vodki, dve seledki, ikry i butylki funta tri' ('44 thousand and half a quart of vodka, two salt herrings, some caviare and three pounds of bottle').[64]

A more interesting role, though, is played by eating at the linguistic level of the text. In *Petrushka*, as in *Punch and Judy*, the device of the comic misunderstanding is used often: one character (usually deliberately) mishears what another has said, and produces an absurd alternative. Nekrylova quotes the conversation between Petrushka and the Gypsy as to the price of the horse:

Tsygan:	Sto pyat'desyat rublei.
Petrushka:	Neuzheli sto vosem'desyat gvozdei?
Tsygan:	Ne gvozdei, a rublei.
Petrushka:	Drozhzhei?
Tsygan:	Ne drozhzhei, a rublei.
Petrushka:	Golubei?

[Gypsy:	A hundred and fifty roubles.

Petrushka: What, a hundred and fifty doodles?
Gypsy: Not doodles, roubles.
Petrushka: Noodles?
Gypsy: Not noodles, roubles.
Petrushka: Strudels?][65]

Such puns or ambiguities are scattered throughout the text. Both Nekrylova and Bogatyrev have pointed them out. What interests me here is their contribution to the carnival comedy of the text. Very many such misunderstandings occur when Petrushka mistakes the name of some object for the name of a food or a drink: above, he confuses (literally) 'roubles' with *drozhzhi*, 'yeast', and then with *golubi*, 'pigeons'. In a version cited by Al'ferov he addresses the Soldier as 'vashe skovorod'e' ('your frying-pan-hour') not as 'vashe vysokorod'e' ('your honour') (*RND*, p. 114). Eremin quotes a version in which, on hearing the Musician introduce the German (*nemets*), Petrushka exclaims: 'Perets? neuzheli on takoi gor'kii?' ('Pepper? Does he get up your nose, then?').[66] In the full variant given by Berkov, Petrushka mistakes the German's faltering Russian 'Was?' for 'Kvas':

Nemets: Va-a-as?
Petrushka: Kva-a-as? Kakoi tut kvas? Poshel von ot nas, my ne khotim znat' vas. [*Vytalkivaet nemtsa von*] Muzykant! Nemets ushel kvas pit'?
Muzykant: Net, Petrushka mus'yu, on skazal: seichas nalivki prinesu.

[German: Wa-a-as?
Petrushka: Kva-a-as? There's no kvas here! Get away with you, we don't want to know you! [*Shoves German away*] Musician! Has the German gone off to drink some kvas?
Musician: No, Petrushka moosewer, he said, I'll just bring you back some liqueur.]

(*RND*, p. 119)

The puns and cases of mistaken identity often have sinister overtones: in what Bakhtin termed the spirit of 'culinary dismemberment',[67] they link eating and drinking with violence and death. In the passage quoted above, it emerges that the German has gone to fetch not *kvas*, and not fruit liqueur, but a club. When Petrushka kills the German and sees him lying on the ground, he exclaims, 'Muzykant, a ved' nemets p'yan!' ('But, Musician, the German is drunk!') (*RND*, p. 119). In some versions, he then slings him over his shoulder and offers him to passers-by as provisions, calling, 'Kartofelyu, kartofelyu! Porosyat, porosyat!' ('Potatoes, potatoes! Sucking pigs, sucking pigs!') (*RND*, p. 114). When collecting money for the German's funeral, he links the German's death with food by using the expression 'on s"el grib', 'he ate a mushroom', figuratively, 'he bit off more than he could chew':

> Pozhertvuite! Pozhertvuite, gospoda, na pokhorony nemtsa-podletsa! On nechayanno na yaroslavtsa-Petrushku naletel da grib s"el i... podavilsya!
>
> [Gentlemen! Gentlemen, give us your pennies to bury the German! He happened to run across Petrushka from Yaroslavl', and bit off more than he could chew and... choked to death!]
> (*RND*, p. 120)

The connection between eating and death is pointed out by Petrushka's own sticky end, eaten by the *Sobaka-barbos*:

> Konchilos' delo,
> Petrushku sobaka s"ela...
>
> [That's all for now,
> Petrushka's been eaten by the bow-wow...]
> (*RND*, p. 123)

The connection between eating and drinking and death is also found in *Punch and Judy*. When the hangman comes to take Punch away, Punch mistakes most of the references to his own execution for food-and-drink words. The point is rammed home more clumsily than in the Russian texts:

> Marwood: Come up here and suffer the penalty of the law.
> Punch: I don't want to go to bed and snore.
> Marwood: Come up and suffer.
> Punch: I don't want any supper.

Marwood:	If you don't come up by fair means you will come up by foul.
Punch:	I don't like it.
Marwood:	Don't like what?
Punch:	Fowl. [...]
Punch:	Here, what's this?
Marwood:	Why, that's your coffin.
Punch:	Coffee pot? [...]
Marwood:	Now Punch, repeat this after me.
Punch:	Eat what after you? [...]
Marwood:	'Ladies and gentlemen, I have been a very bad and wicked man'.
Punch:	I want a slice of bread and jam.
Marwood:	A sentence of death has been passed upon you; you are to be hung.
Punch:	I don't like it.
Marwood:	Don't like what?
Punch:	Don't like a glass of rum.
Marwood:	No! You are to be hung up by the neck!
Punch:	By my feet?
Marwood:	No! By your neck till you are dead, dead, dead!
Punch:	Till I am bread, bread, bread![68]

The conclusion of *Petrushka* also displays carnival ambivalence in another way. Petrushka's death is not final: he will immediately be resurrected, and will begin another performance:

Odno konchaetsya – drugoe nachinaetsya. Pozhaluite, zakhodite, Petrushku posmotrite.

[One thing ends and another begins. Please come in. *Petrushka* will soon begin.]

(RND, p. 123)

The other types of verbal spectacle found at the Russian carnival – for example, the peep shows and the comic sketches – are similarly preoccupied with the physical and the extraordinary, upside-down world. There was no Russian equivalent of 'What the Butler Saw', but favourite peep-show pictures included those of a man 'who tried to put out the Kostroma fire by pissing on it' and the Russian nobles who showered beggars in the streets of

Palermo with gold when it was burning down (*RND*, pp. 125–6 and 128).

Parody was also popular. Eremin mentions that *Petrushka* often included parodies of folk songs, though he gives no details; it is possible that the two songs in Berkov's version were sung to well-known tunes.[69] There are some outstanding examples of the profanation of sacred chants in one of the plays performed at carnivals by live actors, *Tsar' Maksimilian*. Lines taken from the church burial rite were interspersed with food words:

> Svyatisya, svyatisya
> (Pirog ispekisya),
> Novyi Erusalim!
> Slava bo gospodnya
> (Korochka ispodnya)
> Na tebya vossiya.
> (Gorshok kiselya;
> Kaby lozhechka byla,
> Pokhlebal by ego,
> da i net nichego.)
>
> [Holy, holy, holy!
> (The pie is ready!)
> New Jerusalem!
> Glory to God!
> (Hell's pod)
> In the highest.
> (Fine bowl of junket,
> need a spoon to eat it,
> but spoon I have not,
> so I'll do without.)][70]

The carnival nature of *Petrushka* and the other comic fairground texts means that critical statements about structure and political meaning must be reappraised. The oxymoronic structure of *Petrushka* expresses carnival ambivalence: all things embrace their opposites. The Doctor, who is supposed to restore life, sends his patients to an early grave; a dead man becomes food for others, as a sack of potatoes. The political message of *Petrushka* is also double-edged. Many of the values espoused by the play are conservative: it is racist and sexist, and it is intolerant of anything which comes at the wrong end of Petrushka's *dubinka*. The equivocal nature of the play was recognized by the Tsarist authorities; before the Revolution puppeteers were routinely harassed, but their performances were also enjoyed tacitly by the authorities, as Zaitsev, one of the last folk puppeteers, recorded:

> The police prohibited our performances, but the prohibition was often effected only on paper, and if they felt like it, they would come along and watch our plays with enjoyment.

He relates an anecdote of how he once discovered half-way through a performance that he had set up his booth directly opposite the windows of the local police station, and that every official in the place was watching and roaring with laughter as Petrushka whacked the Policeman. Afterwards, Zaitsev records, 'the keepers of law and order made generous contributions to the collection'.[71]

Normal social rules were suspended, not overturned, in the carnival; and the social criticism does not imply profound rejection of the status quo. Krupryanskaya states that in one village the performers and audience suddenly lost their enthusiasm for the parodistic burial rites in *Tsar' Maksimilian* when the local priest suggested that if they really had so low an opinion of church funerals, they might prefer to do without one themselves.[72] The licensed profanity of the carnival did not indicate organized hostility to the political hierarchy either. As Vsevolodskii-Gerngross put it, Petrushka is not an enlightened political campaigner, but an anarchist: 'Petrushka's rebellion has no definite purpose; it is an anarchic rebellion.'[73]

How then was Petrushka to be appropriated by the agitprop theatre, which certainly did not lack a definite political purpose? Obraztsov sums up the problem:

> A sort of 'scissor-effect' came into play. If Petrushka was depicted as a drunkard and a skiver, his charming comic personality would still inspire the spectators' sympathy, and this went against the meaning of the play and its educational purpose. If the author and the producer tried to safeguard their educational purpose by stripping Petrushka of all his attractive qualities, and the spectators were forced to disapprove of his behaviour, then Petrushka would lose his essential characteristic – his role as the public's favourite, whose every action, every word

inspired approval and amusement – in other words, he would no longer be what he was in the folk puppet theatre.[74]

In order to illustrate what was done with the puppet hero, I have chosen the three agitprop puppet plays published by Eremin and meant to encourage village *kul'torgy* in their own *Petrushka* performances. The plays are *Khlop v lob* (*Crack on the Nut*) by Leo Miryanin, *Znakharstvo – debri t'my* (*Witch Doctory is the Debris of the Underworld*) by M. D. Utenkov, and *Predstavlenie lyubitel'skoe* (*An Amateur Performance*) (the full title stretches three lines) by M. Vol'pin.[75] All three plays are of similar length to the average folk theatre performance: they would probably take about half an hour to play. The simplest and closest to the prototype is *Khlop v lob*, in which Petrushka introduces himself, hits a variety of undesirables over the head with his club (including Denikin, Vrangel' and a Bourgeois), and is saved by a Teacher and a Red Army Officer from falling into the jaws of the traditional Barbos, here in a new incarnation as the *Barbos-Negramotnost'* (Cur of Illiteracy). In the second play Petrushka falls into the hands of several charlatans and quacks before being cured of his illness instantly by a Soviet Doctor. In Vol'pin's play Petrushka is peripheral to the action, on which he gives a running commentary. The play depicts the attempt by an unscrupulous merchant to bring the local co-operative into disrepute; whilst the co-operative member in charge of the shop is canoodling with the merchant's daughter, the merchant himself is busy sabotaging all the goods in the place.

The authors of all three plays have aimed to make them authentic. Some old characters, such as the Gypsy, the Doctor and the Barbos, appear; some of the new characters, such as the Merchant in Vol'pin's play, are modelled on old ones. Many of the traditional formulae appear. Miryanin's Petrushka, for example, introduces himself in the traditional manner (though his expressed intention of 'educating' is a novelty):

Ya Petrukha	[I'm Petrukha
po prozvishchu Farnos –	known as Farnose –
krasnyi nos.	the red-nose.
V kamed' igrayu,	I'll show you my comedy
vsekh zabavlyayu,	and make you all happy.
shutki shuchu,	I'll amuse you,

a koli zakhochu, –	and if I choose to
prouchu.	I'll teach you a thing or two too.]

(*TP*, p. 144)

Utenkov's Gypsy and Doctor also use traditional formulae of introduction:

Ya tsygan Mora	[I'm the Gypsy Morus
iz tsyganskogo khora,	from the Gypsy chorus,
poyu basom....	I sing bass...]
Ya znamenityi doktor-lekar',	[I'm the famous doctor-physician,
iz-pod kamennogo mosta aptekar',	the apothecary from Stone Bridge,
akusher i konoval, –	veterinary and obstetrician,
znaet menya ves' Zatsepski val.	known all along the Zatsep ditch.]

(*TP*, pp. 155, 158)

Traditional comic devices are used in all three plays. Foreigners' strange accents are mocked in Miryanin's play (English and French voices rather than the traditional German). There is a comic song to an old tune (Sten'ka Razin) in Vol'pin's play:

> Vse propalo, vse propalo,
> Akh, prikazchik, sukin syn,
> Vmesto myla budet salo,
> Vmesto sala – kerosin.
> Zadadut tebe, brat, strakhu!
> Kooperatsiya, proshchai!
> On podsypaet soli v sakhar,
> On podsypaet perets v chai.
>
> [Everything has gone to pot
> Through that bastard salesman's fault.
> There'll be lard instead of soap flakes,
> Paraffin instead of lard.
> Brother, will our life be hard!

Our co-op is bound to die.
He's mixed up the salt and sugar,
and put pepper in the tea.]

(TP, p. 170)

The imitation of the folk tradition is superficial, however. None of the writers was very skilled in mixing prose and verse in the manner of the traditional *Petrushechniki*. Miryanin's is almost entirely in prose, apart from short verse passages which stand out from the basic texts; the other two are entirely in doggerel, the effect of which is monotonous. What is more, most of the carnival elements have been excised.

The curious and distorted physique of the traditional Petrushka has been modified. In the picture reproduced by Eremin he is humpless, and, though his nose is large, his expression is kindly rather than frenziedly malevolent. The other puppets in the collection have much less emphasis on mouth, nose and cheekbones than the traditional figures of the Petrushka stage (*TP*, pp. 188 ff).[76]

The physicality of the text is played down. Petrushka has no wife, so there is no sexual horseplay. His aggression is also tempered: in Vol'pin's play he loses his *dubinka*, and becomes a passive commentator; in the other two plays he is allowed to keep the club, but commits no murders, and hits out less often than before. The witty euphemisms of the street Petrushka have gone too. Miryanin's hero hits out each time with an inane cry of 'Khlop v lob' ('Whack on the nut'). The motivation for Utenkov's Petrushka's attacks on the charlatan doctors who visit him is fairly convincing, but only once does he precede his blows by innuendo in the traditional style:

Oi, lomaet, oi, korezhit,	[Oh! I'm aching, oh I'm writhing,
Razve eta dryan' pomozhet?	That rubbish does no good at all.
Pogodi zh ty u menya	Just you wait here at my bedside,
Zagovorchik znayu ya.	I know a good spell as well.]

(TP, p. 157)

There are fewer references to physical elements and bodily

functions in these plays than in the traditional text. The prologue to Miryanin's play is self-consciously and embarrassingly vulgar, but it is not representative of the tone of the rest of the play:

> Tak seichas narod sobiraetsya, molodoi da staryi, osoblivo rebyatishki, pridut, kruzhkom stanut, ushi navostryat, burkaly vystavyat – smotryat, smotryat, i izo rta slyunki ot radosti tekut... Kto kushak poteryal, kogo mat' so slezami ishchet, *u kogo stanishki, izvinite, mokrye.*
>
> [I can see them rolling up from here, old and young, especially the kiddies, they come here and stand round me, ears pricked, eyes out on stalks – watching and watching, dribbling with delight... Someone's lost her sash; someone's lost his mother, and someone else (excuse me for saying so) *has just wet his pants.*]
>
> (*TP*, p. 145; my emphasis)

The old Petrushka would never have apologized for such an innocent remark; for the new one it is an isolated lapse from propriety.

In the new plays only the negative characters dance and kiss in the manner of Petrushka and Parashka. In Vol'pin's play Petrushka presents the activities of Nyurka and the Assistant to the public with evident disapproval:

> Ya skvoz' zanaves vizhu p'esku,
> Nedarom ya – Petrushka rasskazchik;
> Vot k lavke podkhodit prikazchik,
> A Nyurka zhdet ne dozhdetsya,
> S nogi na nogu mnetsya.
> Tselovat'sya polez. Shchekochet usami,
> Ne verite? Pozhaluista, smotrite sami.
>
> [I can see it through the curtain.
> I'm not the narrator for nothing, that's certain.
> The salesman's coming to the shop,
> Nyurka's so excited she can't wait;
> From foot to foot she goes hip-hop.
> He's creeping in to kiss her. His whiskers he twirls.
> You don't believe me? Just look, boys and girls.]
>
> (*TP*, p. 169)

In Miryanin's *Khlop v lob*, Petrushka's desire to *flirtanut'* with the Frenchwoman is used to point up the ridiculous snobbery of the White supporters, not to contribute to the characterization of him. The only other characters in this play who attempt physical contact are also negative: Aunt Sabotage and Uncle Famine, who announce their intention of 'caressing' Petrushka.

Eating and drinking are also confined to the negative characters in the three plays. In *Khlop v lob*, Denikin is portrayed as a secret tippler; in *Znakharstvo – debri t'my* the Gypsy introduces himself (as in the street text) with a reference to his favourite foods:

Poyu basom,	[I sing bass,
Zaedayu ananasom,	I wash it down with pineapple slices,
Zapivayu kvasom ...	And a draught of kvas.]

(*TP*, p. 156)

He also invites Petrushka to contribute to his household expenses with a traditional formula:

Pribavlyai rebyatishkam	[Give us a quid
Na molochishko ...	to buy milk for the kids ...]

(*TP*, p. 156)

In *Predstavlenie lyubitel'skoe* the Merchant compares his greedy and giddy daughter to a rat on the prowl:

> Kak krysa k salu, tak ty k pudram.
>
> [You go for face-powder like a rat
> For bacon-fat.]

(*TP*, p. 167)

The only other role played by food in *Predstavlenie lyubitel'skoe* is that food substances are among the goods belonging to the co-operative which Nyurka's father sabotages; but they are not differentiated in value from the other goods, and little comic play is made of them.

In summary: the only carnival elements in the three plays are insignificant, and their presence is incidental. Moreover, there is a new spirit of puritanism. In *Predstavlenie lyubitel'skoe*, physical attraction is punished by a prison sentence:

> Sud nynche strog:
> kuptsa v ostrog,
> Nyurku v ostrog.
> (Ne udalos' sukhim iz voditsy vylezti.)
> Da i prikazchiku ne bylo milosti:
> za veseloe vremyaprovozhdenie,
> za lyubovnoe pokhozhdenie,
> kak sleduet vletelo:
> baba – babo, a delo – delom.
>
> [The law's arm is long.
> The merchant gets sent down,
> Nyurku gets sent down.
> (So they didn't get away with it.)
> The salesman too was hit where it hurts:
> for his flirtations
> and time-wastations
> he got his deserts:
> no use mixing up women and work.]
>
> (*TP*, p. 173)

In *Znakharstvo – debri t'my*, the audience are urged to heed the physical, not in a hedonistic sense, but in the sense of washing behind their ears and taking regular exercise:

> Koli khotite sovsem byt' na lyudei pokhozhi, –
> nauchites' skoree gramote
> da pochashche moite rozhi,
> Ne zabyvaite i tela, –
> i togda v shlyape budet delo.
>
> [If you want to be much better,
> just make sure you know your letters;
> wash your faces every day,
> and your bodies, by the way –
> then you'll make a fine display.]
>
> (*TP*, p. 163)

The political ambivalence of the carnival text has also disappeared. Petrushka has become the mouthpiece of authority, rather than its scourge; in Miryanin's play he even joins forces with a teacher and a Red Army Officer.

In two plays written by Simonovich-Efimova, *Veselyi Petrushka* (*Merry Petrushka*) and *Bol'noi Petrushka* (*Petrushka is Sick*), and in Marshak's play for children, *Petrushka-inostranets* (*Petrushka the Foreigner*), the emphasis is different. In all three, Petrushka retains a shadow of his old anti-social spirit. Efimova's hero is greedy, cowardly and lazy; at the end of the play he celebrates his various successes with a song in praise of eating:

Vot ya i ozhil!	[So I got away!
I chut' do bedy ne dozhil.	Nearly my unlucky day!
Tram-tram-trushki,	Tram-tram-try!
El vatrushki,	I ate a pie!
Tram-tram-trom,	Tram-tram-tried!
S tvorogom.	With cheese inside!][77]

There is a comic scene in which Petrushka is visited by the doctor and, on being asked the source of his pain, mentions an archetypally carnivalesque part of his body – the belly. As in Utenkov's play, though, he displays uncharacteristic reticence, saying 'Excuse me if my language is coarse'.

Efimova's plays, and Marshak's version, have considerable charm as texts for small children. But all of them trivialize Petrushka's anti-social tendencies; he not only loses his spouse and his *dubinka*, but is transformed from a dangerously uncooperative adult into a naughty but finally tractable child. In Marshak's version the quintessence of Petrushka's rebellion is his refusal to go to school:

Sumku shkol'nuyu svoyu	[My school-bag is much too big,
Ya nadenu na svin'yu.	I will hang it on a pig.][78]

Only one new version of *Petrushka* retains the carnival spirit of the old fairground and has a hero who has not been, and never will be, tamed by Soviet society. This is *Van'ka*, performed in Voronezh in the 1920s.[79]

The play was recorded by A. M. Putintsev in 1923. The group of puppeteers who performed it were at that stage the only group in

Voronezh; their leader, M. A. Plotkin, had worked in the *balagany* since the age of nine.

The play has the plotlessness typical of the fairground genres; it is a series of more or less unlinked scenes. Many old motifs are present: Van'ka decides to marry, buys a horse, fights with and kills a series of adversaries before being dragged off by the Barbos. Van'ka's appearance resembles that of the traditional Petrushka, with a clown's hat, a hump and a hooked nose. His character is also little changed: he displays typical priapism towards his wife. One stage direction reads: 'From time to time they stop dancing, embrace, and give each other juicy-sounding kisses' (*VLB*, p. 10). He also displays the same ready aggression: the grand total is four murders in less than six pages of text. He remains quite unrepentant when rebuked by the Feed for his bad behaviour; when no one is left to bury the corpses, he is unperturbed:

Otvetchik:	Vanya! ty ishcho ubil chilaveka?
Van'ka:	[*burchit*] I etava skharanyu.
Otvetchik:	A s kem ty budesh kharanit', vit' ya ni budu.
Van'ka:	S kem? Khot' s chortam.
[Feed:	Vanya! Have you killed another person?
Van'ka:	[*under his breath*] I'll bury this one too.
Feed:	Who can you get to help you, I'm not going to, you know.
Van'ka:	Who? Why, the devil, for all I care.]

(*VLB*, p. 14)

Van'ka remains equally unperturbed when the Devil takes him at his word.

Van'ka also displays the traditional obsession with drinking and eating. As usual he demands his dowry in food and drink. He offers to bribe the Feed with alcohol for information about a horse:

Otvetchik:	A znaish, Vanya, ya znayu, u kavo loshad' kupit'.
Van'ka:	U kavo?
Otvetchik:	Dash na chai, tada skazhu.
Van'ka:	Dam tibe na butylku samagonu, skazhi tol'ka.

[Feed:	You know, Vanya, I know who'll sell you a horse.
Van'ka:	Who?
Feed:	Buy me a cup of tea, I'll tell you then.
Van'ka:	I'll buy you a whole bottle of vodka if you'll only tell me.]

(*VLB*, p. 11)

Perhaps the most outstanding reworking of a traditional motif is the mistaken-identity/food-death link, which is developed here with macabre fantasy. When Van'ka kills the Gypsy, the following exchange takes place:

Otvetchik:	Zachem ty, Vanya, cheloveka pabil. On pomir.
Van'ka:	On povar?
Otvetchik:	Net, ni povar, a pomir: povar na kukhni kartoshku zharit'.

[Feed:	Why did you kill the man, Vanya. He's copped it.
Van'ka:	He's cooked it?
Feed:	No, not cooked it, copped it; cooked it is what you do to spuds in the kitchen.]

(*VLB*, p. 11)

When Van'ka returns from burying the Gypsy and the Doctor, he announces that they have been put to use for food:

Van'ka:	Atpravili na kolbasu.
[Van'ka:	They've bin sent down the sausage factory.]

(*VLB*, p. 13)

The punishment enacted by the traditional Barbos has been made even more vicious than before: Van'ka's nose is bitten off before he is dragged away to Hell.

The politically subversive nature of the text is evident everywhere. This incarnation of Petrushka is not on the side of the angels. He announces as he arrives:

Pozdravlyayu vas s praz'nikom, s savetskim, a ni kadetskim.

[Best wishes for the 'oliday, the Sov-iet 'oliday, not the Kadet 'oliday.]

(*VLB*, p. 9)

But his actions in the play do not express much sympathy with the *savetskii praz'nik* (Soviet 'oliday). His traditional enemies, the Soldier and the Policeman, here appear in Soviet guise as the *Krasnoarmeets* (Red Army Soldier) and the *Militsioner* (Soviet Policeman). When the *Militsioner* appears and pompously enquires how the Doctor and the Gypsy died, Van'ka bribes the Feed to say: 'Eti sami umirli' ('They just went and died by themselves'); then, when he is warned that he will be sent to trial, he takes justice into his own hands:

Otvetchik: Sichas' tibe, Vanya, mil'tsianer sudit' budit'.
Van'ka: Ya iivo rassuzhu pa svoimu [*otpravlyaetsya za shirmy, vozvrashchaetsya s dubinkoi i razmakhnuvshis' ubivaet militsionera*] Vot i vsimu sudu kanets.

[Feed: Now the p'liceman'll come and judge you, Vanya.
Van'ka: I'll give him judge. [*goes off-stage, comes back with his club, whacks the Militsioner over the head and kills him*] There's an end to all judgements.]

(*VLB*, p. 13)

Shortly after liberating himself from the policeman's attentions, Van'ka is taken for a deserter by a Soldier from the Red Army, and is made to take part in impromptu military training. This has predictable results:

Krasnoarmeets: [*pokazyvaya na Van'ku*] Khto eto takoi? Dizirter? [*Van'ke*] Nu-ka stanovis' va khrunt pat ruzh'e.
Van'ka: Ni khachu i ni khachu! [*mashet golovoi i rukami*]
Krasnoarmeets: Biri, gavaryat' tibe, ruzh'e f ruki. Ni to f tribunal zabirem. [*Van'ka beret ruzh'e v ruki*]
Van'ka: Ya ne umeyu!
Krasnoarmeets: Budish umet'. Slushai moei komandi.
Van'ka: Ruzh'e u mine, kaby ni tak. Tiperich ya tibe ni bayus'. Adnim mentam zakalyu. [*Zakalyvaet na smert' krasnoarmeitsa*]

[Red Army Soldier: [*pointing at Van'ka*] Who's that then? A disserter, eh? [*To Van'ka*] Right, stand over there with this rifle, will you.

Van'ka:	Don't want to! No! [*waving his head and arms*]
Red Army Soldier:	I'm telling you to take this rifle, else we'll have you up in front of the tribunal. [*Van'ka takes the rifle*]
Van'ka:	I can't.
Red Army Soldier:	No can'ts. Now do as I say.
Van'ka:	I've got the rifle, ain't that so. Now I'm not scared of you. I'll stab you this minute. [*Bayonets the Red Army Soldier to death*]

(*VLB*, pp. 13–14)

Van'ka's cynicism is so consummate that at the end of the play, when he is seized by the Barbos, he is even prepared to call religion to his aid; and at this point, the Feed reveals that (incredibly) Van'ka has held the position of Church Elder in the parish:

Van'ka:	Atpustitya dushu na pakayaniya.
Otvetchik:	Eta ni pa modi, Vanyusha, kaiitsya. A tibe vprot'chim nada: ty, vit', f zhivetskai tserkvi titaram sastaish.
[Van'ka:	Release my soul that I may repent.
Feed:	Tisn't in fashion, Vanyusha, repentance isn't. But then again, you'd better, hadn't you, after all you're the Parish Church Elder.]

(*VLB*, p. 14)

The neologisms in *Van'ka* add to the comedy. Van'ka has been in Germany, but has returned home to find a suitable bride – a *papova doch'*. Twice when he attempts to bribe the Feed he offers payments of a newfangled sort: 'Ya tibe veksil' vyshlyu pa radii' ('I'll send you a cheque over the radio') and ten roubles 'pa zalatomu kursu' ('at the gold rate') (*VLB*, pp. 10, 12).

The analysis of *Van'ka* has made two important points clear. The puppet theatre cannot be modernized without respect for its innate conservatism. In Russia the modernizations were imposed from outside, by literate authors who had little experience of or respect for the pre-literate puppet theatre, except as a vehicle for their alien political message. In Britain, France and Italy, much more successful innovations have been made by those who have come to the traditional glove puppet theatre from inside, as operators and improvisers. They have heeded one guideline: the subsidiary characters and the puppet hero's adversaries may be modernized, but the protagonist must remain unchanged, or the text becomes unrecognizable.

The second essential of modernization is that the carnival elements should be recognized and respected. The carnival tradition is naturally aggressive and subversive; it is drama for independent adults, who are treated as equals with the puppeteer, not patronized and hectored. It is drama which engages with authoritarian political or literary discourse. The failure of the Russian agitprop puppet theatre was due to a refusal to recognize the absurdity of harnessing the Petrushka text whilst neutralizing its disturbing qualities, a refusal to recognize that, in Dana Polan's words, 'Popular culture, as Bakhtin invokes it and as it operates today, is a complex form that is accessible to logocentrism and monologism only at the cost of critical reduction.'[80] Bakhtin's book on Rabelais, which apparently ignores the Russian carnival, is in fact a monument to it constructed at the moment when the fairground tradition was about to vanish underground, to exist only in overlooked lapses, manifesting its presence insidiously in the texts and actions of authoritarianism.[81]

NOTES AND REFERENCES

My thanks to John Blundall, Director of the Cannon Hill Puppet Theatre, Birmingham, the staff of the Puppet Centre Trust, London, Adam Noble, and John Richmond for *tsennye ukazaniya*.

1. Mikhail Bakhtin, Rabelais and His World, trans. Hélène Iswolsky, Bloomington, Indiana, 1984, pp. 218–19.
2. V. D. Kuz'mina, *Russkii demokraticheskii teatr XVIII veka*, Moscow, 1958, p. 52.
3. On the origins of the dancing bears, mumming shows, and other carnival activities in the displays of the *skomorokhi*, see Russell Zguta, *Russian Minstrels*, Oxford, 1978, pp. 103–21.
4. For a detailed description of the Russian fairs, see A. Ya. Alekseev-Yakovlev, *Russkie narodnye gulyan'ya*, Moscow, Leningrad, 1948,

especially chapter 1; A. F. Nekrylova, *Russkie narodnye gorodskie prazdniki*, Leningrad, 1984; and A. M. Konechnyi, 'Peterburgskie balagany', *Panorama iskusstv*, Moscow, 8, 1985, pp. 383–95.
5. *The Voyages and Travels of the Ambassadors by Adam Olearius*, rendered into English by John Davies of Kidwelly, London, 1662, pp. 81–2.
6. Aleksandr Benua (=Benois), *Moi vospominaniya*, vol. 1, Moscow, 1980, p. 289.
7. Bronislava Nijinska, *Early Memories*, London, 1982, p. 30.
8. Nina Simonovich-Efimova, *Zapiski petrushechnika*, Leningrad, 1980, p. 182.
9. Ibid, p. 181.
10. V. N. Vsevolodskii-Gerngross, 'Nachalo tsirka v Rossii', in *O teatre vremennik otdela istorii teatra Gosudarstvennogo instituta iskusstv*, Leningrad, 2, 1926, p. 71.
11. Simonovich-Efimova, p. 119.
12. Lev Shcheglov, 'Sel'skaya yarmarka i Petrushka Uksusov', *Narod i teatr*, St Petersburg (1911), pp. 109–30.
13. Alekseev-Yakovlev, p. 49.
14. Quoted in *Istoriya russkogo dramaticheskogo teatra v semi tomakh*, vol. 6, Moscow, 1982, p. 289.
15. A. V. Lunacharskii, 'O tsirkakh', in *O teatre i dramaturgii*, vol. 1, Moscow, 1958, p. 458.
16. Lunacharskii, 'O narodnykh prazdnestvakh', ibid, pp. 191, 193.
17. Alekseev-Yakovlev, p. 164.
18. Sergei Obraztsov, *Moya professiya*, Moscow, 1982, p. 74, writes: 'How moribund and false are the works of those amongst our contemporaries who imitate the "primitives" in their painting and sculpture.' On the disappearance of the folk puppet tradition by 1940, see also Yu. M. Sokolov, *Russkii fol'klor*, Moscow, 1941, p. 378.
19. Robert Leach, *The Punch and Judy Show*, London, 1984, pp. 148–9.
20. David Braithwaite, *Fairground Architecture*, London, 1968, p. 20.
21. Tim and Amanda Webb, 'The Puppet Theatre in China Today', *Animations*, 1, 1985, p. 9.
22. Bakhtin, p. xi.
23. On the carnivals of 1918 and 1919, see N. I. Smirnova, *Sovetskii teatr kukol 1918–1932*, Moscow, 1963, pp. 122, 149; a photograph of the Efimovs' *agitfurgon* is reproduced in *Les Cahiers de la Marionette*, 3, September 1985.
24. František Deák, 'Blue Blouse', *Drama Review*, 17/1, 1975, p. 43; Elizabeth Warner, *The Russian Folk Theatre*, The Hague, Paris, 1977, p. 198.
25. Smirnova, p. 249. Smirnova's book is overtly tendentious, indeed at times homiletic, but it is by far the fullest available study of the agitprop puppet theatre.
26. Smirnova, p. 74.
27. For example, G. Tarasov, *Petrushka v shkole i v pionerskom otryade*, Moscow, 1930; Igor' Eremin and Orest Tsekhnovitser, *Teatr Petrushki*, Moscow, Leningrad, 1927; numerous articles by diverse authors in the journals *Klub* and *Krasnaya nov'*.

28. V. Markov and N. Nadezhdin manufactured sets of ten puppets which could be adapted by individual clubs (see Smirnova, p. 273).
29. Smirnova, p. 258.
30. E. Uvarova, *Estradnyi teatr: miniatyury, obozreniya, myuzik-kholly 1917–1945*, Moscow, 1983, p. 132.
31. Smirnova, p. 261.
32. Obraztsov, pp. 199–200.
33. This sketch has been widely reproduced. A clearer reproduction than most is in Sokolov, p. 379.
34. 'Raeshnik po vsem frontam', in *Krasnoarmeiskii fol'klor, sbornik*, Moscow, 1938.
35. For colour reproductions of Zaitsev's string and glove puppet Petrushka, see Obraztsov, pp. 72–3; good colour photographs of some traditional puppets appear also in the guide book to the Moscow Central State Puppet Theatre Museum.
36. The Petrushka most familiar to Westerners, the hero of the Stravinsky-Benois ballet, does not remotely resemble his namesake in either appearance or character; he is based on the French Pierrot – Commedia dell'arte Pedrolino, who is a sad dupe, not an aggressive scoundrel.
37. The only reference to Petrushka and his wife fighting is under the Petrushka entry in *Entsiklopedicheskii slovar' Brokgauza i Efrona*, vol. 23, St Petersburg, 1898, p. 481.
38. For a full list of the characters, see Eremin and Tsekhnovitser, pp. 56–9.
39. Zigfrid (=Siegfried) Ashkenazi, 'Bessmertnyi Petrushka', *Ezhegodnik imperatorskikh teatrov*, 4, 1914, pp. 1–18.
40. Benua, vol. 2, p. 522.
41. P. N. Berkov, *Russkaya narodnaya drama XVII–XX vekov*, Moscow, 1953, p. 21.
42. Maksim Gor'kii, *Sobranie sochinenii v tridtsati tomakh*, vol. 23, Moscow, 1953, p. 494.
43. Smirnova, p. 37; V. Yu. Krupryanskaya, 'Narodnyi teatr', in P. G. Bogatyrev, *Russkoe narodnoe poeticheskoe tvorchestvo*, Moscow, 1954, p. 410.
44. Quoted in Smirnova, p. 25.
45. Bogatyrev, *Cheshskii kukol'nyi i russkii narodnyi teatr*, Berlin, Petersburg, 1923; 'Khudozhestvennye sredstva v yumoristicheskom yarmarochnom fol'klore', in his *Voprosy teorii narodnogo iskusstva*, Moscow, 1971, pp. 450–97; Nekrylova, 'Zakon kontrasta v poetike russkogo narodnogo kukol'nogo teatra Petrushka', *Problemy khudozhestvennoi formy*, 14, 1974, pp. 210–18.
46. Bakhtin, p. 251.
47. Ibid, pp. 309, 423.
48. Simonovich-Efimova, p. 130.
49. Berkov, p. 338.
50. Simonovich-Efimova, p. 129.
51. D. A. Rovinskii, *Russkie narodnye kartinki*, vol. 4, St Petersburg, 1881, p. 212.

52. 'Petrushka, on zhe Van'ka-Ratatui', Berkov, pp. 115–24; all future references to this variant in text (*RND*, p. 115, etc.).
53. Bakhtin, p. 317.
54. As in Obraztsov's performance of Mayakovskii's 'Otnoshenie k baryshne' (see *Les marionettes*, ed. Paul Fournel, Paris, 1982, p. 73).
55. Eremin and Tsekhnovitser, p. 61.
56. Rovinskii, *Russkie narodnye kartinki* (2nd edn), vol. 1, St Petersburg, 1900, pp. 363–4.
57. Nekrylova, 'Zakon kontrasta', p. 217.
58. Ibid, p. 213.
59. Eremin and Tsekhnovitser, p. 70.
60. Bakhtin, p. 281.
61. Warner, p. 114.
62. Nekrylova, 'Zakon kontrasta', p. 218.
63. Eremin and Tsekhnovitser, pp. 70–1.
64. Nekrylova, 'Zakon kontrasta', p. 213.
65. Ibid, p. 216.
66. Eremin and Tsekhnovitser, p. 69.
67. Bakhtin, p. 195.
68. Professor Smith's version, quoted in Michael Byrom, *Punch and Judy, its Origins and Evolution* (2nd edn), London, 1978, pp. 53–4.
69. Eremin and Tsekhnovitser, p. 71.
70. V. Krivonosov and L. Kulakovskii, 'Tsar' Maksimilian', in *Sovetskaya muzyka*, 7, 1939, pp. 37–8.
71. Quoted by Smirnova, p. 39.
72. Krupryanskaya, p. 410.
73. Vsevolodskii-Gerngross, *Russkaya ustnaya narodnaya drama*, Moscow, 1959, p. 115.
74. Obraztsov, pp. 198–9.
75. Eremin and Tseknovitser, pp. 144–74; all further references to this edition in text (*TP*, p. 144, etc.).
76. Photographs of the Petrushki used by various agitprop collectives can be seen in *Les Cahiers de la Marionette*, 3, September 1985; only that belonging to the *Teatr detskoi knigi* recalls the prototype.
77. Simonovich-Efimova, p. 152.
78. S. Marshak, *Skazki, pesni, zagadki* ... etc., Moscow, 1981, p. 175.
79. 'Van'ka' in *Voronezhskaya literaturnaya beseda*, 1, 1925, pp. 5–15; henceforth in text (*VLB*, p. 5, etc.). The Southern dialect forms – *akan'e*, soft-ending third-person verbs, fricative *g* – are given as in Putintsev's transcription.
80. See Dana Polan's contribution to this volume, p. 16.
81. 'Even the outward attributes of the *oprichnina* had some carnival aspects' (Bakhtin, p. 270). This is clearly a subtextual reference to the grotesque absurdity of Stalin's reign of terror, which could indeed be seen as carnival turned on its head.

Part III
Sexuality

6
Text and Violence in Tsvetaeva's *Molodets*

Michael Makin

Marina Tsvetaeva's narrative poem *Molodets* (*The Swain*) has received relatively little critical attention.[1] Yet it is the second longest work of narrative poetry completed and published by the poet; it was written at the height of her powers; and it displays some of the most important features of her poetics and her relations to traditions and genres. Commentators who have paused over it have described those features only in general terms, concluding that *Molodets* is an original but unproblematic example of a traditional form. Such a conclusion, emphasizing the continuity of tradition, ignores the radical modifications of familiar elements and the moments of dislocation and discontinuity (thematic and formal) which can also be seen in *Molodets*. If these features are examined, a quite different reading can be produced.

As the stress (*Mólodets*) and the subtitle (*skazka* (*folk tale*)) suggest, it is based on Russian folk motifs. Russian folk literature (that is, literature composed, transmitted, and performed orally), ranging from the epic *bylina* (heroic narrative poem) to the aphoristic *chastushka* (rhyming, comic verse), has long attracted producers of *belles lettres* (that is, the work of literate authors, writing for an educated and literate public). The incorporation of folklore, with its vitality and popular, often specifically national, features, into written, 'high' literature has played an important part in the development of Russian prose and poetry. The forms of incorporation have been determined by the ways in which the poetics of folklore have been understood, and by the changing attitudes to its apparently lowly and naïve forms. As knowledge of folk literature has increased, so the tendency to imitate closely or to distort self-consciously has grown.

In the early nineteenth century there was intense interest in folk literature, exemplified by such appropriations as the literary ballad.[2] Another product of this interest was the *poema-skazka* of the 1830s which amalgamated the *poema* (narrative poem) of *belles lettres* with the *skazka*. The *poema-skazka* was distinguished from other contemporary treatments of folklore by its more scrupulous attention to the specific devices and narratives of its popular prototype.[3] It flowered briefly. The main examples of the 'classical' *poema-skazka* were, with one exception, written in the early 1830s, and by three writers: Pushkin's 'Skazka o pope i o rabotnike ego Balde' ('Tale of the Priest and his Worker Balda') (1830), 'Skazka o tsare Saltane' ('Tale of Tsar Saltan') (1831), 'Skazka o rybake i rybke' ('Tale of the Fisherman and the Fish') (1833), 'Skazka o mertvoi tsarevne i o semi bogatyryakh' ('Tale of the Dead Princess and the Seven Warriors') (1833), 'Skazka o zolotom petushke' ('Tale of the Golden Cockerel') (1834); Zhukovskii's 'Skazka o tsare Berendee' ('Tale of Tsar Berendei') (1831), 'Spyashchaya tsarevna' ('The Sleeping Princess') (1831), 'Skazka o Ivane-tsareviche i o Serom Volke' ('Tale of Tsarevich Ivan and the Grey Wolf') (1845); Ershov's 'Konek-gorbunok' ('The Hunchback Horse') (1834).[4]

There were, of course, narrative poems employing motifs from folk tales both before and after this period, but they were quite different in character. The 'classical' *poema-skazka* discussed here can be distinguished from earlier and later versions by its coherence of tone and purely literary motivation. Its principal purpose was to turn folklore into *belles lettres* – to make the popular acceptable, indeed, recognizable as literature. Earlier works such as Pushkin's 'Tsar' Nikita i ego sorok docherei' ('Tsar Nikita and his Forty Daughters') (1822), or the later works of Yazykov, Nekrasov, Basov-Verkhoyantsev, and others, are quite different in character: folk motifs (or, in some later works, borrowings from earlier *poemy-skazki*) are used to motivate pornography, parody, or political commentary (in other words, such works state their peripheral literary function by resort to the folkloric).[5] The classical version aimed to reproduce the simplicity of the folk tale as manifested in its obvious devices (repetition, parallelism, etc.), but in literary form. The charming but crude naïveté of the folk tale was ennobled by verse, and by the removal of embarrassing inconsistencies. The folk tale, frequently combining quite disparate elements and in no sense the fixed work of a single author, was converted by judicious editing and the application of the aesthetic criteria of *belles lettres* into an apparently seamless work.

Both supporters and detractors of these first *poemy-skazki* commented on what they saw as the close resemblance of the new works to authentic folk tales.[6] Pushkin's works, when first published, were regarded by many as 'too authentic' – as mere reproductions of the original. But this was because they were perceived against the background of previous, more cavalier treatments of folklore. In fact, the works of Pushkin, Zhukovskii, and Ershov combine many different stories, use plots from the folklore of other nations, and radically modify the originals to render them acceptable high literature.[7] Indeed, the verse which contributes most to the ennobling of the lowly, popular form underlines how far the *poema-skazka* has strayed from its folkloric sources: Russian folk tales are recorded almost exclusively in prose. Zhukovskii's hexameters in 'Tsar' Berendei' are but an extreme version of the use of literary metre to render the original material more regular and acceptable. Of the works listed above only Pushkin's 'Pop i Balda' uses a genuinely popular verse from (the *raeshnik*).[8] By the modification of incoherent plots, and the addition of complex, psychological motivation, the original was absorbed into literature, was made palatable. The attention paid to popular devices certainly marked these works as novel treatments of folklore, but they remained unashamedly literary.

However, attitudes to folklore were changing fast, and the *poema-skazka* was soon superseded. Writers with a native familiarity with folklore (Kol'tsov, for example) were emerging; folklore was receiving more scholarly attention. Vladimir Dal', who recorded and collected many folk tales in the 1830s and 1840s, had felt unable to publish them as they were, but, in the 1850s and 1860s, Afanas'ev, using the manuscripts of Dal' and others, brought out his *Narodnye russkie skazki* (*Popular Russian Tales*), reproducing the originals with relatively few modifications.[9] By then it was harder to treat folklore simply as an impoverished relative of *belles lettres*, obliged to regard any attention as an honour. Mei, for example, when imitating folkloric poetry in his 'Predanie otchego perevelis' vityazi na svyatoi Rusi' ('Legend about how Knights Died out in Holy Russia') (1856), employed explicitly popular irregular versification and plot motifs and equipped his version with footnotes.[10]

Close, semi-scholarly imitation became the dominant means of appropriating folklore to *belles lettres*. Literary reworking aimed to remove the inconsistencies and *lacunae* of the original, but not to change radically the overall form of the source, nor to add literary complexities of plot, psychology, or device. Tsvetaeva's contemporaries provide apposite examples: Remizov's tales in *Posolon'* (*By the Course of the Sun*) (published 1907) are in prose and match their popular prototypes in brevity and psychological simplicity, adding only the literary virtues of greater stylistic and narrative coherence; Kuzmin's 'Dukhovnye stikhi' ('Spiritual verses') in *Osennie ozera* (*Autumn Lakes*) (published 1912) are a similar example from contemporary poetry, being very close imitations of folk works. Conversely, Sologub's *Nochnye plyaski* (*Night Dances*) (1908) takes great liberties with its popular source, turning a folk tale into a three-act drama with complex plot and characterization. But the play self-consciously exploits the distance between itself and its source, with pantomime references to the twentieth century and the introduction of elements inconsistent with the never-never-land of the folk tale.[11]

In other words, by Tsvetaeva's time the innocent *poema-skazka* of Pushkin, Zhukovskii, and Ershov was an 'impossible' genre. Too much was known of folklore for such an unselfconscious literary form to continue to exist. Contemporary literary versions of folklore tended either to preserve the form and style of their sources with care, disposing merely of the untidiness characteristic of oral works, or else to rework them self-consciously for parodic or similar effects.

Tsvetaeva, however, does the impossible. *Molodets* is a long treatment in verse of a short source recorded in prose; it incorporates disparate materials and devices; its subtitle, *skazka*, implies the abolition of the problematic differences between folklore and *belles lettres*, and suggests that the innocent appropriation of a popular source is as natural in the 1920s as in the 1830s. Thus, it invites a reading through the original *poemy-skazki* and against contemporary treatments of folklore. At the same time, it is as different from those literary prototypes as from the meticulous latterday versions of folklore by Remizov and Kuzmin. The appeal to tradition is accompanied by a subversion of tradition; the conflict with modernity by many features of modernism.

Molodets was written in 1922, the year when Tsvetaeva left Russia, and was published in Prague in 1924.[12] It has since appeared in two Western photo-reprints, and in the fourth volume of her American collected works, but it has never been published in the Soviet Union.[13] It is the last of her three completed narrative poems based on Russian folklore. These three works (the other two are *Tsar'-Devitsa* (*Tsar-Maiden*) (1920), her first *poema-skazka*, and 'Pereulochki' ('Sidestreets') (1922)) represent the culmination of her interest in folklore, an interest first expressed in her third major lyric collection, *Yunosheskie stikhi* (*Juvenilia*), containing poems written between 1912 and 1915.[14] In 1920–21 and again in 1928 she worked on another narrative poem based on Russian folklore, the lengthy 'Egorushka', but she never completed it, and only fragments have been published.[15]

All of Tsvetaeva's folk-based work illustrates the contradictory relationship between her poetry and the literary traditions and conventions to which it refers. *Molodets* is of particular interest, as a vivid and sophisticated example. Whereas the other three texts refer specifically to Russian folklore and *belles lettres*, *Molodets* is based on a story encountered throughout European folklore, and in many literary adaptations, thus emphasizing the eschewal of scholarly obscurity, and the choice of canonical themes. *Molodets* is, moreover, a significant example of the revision of other literary and sexual conventions.[16]

Its story is that of the vampire, and the version used as a source is the tale 'Upyr'' ('The Vampire') in Afanas'ev's collection.[17] This tale combines the basic vampire story with another motif: the flower which turns into a beautiful girl. Stories of diabolical or predatory fiancés and lovers are found in Russian *belles lettres*: Zhukovskii's 'Svetlana' (1812) is the most famous. Vampire tales are also common, as in Pushkin's free translations of Mérimée, 'Marko Yakubovich' and (a comic version) 'Vurdalak' in 'Pesni zapadnykh slavyan' ('Songs of the Western Slavs') (1834). The combination of the two produces a sexual myth frequently exploited in romanticism, and later, as will be shown.

'Upyr'' tells of a village girl, Marusya, who is betrothed to a *dobryi molodets* ('good swain') whom she meets while celebrating the feast of St Andrew the Apostle. He lavishes gifts on Marusya and her friends. Marusya, on her mother's advice, follows her new fiancé after their next meeting. He goes to the church, where, to her horror, she sees him eating a corpse laid out there. She rushes home in terror, but does not reveal what she has seen. Persuaded by her mother and her girlfriends, she spends the following evening with the young man. As they part at the end of the evening he asks her if she saw him in the church. Upon hearing her denial he says that her father will die the next day, and then vanishes. After her father's death she again rejoins her girlfriends, and again encounters the young man (now described as 'nechistyi' ('ungodly'). At the end of the evening he asks her the same question, and she gives the same reply. He foretells her mother's death and vanishes. Her mother dies, Marusya sees him again, and this time he predicts her own death. She seeks the advice of her aged grandmother, who tells her that after her death her body must be carried out of the *izba* beneath the threshold and buried at the crossroads. Marusya instructs the village priest accordingly, goes home, and dies. Shortly afterwards a young nobleman passes her roadside grave and sees a beautiful flower on it. He instructs his servant to dig it up and they take it home. One night the servant sees the flower fall off the plant, turn into a beautiful girl, and wander round the house. She helps herself to food, and then resumes floral shape. The next night the nobleman joins his servant to keep watch. When the same transformation takes place he seizes the girl. He decides to marry her. She consents on condition that she does not go to church for four years. After two years of conjugal bliss the nobleman ill-advisedly boasts of his wife's beauty to some guests. They object that she is not baptized. He orders her to accompany him to church. There she encounters the *nechistyi* again. After the usual dialogue he predicts the death of both her husband and her son. She rushes off to consult her grandmother, who provides the necessary holy and 'living' water. When husband and son both die, as predicted, the vampire flies in and asks his usual questions. This time Marusya answers that she was at the church, and did see what he was doing ('mertvogo zhral! ('you were munching the dead!')). She destroys the vampire by splashing him with holy water, revives her husband and son with the 'living' water, and lives with them happily ever after.

As this account illustrates, the folk tale itself is indifferent to the literary values of verisimilitude, causality, and narrative unity. There is no motivation for the vampire's insistent inquiries, nor for Marusya's silence, which is a 'retardation device', prolonging the story by postponing the inevitable conclusion. The grandmother, for example, is introduced without any preparation, after Marusya's father and mother have already died:

Marusya perenochevala s podrugami, poutru vstala i dumaet: chto ei delat'? Vspomnila, chto u nei est' babka – staraya-staraya, uzh oslepla ot dolgikh let. 'Poidu ya k nei, posovetuyus''.[18]

[Marusya spent the night with her girlfriends, rose in the morning and thought: what should she do? She remembered that she had a grandmother, very old, blind from age. 'I will go to her for advice.']

No explanation is given for the apparent links between the vampire and the deaths of the various characters: his predictions are simply fulfilled the next day. The priest carries out Marusya's instructions about her burial without comment, even though they mark her as *nechistaya*. One night she turns back into a flower, the next she remains in human shape with the *barich* (lordling). Such 'problems' do not exist for the folk tale – they stem from questions which it does not ask itself.

Molodets follows the outline of the source very closely (in contrast to *Tsar'-Devitsa* and 'Egorushka'), leading Karlinsky to speak of its 'utmost fidelity' to its source.[19] However, many of the familiar operations of literary appropriation are performed on details.

Molodets is divided into two parts, each of five cantos. The first part tells the story of Marusya's meeting with the vampire and the consequent deaths, concluding with her burial. The second tells the story of Marusya and the nobleman. The plot is tidier than the folk tale's: redundant details are removed; explanation added. The vampire's role in the three deaths is made explicit: he kills his victims in the time-honoured way. The grandmother is removed, her burial instructions to the heroine now provided by the vampire himself. The *barich* prevents Marusya's return to floral form by making the sign of the cross over her. Most important of all, psychological motivation is added: in the folk tale things 'just happen'; in *Molodets* they are explained. Thus, the silence of the heroine and the persistence of the vampire are motivated: she will not reveal the truth for love, he is attracted to her for the same reason, therefore offering her every opportunity to save herself, and then escape damnation. Tsvetaeva herself explained what she did to the story in her article 'Poet o kritike' ('A Poet on Criticism'):

I read Afanas'ev's tale 'The Vampire' and wondered why Marusya, who feared the vampire, so stubbornly refused to acknowledge what she had seen, knowing that to name him is to be saved. ... Fear? ... No, not fear ... Love. Marusya loved the vampire, and that is why she did not name him ...

That was my task, when I was working on 'The Swain'. To reveal the essence of the folk tale, which it gives in outline. To undo its spell.[20]

From this account it might be assumed that the folk tale had been reworked in the standard literary way: causality is introduced, although the outline of the story remains the same. But this apparently conventional approach leads in fact to a radical subversion of the conventions on which it draws. The standard vampire tale is the tale of a predatory or diabolical lover, whose prey is an innocent girl. In literary versions such tales become accounts of sexual power, repression, and anxiety: the heroine's loss of virginity is represented as a male bloodsucking, facilitated by diabolical bewitchment, and leading inevitably, and, in terms of the sexual myth, appropriately, to death.

In *Molodets* this sexual myth is subverted: Marusya, far from being a passive victim, is a willing lover, more open to desire than the hesitant vampire. She welcomes physical attraction throughout the story, while the vampire resists it in maidenly fashion. Subversion and rebellion culminate in the final episode, when *Molodets* parts company from its source and from its literary archetype: the heroine, far from destroying the vampire (acting on the advice of her elders and betters) and living happily ever after with her husband, as the original has it, or finding herself eternally damned at the very least, rejects conventional solutions: she prefers the vampire to her nobleman, and flies off with him 'v ogn' sin'' ('into the blue'). In other words, the very logic of literary rewriting, which demands the addition of psychological motivation, leads not to the elaboration of the story in terms of the usual sexual and literary stereotypes, but to a violent subversion of those stereotypes. A tale which provides a myth of sexual repression and male fantasy (with the subliminal message that women are the objects of uncontrollable male desire, losing their lives with their virginity when they fall victim to that desire) has been reversed by the very features which might have been expected to elaborate the basic myth.

The radical nature of this rewriting can be illustrated by comparing *Molodets* with Remizov's literary version of a vampire tale. His 'Upyr'' in *Posolon'* takes no such liberties. The form and style of a folk tale are closely followed: 'Upyr'' is brief and in prose. The status of this treatment was clearly established when 'Upyr'' appeared with a short scholarly note about vampires in Remizov's collected works.[21] Remizov's tales are tidy, literary versions of the folk original: as Shane writes, 'Remizov frequently amplified details or inserted additions which unified and emphasized the sense, imagery and setting of the original text'.[22] In other words, the literary reworking helps the tale to state more clearly what it is supposedly struggling to say in the original form: such is the purpose of the traditional literary appropriations of folklore to which *Molodets* refers in form and theme, but which, simultaneously, it subverts. In Remizov's 'Upyr'' genteel eroticism is emphasized: the heroine, Princess Chuchelka, is the vampire's passive victim:

> I nadela tsarevna belye plat'ya, zhemchug, – vyshla. Vyshla tsarevna. I v krugu mertvetsov zamerla.
> A! kak obradovan mertvyi zhivomu!
> – Ya tebe veren za grobom, tseloval tsarevnu mertvyi tsarevich i s potseluem zhivaya krov' ubyvala – teplaya krovka tekla v ego kholodnye zhily.

[The princess put on her white robes and pearls and went out. Out she went. And froze among the corpses.
Ah! how the dead delight in the living!
'I am faithful to you beyond the grave', said the dead prince, kissing the princess, and with his kiss her living blood departed – warm blood flowed into his cold veins.][23]

The eroticism of *Molodets* is quite different: after a moment of hesitation Marusya welcomes the vampire. Far from a cowering victim, she is an active participant in the resolution of her own destiny:

> – Splyu, ne trozh'!
> – Zhzhem-ne zhdem!
> Vkrug roskoshestva –
> Shmelem.
>
> Chas da nash,
> Ad moi al!
> K samoi chashechke
> Pripal.

– Konets tvoim rudam!
– Gudom, gudom, gudom!

– Konets tvoim alym!
Zhalom, zhalom, zhalom!

– Ai – zhal'?
– Zlei – zhal'!
S dnom pei,
Ai, shmel'!

Vo – ves'
Svoi – khmel'
Pei, shmel'!
Ai, shmel'!

[– I sleep, hands off!
– We buzz, won't wait!
As round luxuriance
A bumble-bee.

The hour is ours,
My scarlet hell!
Upon the goblet
He fell.

– An end to your deposits!
With humming, humming, humming!

– An end to their scarlet!
With stinging, stinging, stinging!

– Ah – you're sore?
– No, sting – more!
Drink all
My bee!

Quaff – deep
Be – drunk
Drink, bee,
Ah, bee!]   (pp. 109–10)

Sexual pleasure is asserted against the conventions of familial and social order. Marusya refuses to obey conventional demands, sacrificing her family to her sensual love for the vampire.

A small but significant change has been made to the source here: in *Molodets*, Marusya sacrifices her brother, not her father (as in the folk tale): there is no mention of her father at all. The removal from the story of the traditional source and agent of family power, whose role in restricting and defining a daughter's character is especially large, suggests that a psychoanalytical reading would also conclude that in *Molodets* female sexuality is freed from its conventional restraints.[24]

Aikhenval'd, whose criticism of *Molodets* annoyed Tsvetaeva, complained of its 'alogika smysla' ('alogism in meaning'): linguistic virtuosity ('logika zvuka', 'logic of sound') had taken the place of meaning as conveyed in the transparent language of the classical *poema-skazka*.[25] Here it has been argued that the story of *Molodets* is, on the contrary, very logical (the rewriting has rendered the source 'literary', neat and tidy, with all the necessary motivation and psychological explanation), but, of course, the logic is subversive, and ironic (disappointing the expectations which literary reworkings of this theme excite), and is allied with, not opposed to, Aikhenval'd's *logika zvuka*. Just as the heroine frees herself from the constraints of social and sexual conventions, explicit in her marriage to the *barin* (lord, master), so too the language of *Molodets* frees itself from the demands of conventional linguistic order. No longer a transparent (and, therefore, passive) conveyor of meaning, language itself is a sensual object, to be enjoyed in its own right, on its own terms.

Whereas the plot and story of *Molodets* are simple and linear, the narration is indirect and difficult. Verbs are omitted, parataxis and parallelism replace the standard expressions of narrative causality; where verbs are present, conjunctions are missing, and so on. This is especially evident in such climactic scenes as the consummation, quoted in part above. In the twelve lines from 'Konets tvoim rudam' to 'Ai shmel''! there are no finite verbs. The passage also illustrates the disturbing polyphony of *Molodets*: the narrative voice is but one of many, and is often submerged by others, some choral, some clearly belonging to participants in the story. Dismembered, unidentified voices often interrupt and contradict one another, subverting the putative fixity of the narrative. At other times, as in the extract above, the passage from one voice to another is not announced, nor marked typographically. The first and second lines of the first and second stanzas, for example, are evidently spoken by Marusya and the vampire, the third and fourth lines belong to the narrative. But this is not clear until the fourth line of the second stanza, with its narrative statement 'pripal' ('he fell').

Another illustration of the association of the breaking of linguistic constraints with the transgression of other norms is provided by the culmination of the second part of *Molodets*, when the heroine travels to church, meets the vampire again, and abandons her husband and son. Indeed, her final words to her husband explicitly announce her rejection of him as the conventional choice: 'proshchai syten'kii' ('farewell well-fed') (p. 149). On their way to church, and during the service, voices belonging to or suggestive of the vampire are heard, mocking the world of the *barin* and of the orthodox liturgy.[26] Moreover, it is made clear that Marusya's rebellion is social, as well as sexual, by the claims of ownership made by her husband during the journey to church:

> Pishi, idoly, belo:
> Nashei milosti – selo!
> Kivni, milaya, v bobry!
> Nashei milosti – raby!
>
> Ch'i khaty? – Barinovy!
> Lo-paty? – Barinovy!
> Za-platy? – Barinovy!
> Re-byaty? – Barinovy!
>
> Moi – khaty,
> Moi – traty,
> Ottsom vzyato,
> Bogu svyato.
>
> – Sapozhki valenye!
> Ch'i nozhki? – Barinovy!
> – Se-rezhki darenye,
> Ch'i nochki? – Barinovy!
>
> Moi strakhi,
> Moi khripy,
> Tsarem shito,
> Bogom kryto.
>
> – Ei, gusi zharenye!
> Ch'i gusi? – Barinovy!
> – Ei, ruki rzhavlennye!
> Ch'i Rusi? – Barinovy!

[Write, you fools, in black and white:
Of our indulgence – this the site!
Bow, my dear, in beaver furs!
Of our indulgence – these the serfs!

Whose hovels? – Master's!
Whose sho-vels? – Master's!
Whose pa-tches? – Master's!
Whose la-ddies? – Master's!

Mine – the hovels,
Mine – the losses.
Father wrested
God blessed them.

– Booties of felt!
Whose legs? – Master's!
– Earrings presented
Whose nights? – Master's!

My fears,
My moans,
Tsar-sewn,
God-smeared.

– Hey, fried ganders!
Whose ganders? – Master's!
– Hey, rusted members!
Whose Russias? – Master's! (p. 144)

Similar disruptions are worked on the fabric of language itself: non-standard stresses and morphological forms are common. Such disruptions are often given especial prominence, for example, by providing the standard form in the same line:

Pòkatim-pokàtim
K obedne-k obedne!
Pòkatim-pokàtim
K prìchast'yu-k prichàst'yu!

[Lèt's go-let's gò
To mass-to mass!
Lèt's go-let's gò
To còmmunion-commùnion!] (p.141)

In these lines another device common in *Molodets* is seen: the joining of words by the dash. It is distantly reminiscent of folk literature, but is employed here to join disparate (not similar, as in folklore) elements. Furthermore, its disruptive function is emphasized by the fact that the same typographical device is also used (sometimes in adjoining lines or stanzas) to divide words into their constituent syllables (implying a multiple stress, impossible in standard Russian):

> – Polno-grudye!
> Kruto-plechie!
> – Pona-dumalos',
> Pri-mereshchilos'!
>
> Vstavai prakhom, vstavai pyl'yu,
> Vstavai pamyat'yu so lba!
> Uzh ty krest-raz"ezd-razvil'e-
> Razdorozh'itse-sud'ba!
>
> [– Full-breasted!
> Tight-shouldered!
> – Just o-ccurring,
> Just su-ggested!
>
> Rise in ashes, rise in dust,
> Rise in memory off the pate!
> Oh, you cross-dispersal-forking-
> Intersection-fate!] (p. 143)

Verbless narration carried forward by grammatical distortion and neologisms is also encountered:

> V okonnye rzhavi
> Rassvetnye tsveli. . . .
>
> Rassvetnye sedi,
> Rassvetnye skvozi.
>
> [Into window rusterings
> Dawn moulderings. . . .
>
> Dawn greyerings,
> Dawn througherings.] (p. 138)

The tendency towards 'trans-sense' language (facilitated by the gesture to folkloric form) is further encouraged by the frequently polyphonic chorus, most notably when Marusya's husband is challenged by his diabolical guests to show his wife and child. Words first describe and then become simple units of sound:

> Khristom prosyat,
> Slyunoi pryshchut.
> Tot po pes'i,
> Tot po krys'i.
>
> . . .
>
> An:
> Zga!
> Petushinyi klich!
> Chud', dich',
> Nezhit' – v brega!
> Ai –
> da!
>
> [They ask in Christ
> Splash in spit.
> Some as dogs,
> Some as rats.
>
> . . .
>
> Look:
> Nolight!
> Cock crow!
> Filth, fowl,
> Ungod – overflow!
> Ah –
> yes!]
>
> (pp. 132, 138)

In the final canto of *Molodets*, disembodied voices struggle for possession of the heroine, adding further to the fragmentation and dissolution of the narrative:

Khleshchi, stuzha!
Terpi, krotost'!
Zhena s muzhem –
Odna propast'!

Gde dvoe – ne lez',
Besshtannaya blud'!
– 'Ei, barskaya spes'!
Rodstva ne zabud'!'

Proch'! Ne do brat'ev!
Chto bylo – proshlo!

[Lash, chill!
Endure, mildness!
Wife and husband –
One wildness!

With a pair – don't tread,
Unpanted begetter!
'Hey, lordly pride!
Roots-forgetter!'

Away! No brothers matter!
What was – is shattered!]

(p. 142)

Throughout *Molodets* the narrative is elliptical, denying the transparency and ease of consumption which the genre leads the reader to expect, just as the literary reworking of plot leads not to conventional, but unconventional and challenging resolutions. The story shows Marusya actively enjoying and welcoming her diabolical lover; so too, language offers itself as a sensual object, and welcomes the participation of the reader. The text, far from surrendering easily, offers a challenge and an invitation to participate in its own construction: for example, words are often omitted, or merely suggested, so that the narrative requires an active response:

Goryat, yarki,
Goryat, zharki,
Zharom barkhacheny –
Ekh!

> Moi – zharche,
> Tvoi – zharche,
> U Marusi – zharche vsekh!
>
> [Bright ones burn,
> Hot ones burn,
> Veloured in heat –
> Oh!
> Mine are hotter,
> Yours are hotter,
> Marusya has the hottest yet!]
>
> (p. 92)

In this example, linguistically and semantically sensual, the word omitted is *shcheki* (cheeks). At other moments in *Molodets* the omission of words or parts of words is emphasized by rhyme:

> Lyut brachnyi tvoi pir,
> Zhenikh tvoi u-
>
> [Wild is your wedding feast,
> Your groom's a deadly b-]
>
> (p. 101)

The reader of the Russian is invited to intervene, and to complete the line with the syllable *pyr'*, forming the word for 'vampire'. This device, like so many in the work, emphasizes the literary structuring of poetic discourse, and emphasizes its reliance on conventions, in this case subverted by knowing omission, while at the same time coinciding exactly with the narrative requirements of the story (the revelation – from the heroine's brother – is cut off by the vampire himself as he commits his murder).

The metre of *Molodets* is equally unsettled and unsettling. Individual metrical patterns (often 'compound' or 'logaoedic') predominate only for short periods. The work is aggressively polymetrical, consisting mostly of short lines in irregular strophic patterns. Its metrical fabric is roughened by lines of irregular length, adjacent stresses, heterotonic rhyme, violent enjambment, and so on. It is, however, not written in *dol'niki*.[27] Its metrical effects depend (like its narrative and linguistic effects) upon the disruption of regular and familiar forms, not on the establishment of novel irregular ones. The metre gestures towards the neat literary closure of the traditional *poema-skazka*, only to emphasize its own openness. In this respect it is typical of the work as a whole, which invites comparison with inherited classical forms, but in doing so underlines its own divergence from them.[28]

Molodets has been read by some critics as a modification of the original *poema-skazka*, bringing it closer to the devices and interests of folklore than were its literary antecedents.[29] Others consider it an example of *style russe*, the nostalgic, decadent, and self-conscious imitation of the national content and vital style of folklore.[30] Both approaches show the anxiety experienced by critical readers when faced with a work which gestures so strongly towards continuity (in genre, theme, and, at times, devices), only to reveal its radical discontinuity (the expectations raised by genre and story are subverted; conventional sexuality and narrative are revised; language and semantics join the heroine's rebellion against ossified forms and notions of ownership). The reading proposed here has examined the text through and against the forms with which it is, supposedly, continuous, in an attempt to recognize the moments of discontinuity within this text, and between it and others, thereby acknowledging its problematic employment of textual violence.

NOTES AND REFERENCES

1. The only substantial recent accounts of *Molodets* are in S. Karlinsky, *Marina Cvetaeva: Her Life and Art*, Berkeley and Los Angeles, 1966, pp. 227–30, and *Marina Tsvetaeva: The Woman, Her World, and Her Poetry* (Cambridge Studies in Russian Literature), Cambridge, 1985, pp. 142–4; F. Scholz, 'Das Volksmaerchen in der russischen Literatur. Die Literarischen Versmaerchen Marina Cvetaevas', *Colloquium Slavicum Basiliense: Gedenkschrift für Hildegard Schroeder*, ed. H. Riggenbach, Berne, 1981, pp. 697–719, especially 703–6; R. Pauli, *Das russische Versmärchen von Puškin bis Cvetaeva: zur Geschichte und Analyse des Genres* (Dissertationen der Universität Wien 140), Vienna, 1978, pp. 197–207. All these accounts tend to present *Molodets* as a modification of traditional literary appropriations of folklore, closer to the popular originals than previous such appropriations. Also of interest are two perceptive reviews of the first publication: V. Khodasevich, *Poslednie novosti*, 11 June 1925, reprinted in *Marina*

Cvetaeva: Studien und Materialen, ed. H. Lampl and A. Hansen-Löve (*Wiener Slawistischer Almanach*, Sonderband 3), Vienna, 1981, pp. 262–6, and D. Svyatopolk-Mirskii, *Sovremennye zapiski*, 27, 1926, pp. 569–72. Tsvetaeva's comments on the hostile reception of *Molodets* by such critics as Aikhenval'd, whose comments are discussed below, can be found in her 'Poet o kritike' and 'Tsvetnik' (M. Tsvetaeva, *Izbrannaya proza v dvukh tomakh*, vol. 1, New York, 1979, pp. 221–50).
2. For an account of the literary ballad, see M. Katz, *The Literary Ballad in Early Nineteenth-Century Russian Literature* (Oxford Modern Languages and Literature Monographs), Oxford, 1976.
3. For an account of the novelty of Pushkin's *poemy-skazki*, see M. Azadovskii, *Literatura i fol'klor: ocherki i etyudy*, Leningrad, 1938, pp. 5–105.
4. Here and throughout, the dates given within the main text are for completion of a work, unless otherwise stated.
5. For more details of the history of the *poema-skazka* and for views conflicting with mine, see Pauli, especially pp. 137–84; T. Leonova, *Russkaya literaturnaya skazka XIX veka v ee otnoshenii k narodnoi skazke (poeticheskaya sistema zhanra v istoricheskom razvitii)*, Tomsk, 1982, especially pp. 124–45.
6. Gogol' was especially enthusiastic about the national, popular form of the *poemy-skazki* of Pushkin and Zhukovskii. Baratynskii was equally unenthusiastic for similar reasons (N. Gogol', *Sobranie sochinenii v semi tomakh*, vol. 7, Moscow, 1978, pp. 72–3 (letter to Danilevskii, 2 November 1831); 'Pis'ma E. A. Boratynskogo k I. V. Kireevskomu (1829–1833)', S. Rachinskii, *Tatevskii sbornik*, St Petersburg, 1899, pp. 48–9 (letter of (June?) 1833)).
7. For an account of Pushkin's use of sources for his *poemy-skazki*, see Azadovskii, especially pp. 65–105.
8. The *raeshnik* is a metre encountered in folk theatre, satirical rhymes, and other genres very distinct from the narrative of the folk tale.
9. See M. Azadovskii, *Istoriya russkoi fol'kloristiki*, vol. 2, Moscow, 1963, pp. 19–26, 73–84.
10. L. Mei, *Izbrannye proizvedeniya*, Leningrad, 1972, pp. 154–60. I leave aside here the prominent use of elements of the folk tale in the prose of Saltykov-Shchedrin, Tolstoi, Garshin, and others in the last decades of the nineteenth century, since their appropriations of folklore are motivated largely by the requirements of didacticism, 'Aesopian' political commentary and so on, and therefore belong, *mutatis mutandis*, with the marginal works of the early Pushkin, Nekrasov, Basov-Verkhoyantsev, and Sologub, and do not contribute much to the development of the literary stylization of folklore examined here.
11. The hero, a court poet, sets out to discover the truth about the mysterious, nightly disappearances of all the royal daughters of the (fairy-tale) king. Eventually, he is able to tell the king that they descend to an underground kingdom where they 'ispolnyayut tantsy v stile znamenitoi Aisedory Dunkan' ('perform dances in the style of the famous Isadora Duncan') (Sologub, *Sobranie sochinenii*, vol. 8, St Petersburg, *c*. 1911, p. 254).

12. Marina Tsvetaeva, *Molodets: skazka*, Prague, 1924.
13. Marina Tsvetaeva, *Nesobrannye proizvedeniya* (Slavische Propyläen, Band 70), Munich, 1970, pp. 279–381; *Molodets* (Russian Titles for the Specialist, 18), Letchworth, Herts, 1971; *Stikhotvoreniya i poemy*, vol. 4, New York, 1983, pp. 91–151. All subsequent references to *Molodets* are given in the text, and are to this last publication.
14. For details of folkloric motifs in Tsvetaeva's lyrics, see Karlinsky, *Marina Cvetaeva*, p. 37; A. Flaškova, 'Die Rezeption der Folklore in der Dichtung Marina Cvetaevas', unpublished Ph. D. dissertation, University of Vienna, 1975.
15. The extracts of 'Egorushka' are now available in *Stikhotvoreniya i poemy*, vol. 4, pp. 341–8. 'Pereulochki' and 'Egorushka' are not, strictly speaking, *poemy-skazki*: neither is based on a folk tale ('Pereulochki' is based on a *bylina*; 'Egorushka' loosely on motifs from religious works) and neither has the narrative structure of the classic *poema-skazka* ('Pereulochki' deals with a single episode, not a whole story; 'Egorushka' is disjunctive and episodic).
16. For details of the other three texts, and of this feature throughout Tsvetaeva's poetry, see my unpublished D.Phil. thesis, 'Rewriting the Inherited Text in the Poetic Works of Marina Tsvetaeva', University of Oxford, 1985, pp. 123–58 and *passim*.
17. A. Afanas'ev, *Narodnye russkie skazki*, vol. 3, Moscow, 1957, tale no. 363, pp. 124–6. For the popularity of vampire motifs, see, for example, Azadovskii, *Literatura i fol'klor*, p. 42.
18. Afanas'ev, p. 126.
19. Karlinsky, *Marina Cvetaeva*, p. 226.
20. Tsvetaeva, *Izbrannaya proza*, vol. 1, p. 240.
21. A. M. Remizov, *Posolon'*, photo-reprint of vol. 6 of collected works (St Petersburg, 1910–12) (Slavische Propyläen, 76), Munich, 1971, pp. 204–7, 264–5.
22. A. Shane, 'An Introduction to Alexei Remizov', in *The Bitter Air of Exile: Russian Writers in the West 1922–1972*, ed. S. Karlinsky and A. Appel, Berkeley, Los Angeles, London, 1977, p. 12.
23. Remizov, p. 206.
24. This would be consonant with the poet's own biography, especially her difficult relations with her father and domination of her husband and son. Writing to Pasternak about *Molodets*, she unequivocally identified Marusya with herself (letter of 22 May 1926, published in full only in translation: English version in B. Pasternak, M. Tsvetayeva, R. M. Rilke, *Letters: Summer 1926*, San Diego, New York, London, 1985, pp. 107–8).
25. Yu. Aikhenval'd, review of *Molodets*, *Rul'*, 10 June 1925; this article is cited in L. Mnukhin, 'M. I. Tsvetaeva: bibliograficheskii ukazatel' literatury o zhizni i deyatel'nosti (1910–1928)', in *Marina Cvetaeva: Materialen und Studien*, p. 293, and in I. V. Kudrova, 'Polgoda v Parizhe (k biografii Mariny Tsvetaevoi)', ibid, p. 151. See also note 1 above.
26. See Scholz, 'Das Volksmaerchen', and "'Ty prokhodish' na zapad solntsa". Kirchenslavisches bei Marina Cvetaeva', *Orbis Scriptus (Festschrift für D. Tschizewskij)*, ed. D. Gerhardt, W. Weintraub, and H.-J. zum Winkel, Munich, 1966, p. 675.

27. The term *dol'niki* refers here to 'verse in which the inter-ictic intervals vary within minimal limits of one or two syllables' (M. L. Gasparov, 'Quantative Methods in Russian Metrics: Achievements and Prospects', in *Metre, Rhythm, Stanza, Rhyme,* (*Russian Poetics in Translation,* 7), edited, translated, and with an introduction by G. S. Smith, Oxford, 1980, p. 11.
28. For a fuller discussion of the metre of *Molodets*, see Makin, pp. 176–80.
29. This is implied in Karlinsky's discussion of *Molodets* and the other folklore-based *poemy* (*Marina Cvetaeva,* pp. 228–30).
30. Aikhenval'd, for example, referred to 'chrezmernyi russizm' (cited in Kudrova, p. 151).

7

Radical Sentimentalism or Sentimental Radicalism? A Feminist Approach to Eighteenth-Century Russian Literature

Joe Andrew

Since its re-emergence as an important cultural and political force in the late 1960s, feminism has presented 'incontestably the most important challenge'[1] in recent years to accepted academic approaches to literary studies. In the course of the last two decades several 'feminisms', indeed, have emerged, but each in its own way may be said to have the aim of radically reinterpreting established literary practices, strategies and analyses. The purpose of this present study fits into this tendency, namely, to reinterpret three influential texts from late eighteenth-century Russian literature from a feminist perspective. Central to this enterprise will be the notion that literary texts have an impact on contemporary and later audiences' perceptions about the perceived world, including such matters as the roles of women in society. This impact occurs irrespective of the author's intentions. By re-reading the 'classics' in this way we achieve two things: we see the image of women in a particular culture, and we derive a new perspective on the world of the work concerned and, consequently, on the effect it had, and has, on women's roles, expectations and so on.

It is important to re-evaluate works in this way, especially those which have been 'canonized'. 'Representation of the world, like the world itself, is the work of men; they describe it from their own point of view which they confuse with absolute truth.'[2] We read the works of our cultural history as if they were 'universal', whereas, with very few exceptions, they are partial, if not highly distorted representations of humanity.

However, this approach to literature begs other, underlying questions, in particular, the relationship between an artistic product and the society for which it is produced. Assuming, as I do, that art does have some effect on its consumers, we may see art as having one of two relationships with society. Art either challenges existing patterns and models, it acts as 'an alternative government',[3] even undermines accepted notions of reality itself and creates other worlds, 'anti-worlds'; or else, art operates as an instrument in the process of social control. My argument will run along these latter lines. For these purposes, I will consider literature as part of the ideological processes in society by which a group, or class, maintains its power over other groups. In our present case, the dominant group is the patriarchy.[4]

In his essay 'Ideology and State Apparatuses', Althusser offers an analysis of how ideological institutions act as buttresses to the power of the state which relies, of course, not only on actual force to maintain itself.[5] His arguments apply primarily to a politically constituted state but can be reapplied, in general terms, to other socio-political formations, such as the dominant patriarchal grouping, given that 'The function of an ideology is to justify the status quo and to persuade the powerless that their powerlessness is inevitable.'[6] Through the mechanisms of the political superstructure, the ruling class or group persuades the subservient group(s) that the interests of the ruling and the ruled are synonymous. The family (especially relevant in the feminist case, of course), legal institutions, communications, such as the press, radio, television, and cultural activities, including literature – all these form the ideological state apparatuses (ISAs). Education, in the broadest sense, which would include the arts, is absolutely central to the functioning of the ISAs.[7] Reading and the study of literature can therefore be seen as part of the individual's socialization, and women (and men) learn what it is to be a woman from novels as well as from their earlier training.[8]

Althusser's concept develops Gramsci's idea of 'hegemony', which is equally appropriate for our understanding of the psychological mechanisms in the reading of literature. Power is exercised in what Gramsci terms 'civil society' by consent,

> through the myriad ways in which the institutions of civil society operate to shape, directly or indirectly, the cognitive and affective structures whereby men [sic] perceive and evaluate problematic social reality.[9]

Consequently, images of women in literature, however 'universal' they may appear, and (predominantly male) critics claim them to be, equally insist that the roles allotted to women (predominantly inferior or powerless) are unavoidable or even necessary. In accepting these analyses of culture, we must see literature as part of the 'hegemony' of patriarchy, however subversive or 'alternative' it may seem or be made to seem to us. Accordingly, it will be my contention in the ensuing pages that the works of Fonvizin, Radishchev and Karamzin may appear to humanize and support the cause of the oppressed (especially the Russian peasantry), but that if we apply a feminist analysis to their works, then it emerges that they in no way advance the cause of the most oppressed group, namely women. Each writer illustrates a common pattern: an apparently sympathetic portrayal of women masks a profound, admonitory misogyny.

The methodology used in this study is that first formulated by L. Michael O'Toole and developed by myself and others, analysing narrative structures on the following levels: theme, fable, plot, narrative structure, setting and character; although the basic method is modified where appropriate.[10]

For most of the second half of the eighteenth century Russia was ruled by a woman, Catherine II. Her reign opened with liberal hopes but, particularly after the shocks of Pugachev and 1789, ended in reaction. It also saw the flourishing of the arts and sciences conventionally known as the Russian Enlightenment.[11] In literature, cautious criticism became emboldened as, on the one hand, the reading public increased rapidly and, on the other, political repression precluded most other forms of civic expression. Loyal Classicism shifted gradually into a kind of proto-realism (Fonvizin, Novikov, Derzhavin) and a more fully formed pre-Romanticism, or, to use the more traditional term, Sentimentalism (Radishchev, Karamzin).[12]

FONVIZIN

Theme

Denis Fonvizin's second major play *The Minor* was written in 1781, six years after the *Pugachevshchina* and at a time of growing reaction.¹³ Fonvizin himself has been termed 'the bold lord of satire ... the friend of freedom';¹⁴ and this play is conventionally seen as the first original Russian comedy and the first *political* Russian comedy, especially in terms of its exposure of corruption and serf-abuse amongst the provincial nobility, as represented by the vicious Prostakov family.¹⁵ However, another reading seems just as plausible. Even taking into account the possibility of self-censorship, much more emphasis is laid elsewhere. The play's opening situation may be seen, in the Prostakov family relationships, as an inversion of the natural patriarchal order, which is restored through the intervention of the Wise Father, Starodum.¹⁶ In the opening situation power lies in the hands of Prostakova (who abuses it), and by the end she has it taken away: she can be seen as an archetypal figure, the demon woman, the shrew, whose 'own men' are unable to tame her, and so the Law of the Father must be reinstated from outside. (By inference, this may also be seen as an allegorical discussion of the 'unnatural' order within Russia whereby a woman has usurped a rightfully male crown.) One important sub-theme within this is that of language and knowledge: Prostakova abuses the correct patriarchal discourse, as expounded by Starodum, and, again, she is defeated and the power that knowledge confers is restored to its rightful male hands. (I shall return in more detail to this in the discussion of point of view.)

Narrative Structure

Although partially original in content the play follows the conventional Neo-Classical pattern of the three unities and five acts. Moreover, its structure charts the ancient five-part schema of prologue/exposition–complication–peripeteia–dénouement–epilogue, the last being extremely brief.¹⁷ This schema is parabolic in both senses of the term.

The prologue and exposition provide the setting of the play: Act One mainly concerns itself with delineating the foolishness and stupidity of the Prostakov men and the violence of Prostakova. Sof'ya, the demure heroine, is clearly set apart from this, by her silence, and her relatively late appearance, in scene 6. Her quiet virtue is set in relief at once, but equally one of the variations on the theme of abuse of power, and of violence, is adumbrated in that it is precisely Sof'ya's virtue which makes her vulnerable to the rapacious evil embodied in Prostakova.[18] Act One, particularly in the coarse, violent execrations of Prostakova, gives ample illustration of the 'false discourse' which too will be remedied in the latter parts of the play. Act Two sees the complication, with the gathering of the younger men of virtue, Pravdin and Milon, who guard Sof'ya as they await the coming of their 'leader' Starodum. His arrival at the opening of Act Three precipitates the peripeteia as the forces of good score an easy and, indeed, predetermined victory. This victory is marked by Starodum's initial anger, and then scornful laughter at the violent, noisy behaviour of his hostess (p. 135). Acts Four and Five provide minor renewed complications in the attempted abduction of Sof'ya by Prostakova, but essentially the play, which eventually ends with its sententious lines on '[female] vice punished' and 'virtue rewarded', in terms of its narrative structure, could have ended two acts earlier. The delay is occasioned by the lengthy discourses, primarily between Starodum and Sof'ya, to which too we may return. For the moment it should be noted that they are clearly foregrounded by the way in which they interrupt the otherwise schematic structure.

Plot[19]

As in many literary works which are still close to relatively primitive, unsophisticated origins, the plot of *The Minor* is predetermined, or even overdetermined, in this case by the device, common in eighteenth-century Russian theatre, of 'telling names'.[20] Even before the action opens the grouping of characters into the good (Starodum, Pravdin, Milon and Sof'ya) and the bad (Prostakov, Prostakova and Skotinin) implies that the action will revolve around the disposition of the virtuous, unindividuated heroine, Sof'ya. Traditionally, the evil world could be represented by her parents (in this instance, her temporary guardians). Significantly, however, for the play's sexual politics, all the evil emanates from the female, Prostakova: she is the main motive force behind the scheme to cheat Sof'ya, and it is she who later plots her abduction, while her husband is merely stupid. In these terms, Prostakova is a curse to *all*, including her beloved son Mitrofan. Once more, *she* is the organizer of his appalling education, a significant factor given the centrality of enlightenment and knowledge in general in this play, as well as Fonvizin's other works. Prostakova it is who is the one to be punished – not simply for malfeasance on her estate, but for attempting to gain power over men.

She may be the source of all evil, but, otherwise, it is only the male characters who could be termed *actants*. All the active destinies are theirs, and it is they who organize and control the destinies of the women, including Prostakova in the end. The plot is, indeed, remarkably simple: as the military metaphors suggest, it is a battle between Absolute Evil, as represented in the traditional shrew/witch figure of Prostakova, and Absolute Good, whose chief champion is predictably male, namely Starodum. The subplot concerns the surface action of the struggle for the bride's hand. Significantly, both plots reveal another typical motif of patriarchal literature: the disposability of the virtuous heroine. In contrast to much of the literature of the period, there is no seduction theme as such, but virtue is shown to be vulnerable. Although the extended disquisitions of Act Four may suggest that Sof'ya is free to act as she pleases, the plot shows the opposite to be true: her destiny is fought over, with the forces of Good and Evil each rivalling the other to control and dispose of her destiny. Sof'ya herself, despite, or perhaps more accurately, *because of* her virtue is powerless. She may be given (by Starodum) or taken (by Skotinin, or Prostakova for her son) but that is all.

On another level, the plot is even more primitive in that its basic subject-matter is closely linked with the world of the fairy-tale. Sof'ya is the Sleeping Beauty who must be rescued from the Evil Step-Mother. Interestingly it is the *Father*-figure, rather than the younger men of virtue, who plays the part, comically enough, of St George against Prostakova the Dragon. In the end, Evil is, of course, conquered, and the Law-of-the-Father is restored.[21]

An important sub-section of the plot is the picture given of male/female relationships, and, to a lesser extent, that of male/male relationships. As in other aspects of the play, the Prostakovs offer a picture of all that is evil in family relationships, while those relationships revolving around Starodum both implicitly and explicitly provide a model to be emulated.

Prostakova's relationship with her husband is a travesty of the marriage of mutual trust which Starodum outlines in Act Four (pp. 153 ff.). Her very first words denote an 'unnatural' domination of her husband, whom she nags and berates on every occasion, while he is reduced to a nervous stammerer. Arguably, her greatest crime is her inversion of patriarchal Law, particularly as the most positive character is depicted as a true, superhumanly virtuous patriarch, and much of the 'foregrounded' discussion in the second half of the play is devoted to marital relationships of the 'correct' kind.[22] Equally, her maternal love is a grotesque parody of this traditional virtue: Mitrofan is crushed and he too is reduced to a will-less male by this 'castrating' female.

Even before he appears, Starodum stands for the Law, the honourable, genuinely patriotic Father (at least a surrogate one) to whom all the junior males pay their respects. The 'sons' in this instance are profoundly deferential and never once dare contradict the fount of all wisdom. In turn, Sof'ya, the obvious embodiment of female virtue and wisdom (as her name suggests), is dependent and an utterly dutiful daughter. Initially she is under the protection of *two* men, Pravdin and Milon, and once Starodum has arrived to rescue her she asks for nothing but to be told what to do. Indeed, she explicitly asks him to speak his Law, to give her 'instructions': 'Give me rules, which I must follow. Guide my heart' (p. 150). She wishes only 'to obey', and the message is clear: the woman of virtue is she who will be subordinate to the wishes of the Father, in either the literal, or as here, the even more powerful, *symbolic* sense. The ideal male/female relationship is that of Master/Pupil.[23] The actual discussion which ensues in Act Four, and which provides the key to the centrality of this theme to the play, may appear rather more egalitarian and even 'feminist' in tone, but these tendencies are profoundly undermined by Sof'ya's plot situation, her lack of self-determination and her wish for subordination.

Images of Woman

All the above makes it clear that although Fonvizin may appear somewhat liberal in his social thinking, his images of female characters were stereotyped and the overall implications of the play are unmistakably misogynist. A little more elaboration will make this clearer, I think. Both female characters cannot strictly be termed 'characters': both are overdetermined signifiers, symbolizing Absolute Evil and Absolute Good.[24] (It is, of course, traditional to use women as mere symbols, rather than as rounded, developing characters.) In the completeness of the stereotyping both verge on caricatures: Sof'ya symbolizes what is most valuable in the female character (and therefore, what is most to be risked), while Prostakova accrues virtually every recorded negative female characteristic.[25] This level of the play is even more overdetermined than the plot – indeed, to a farcical degree. Prostakova is described as a 'most evil *Fury*, whose *Hellish* character makes the rest of the house unhappy' (p. 117). Elsewhere we are told several times that she is soulless, mad and like an animal. In more 'human' terms, she is hypocritical, vicious, a tyrant, and ignorant (she cannot read or write and does not know the meaning of the word 'geography'). Most notably, in terms of the play's value system, her language is coarse and violent, a desecration of the linguistically pure patriarchal code.

By contrast, Sof'ya, when she is not demurely silent, speaks the almost archaic language of Starodum, and by her very speech pattern allies herself with the triumphant and dominant male group. She is virtuous, innocent, 'feminine', sensitive, and, as we have seen, a truly dutiful daughter. The symbolic relationship between the two women (and it is largely symbolic, as they rarely address one another) dramatizes the twin poles of the loathsome, disgusting shrew, and the adorable, immaculate virgin. Their relationship, though, has another dramatic imperative, namely one of the central issues of the play – power and who wields it. Prostakova seeks power, is shown to be evil by so doing and is finally stripped of it. Conversely, Sof'ya's very powerlessness is seen as a weakness, in that it necessitates her being protected, but is also to be regarded as estimable. In the end, the play pivots on this issue of power, especially that afforded by knowledge, as a discussion of point of view illustrates.

Point of View

As Foucault has argued: 'power and knowledge directly imply one another ... there is no power relation without the correlative constitution of a field of knowledge, nor any knowledge that does not presuppose and constitute ... power relations'.[26] Power, knowledge and their expression in language, or modes of discourse – these can be seen as the central themes of the play and amongst the main criteria by which the characters may be arranged. It may seem strange to speak of 'point of view' in a play, yet dominating almost every utterance, lurking unseen and expectantly awaited, like Gogol's *Revizor*, implicitly watching all other characters, like Foucault's panopticon, stands the central moral referent, the figure of the true, benevolent, yet punishing Father of the Freudian Archetype, namely Starodum.[27] It is he who has the true knowledge of the true Enlightenment, and it is, consequently, he who has the power, whether over his dutiful 'daughter' Sof'ya, or the parody wife and mother, Prostakova.

This symbolic role of Starodum emerges some time before he appears on stage, significantly in the form of the written word, the letter that heralds his arrival and his intentions to control Sof'ya's estate and her destiny. It is as if the Father's Word, his Law is laid down as a harbinger of his avenging justice. Henceforth it is to be *his* utterances which direct the course of the play – his 'word' in a double sense, in that, as we have already seen, the linguistic theme, the theme of correct discourse or linguistic purity, is an important point of reference for assessing the two female polarities. Indeed, all the characters are grouped according to this central signifier. Pravdin, Milon and Sof'ya all ally themselves with the Father's Word by speaking his language, while Prostakov, Skotinin and, most notably, Prostakova desecrate (the word is not too strong) this lapidary code (p. 144 ff.).[28]

Of all the characters Starodum alone speaks with the true authority of the self-determining man. Others listen dutifully to his utterances or ignore them. If control of language leads to control of knowledge, and therefore to power, Starodum should be viewed as the exemplary figure, the true Patriarch. Indeed, one of Prostakova's many crimes is signalled by her misappropriation of the right to label: her husband, son and brother all introduce themselves in terms of her, and not as autonomous self-uttering males (p. 137).[29] Starodum, their antithesis, has been sent to return the patriarchal order to its primary, 'natural' state. Among his first remarks, when he arrives at the opening of Act Three, is a reference to Peter I, and to the linguistic corruption that has occurred since those days. Language, knowledge and power, then, are signs of the overall themes of the play. Prostakova, the shrew, the witch, the Fury from Hell, has misappropriated them and reduced her men to timorous stammerers. Starodum, the man of the old ways, arrives to return the knowledge and power to where it properly lies, and in the end the woman of wisdom, Sof'ya, is elevated to her proper sphere – a happy marriage. Female evil is punished and the patriarchal order is restored.

RADISHCHEV

Themes and Values

Aleksandr Radishchev is the most famous, although not the best, writer of eighteenth-century Russia. He was exiled for his subversive book *Journey from St Petersburg to Moscow* (1790) and has been celebrated ever since as the first inspiration of the Russian radical tradition.[30] Yet his overt espousal of the cause of the Russian peasantry, whether for reform or revolution, does not disguise a misogyny which is both profound and far-reaching. Few of the many encounters in the *Journey* feature women, which is revealing in itself, and those that do, do not depict them in a very favourable light. (Because the *Journey* is not a narrative work proper, O'Toole's scheme will be severely modified, 'Theme' is retained, 'character' is replaced by 'Images of Women' and 'plot' by 'male/female relationships'.)

As Pushkin was perhaps the first to note, Radishchev's thinking has many sources in the different currents of eighteenth-century philosophy.[31] Among his chief mentors was Rousseau, whose ambivalence towards women he shares. He also takes from Rousseau the 'religion of the heart': from the first page, Radishchev's appeal is to the feelings. At the same time, he makes frequent reference to so-called 'natural justice' and 'natural law', most notably in the defence of peasant revenge for the masters' rape of one of 'their' women (pp. 275 ff.). Elsewhere he discusses the nature of freedom and equality: perhaps the cornerstone is the reprinting of his ode 'Liberty'. Yet in all these appeals – to the feelings, to nature, to justice, for liberty – a discussion on the rights of women is absent, although there is a long discussion of sexual matters. Clearly the work was intended to be an *Encyclopaedia* in its own way, but this crucial topic is omitted. As for Rousseau, so too for Radishchev, it is *men* who are born free.

Images of Women

When women do appear in the text, they almost always fit into the familiar, traditional stereotypes, usually reinforced by a prurient sentimentalism that verges on the Sadeian. As already noted, women are not really very important in Radishchev's thinking. They are peripheral to his main concerns, and when they do appear it is as objects for male pleasure, violence or violation: indeed, there is an unnerving and rather distasteful emphasis on this last matter. Not once is a female character depicted as a desiring subject, and women's image is almost uniformly dystopian. Women are unable to live without men, as in the recruiting scene at Gorodnya (p. 362): the old wonder who will care for them once their men are taken, while the young *devka* is equally hopeless. The very first image of a woman in the text is the wife of the victim of injustice. While he is a mixture of stoicism and bitterness, she is fainting, and later dies after childbirth. Realistic, perhaps, but our first impression of the fair sex is of a frail, suffering, oppressed and, indeed, a weaker species.

The next woman we meet is the raped peasant girl, whose men avenge her. Once more the female is suffering, in the best traditions of Sentimentalism. She fits neatly into the stereotype of 'defiled maiden', and indeed the scene is described in near pornographic detail. Her virtuousness is especially emphasized, and it is a gang rape. Equally noticeable is that it is precisely this action which incenses the male peasantry. 'Their' woman is defiled, so they must seek retribution: males compete over the virtue of women in a tradition going back to *Clarissa*. Later we encounter another favourite *frisson* of the darker side of Sentimentalism as our noble narrator laments the death of his wife whose 'pure body' had been destroyed by the corruption his debauchery had introduced into it. The Sadeian echoes are only just below the surface.[32] Defiled femininity is everywhere – as in the grotesque instance of the sixty-two-year-old, and recently married, Madame.

Radishchev's ambivalence towards these strange creatures who flicker on the margins of his vision is best exemplified in the depiction of the town of Valdai, which would appear to have been a large-scale brothel (pp. 300–2). (Once more, women as objects for male gratification.) The emphasis now shifts from defiled virtue to unashamed, and unadmired, sensuality. Valdai is populated by sirens who deprive the weary traveller (male, of course) of his money, time and – again, the gruesome obsession – his health. Moreover, these shameless harlots are faithless, as in the admonitory tale of the brave monk who died while striving to reach his beloved: she was probably entertaining another traveller at the time. Women do not die of love in Valdai, or elsewhere in Radishchev's quasi-Sadeian world: they die in painful childbirth, from violent violation or disease.[33] Women are pure, or shameless, but either way they are punished for their loathsome sexuality.

Twice more, positive stereotypes emerge, but they are stereotypes none the less. In the *Spasskaya Polest'* section (p. 241 ff.) there is the famous dream in which a visiting female wanderer removes the cataracts from the eyes of the self-deceiving ruler: woman as symbol of spiritual inspiration. Later, our world-weary narrator encounters Anyuta, the only woman to be treated in any way as an individual (p. 304 ff.). Certainly she is relatively independent, wishes to organize her own life, and even, with her equally staunch mother, refuses the sentimentalist's charity. Yet profound reservations must remain. Anyuta is completely unindividualized and remains a figment of the Rousseauesque vision of the pure country maiden (at least undefiled!). Indeed, she is explicitly contrasted with the perversions and hypocrisies of urban women, and the narrator sighs that if only he had met Anyuta fifteen years earlier, he would have been rescued from debauchery, corruption of his wife's flesh and so on: Anyuta is simply a variation on the theme of the Pure Angel as Redeemer. In no way should she be seen as an autonomous character, and there is no 'heroine's text' to be found in the *Journey*.[34]

Male/Female Relationships: A Reformed Rake's Point of View

Our Sentimental Traveller clearly found dealings with 'the sex' somewhat problematic. Women exist in the *Journey* for him, as for the other male characters (as indeed was typical for the eighteenth century in general), as objects, moreover, for male rivalry and competition, as the rape incident illustrates, and as was paradigmatic in the novel of seduction.[35] Even the chaste and independent Anyuta, initially at least, is treated in this way – the target for an amorous *baiser volé*, which the narrator, hypocritically, claims to be a token of his esteem and respect. Anyuta might have been his salvation, he continues: implicit in this assertion, and throughout, was another typical male view of the time, namely that women were necessary for the urgent sexual needs of men, and better the innocent country girl than the corrupt (and diseased) city whores. Equally, following the Pauline view, marriage is a 'sacred union' which too may rescue the unfortunate errant male from his baser instincts.

This is the present view of our narrator. However, there are many hints, some more explicit than others, of dark and murky secrets hidden in his 'mis-spent youth' – although not so mis-spent that he does not justify it now.[36] Sexual self-indulgence is generally viewed as part of the male's normal, 'natural' self-expression when young. There are lamentations for the disease this may bring to 'pure wives', concern for healthy heredity, but *no* anxiety for the whorish recipients of these lusts. Indeed, the loudest plaints are the somewhat distasteful and usually hysterical (a female complaint!) outbursts of self-pity and hypocritical self-lacerations over his sinful past. Apart from the regret he expresses over his wife's untimely death, he usually talks of his erstwhile female associates (anonymous and, indeed, interchangeable, of course) with disgust and loathing: 'You have rouge on your cheeks, rouge on your heart, on your conscience rouge, on your sincerity ... soot' (p. 303). This openly misogynist view is paralleled by an admiration of the 'pure' country girls, the language of which speaks for itself: 'Look how the limbs of *my* beauties are round, developed, undeformed, unspoiled' (ibid; my italics). The language of the horse fair.

So, Aleksandr Radishchev, celebrated for his passionate defence of the rights of Man, finally reveals himself as a typical defender of the rights of men to use and abuse women. The women are unindividualized, there are no female narrators and women are shown to exist purely for men, and impurely for the destruction of their health and well-being.

KARAMZIN

'Perhaps the most famous line ever written by Karamzin was "for even peasant women know how to love".'[37] Nikolai Karamzin's *Poor Liza* (1792) may also seem to champion the cause of the oppressed group of peasant women, but a close reading of his most famous work reveals it to be a naive and admonitory little tale which does nothing for the rights of women, peasant or otherwise.[38]

Plot

From its very title onwards *Poor Liza* can be read as a paradigmatic dysphoric heroine's text.[39] Even before we begin *any* reading we know that the eponymous heroine will come to an unfortunate end, which, as it turns out, involves *beda* (disaster) as well as the already doubly signifying *bednost'* (poverty/pitiableness): consequently, Liza, like most heroines of this paradigm, has no control over her destiny, which is predetermined by her situation within the patriarchal world in which she is located. Indeed, her character (such as it is, beyond the ludicrous degree of stereotyping) becomes largely irrelevant. For the most part she exists merely at the level of a plot function. Mechanically she follows the paradigm of virginal virtue leading to seduction. Unlike her celebrated predecessors, most notably Clarissa Harlowe, Liza offers no resistance. At each stage, she complies with Erast's wishes and, indeed, delights naively in her 'love'. The procession is automatic, without the slightest variation on the predictable tradition. Once she has given her all she has nothing left to exchange in this rake's economy. Consequently, the inevitable next stage ensues, betrayal. This, tediously, is rapidly succeeded by abandonment and finally her death.[40] The law of this particular theorem is that lost innocence must be redeemed, and the only currency available is her now worthless life. Significantly, death is by suicide: as so often in this version of the story this is the only self-determining action the heroine is allowed.

As in *The Minor*, echoes of even more traditional plots are not far beneath the surface. Liza is simultaneously Cinderella, Sleeping Beauty and Little Red Riding Hood, Erast a comical version of the last's lupine grandmother. Prince Charming does not rescue her from the kitchen: the kiss, instead of awakening Liza, sends her to what Raymond Chandler was to call the 'Big Sleep'.

Narrative Structure

This level of our reading merely reinforces the predictability of the plot and, as in *The Minor*, follows the parabolic five-part curve. The curve rises, and then descends, to reinforce the already obvious implications. In terms of the narrative structure the title of the story has an even more crushing impact: even before Liza appears we can hazard a very shrewd guess at the dénouement of the structure. These predetermining premonitions are exacerbated by the lengthy, gloomy, gothic prologue/exposition with its emphasis on morbidity, death and desolation. Doom and foreboding herald the appearance of our poor heroine: like all stages of the narrative structure, the prologue is heavily marked, to the extent that its function becomes ludicrously overdetermined.

The complication, too, is *announced* with the first change in scene (ominously, from idyllic pastoral to corrupting city – the same naïve correlation as in the equally Sentimental Radishchev), and by the introduction of a new character, the duplicitous hero, Erast. The peripeteia has several stages, each in turn marked by a new event: each signifies a downward step in the curve to disaster (*beda*). Liza sells her flowers to Erast alone, she ceases coming to Moscow, cannot sleep, and she responds to his first kiss. The encroachment of the dénouement is as heavily underscored: the trysts move to the more sombre setting of the evening (the *decline* of the day), and when Liza finally gives the rest of her chaste body (to follow her already doomed heart) the momentous occasion is accompanied by the banality of thunder and lightning. In case any reader should miss the significance of the moment, the narrator tells us, as Liza returns home, 'but how everything had changed'(!) (p. 616).

The extended dénouement concludes with a neat framing device of plot rhyme: Liza returns to Moscow for the first time since her story entered its fateful downward journey. This structural parallel merely emphasizes the profound change (for the worse) since the starkly worded dénouement. Equally, the Epilogue, although much shorter, exactly parallels the Prologue, by a return to the same scene of desolation. Certainly the construction is neat. This craftsmanship has a telling point, in that the parallels, the rhymes and slow inexorable march up and down the traditional parabola merely emphasize the inevitability of the plot, and hence, transform it into an immutable law. The paradigm is reproduced in an exemplary form.

Male/Female Relationships

The male/female relationships of the story also have an air of predetermination from the Prologue's implicit reference to the specific literary tradition of seduction – betrayal – death. Karamzin proceeds, again, to overdetermine what is already predetermined. His first move in announcing the game of seduction, which will be played to the death (of the heroine only, of course), is to locate Liza quite explicitly in the patriarchal world. Her father has died before the story begins, and it is this fact which has left Liza in the position the title announces: 'But soon after his death his wife and daughter *became poor*' (p. 607; my italics). Women without male protection are defenceless: we are told that Liza's only hope for the future is to find 'a good man'. He only appears after Liza's heart has been lost, in the shape of a decent shepherd who wishes to marry her. However, he too acts as a mere plot function. His rivalry in the battle for the virgin's maidenhead is precisely what precipitates Liza's final fall into the state of virtue lost: men compete for women in this world.

The unequal male/female relationship is doubly underscored in this story. Firstly, of course, Liza is a peasant girl (only fifteen, incidentally), while Erast is a *barin*, a master. The class division, while exciting maximum pathos and lyricism, also emphasizes the vulnerability of our heroine. Secondly, the couple first meet in a relationship which makes the inequality even more glaring: Liza is the seller (of the virginal lilies of the valley) and Erast the buyer. Female:male; servant:master; seller:buyer – the precise social interface could not be made more obvious. However, for the writer of a Sentimental tale in the eighteenth century, this triple overdetermination was not yet enough: an added, darker *frisson* was needed. Occasionally this might be incest (as in the same author's *The Island of Bornholm*). Here it is prostitution. Liza sells 'her flowers' to Erast way over the odds, and the symbolic motif of prostitution is further transmogrified when she becomes a 'kept woman'. She first sells her flowers to him alone, and then Erast buys her even more completely by paying her to stay at home. Now Liza is bound: she waits passively for her Master to call. At the end of the story, this motif is completed when Erast pays her off with the lordly price of one hundred roubles.

Liza is not alone in her position of powerlessness in the patriarchal world. Her mother, too, had 'become poor'. Regrettably, she shows little maternal care for her naïve daughter: instead, she connives at her daughter's seduction and is as foolishly duped by Erast's good looks, masterful graces – and money. This too is a common motif in literature, in that 'the feminine heroine grows up in a world without female solidarity, where women in fact police each other on behalf of patriarchal tyranny'.[41] Even this is not the end of the picture. The third woman in the story is the rich, older widow whom Erast marries to pay off his gambling debts. In the patriarchal world of which Karamzin has given such a faithful picture, *all* women are, like the lilies of the valley, commodities to be bought, used up and then thrown away.[42]

Images of Women

As already indicated, Liza's character is largely irrelevant to the plot, of which she is a mere function. Her portrayal, like everything else, is overdetermined and is a bizarre collocation of stereotypes, a truly identikit heroine. Liza is passive, virtuous and sensitive, and, as is traditional, closely linked with Nature, with which she communes whenever possible. Moreover, she is incredibly naïve (read: stupid), trusting Erast implicitly. For all the forebodings she is deliriously happy in her 'love'. Yet, and this is a common trick, she is *simultaneously* a whore.[43] She sells herself to the first bidder, and poutingly throws her flowers into the Moscow river when Erast fails to appear. The clash of stereotypes, common in misogynist literature, is ludicrous, and maintained throughout. Liza is 'timid', but eagerly awaits Erast's every coming. Once she is a 'fallen woman' she is none the less described 'as an angel'. Her behaviour is, if anything, even more predictable than the plot. At the first kiss, her response is *automatic*: she blushes, her heart flutters, her gaze is cast down. When Erast leaves her, she swoons; when he finally abandons her, she does indeed faint. Her little tragedy is so admonitory precisely because she is so predictable, and her behaviour is so ordinary. Her mother, as we have seen, is no less gullible. One's response recalls that of a recent reader of *Little Red Riding Hood*, to which, as I have noted, *Poor Liza* has certain similarities. For 'cakes' read 'flowers', for 'wolf' read 'seducer': '"Little Red Riding Hood" is the story of a girl, bordering on mental deficiency, who is sent out by an irresponsible mother through dark, wolf-infested woods to take a little basket full to the brim with cakes, to her sick grandmother. Given these circumstances her end is hardly surprising.'[44] *Poor Liza* is, in terms of plot and character, little removed from the fairy tale.

From the first page of *Poor Liza*, Death lurks, and later we see that, in the Sentimentalist vogue, Love and Death are inextricably linked, for women at least.[45] The story plays a clever trick on the gullible reader. Peasant women may indeed know how to love, but they are certainly not humanized: every level of the story, the title, the setting, exposition, symbolism, reduces them to mere functions of the generic 'tale of pathos'. Erast escapes with a troubled conscience while Liza perishes at the bottom of her celebrated pond. The little tragedy of poor, poor Liza conveys a series of grim warnings. Women are 'natural', passive and stunningly stupid. They are defenceless without male protection. They flatter to deceive because they are simultaneously virgins and whores (men beware the wiles of women!). Women actively seek their own destruction, in which their far from maternal mothers connive. Most generally, and most threateningly, to be awoken sexually is to be condemned to death. This heroine's text could hardly be more dysphoric: 'If you go down to the woods today you're sure of a big surprise.'

NOTES AND REFERENCES

1. K. K. Ruthven, *Feminist Literary Studies: An Introduction*, Cambridge, 1984, p. 7. See this work *passim* for a general discussion of the developments in feminist literary criticism.
2. S. de Beauvoir, *The Second Sex*, London, 1972, p. 162. The relevance and power of a feminist analysis is admirably conveyed by Ruthven: 'To read a canonical text in a feminist way is to force that text to reveal its hidden sexual ideology which ... tends not to be mentioned in non-feminist criticism' (p. 31).
3. This is a common view of literature, which has been particularly applied to nineteenth-century Russian literature. See, for example, my *Writers and Society During the Rise of Russian Realism*, London,

1980, and *Russian Writers and Society in the Second Half of the Nineteenth Century*, London, 1982.
4. The best analyses of the origins and theory of patriarchal hegemony are probably still those of J. S. Mill and Engels: J. S. Mill, *On the Subjugation of Women*, London, 1869, and F. Engels, *The Origin of the Family, Private Property and the State*, London, 1972. See also de Beauvoir.
5. L. Althusser, 'Ideology and State Apparatuses', in *Lenin and Philosophy and Other Essays*, London, 1977, pp. 121–73.
6. Ruthven, p. 31.
7. Althusser, p. 147.
8. An excellent, and personal account of this process is given by Rachel M. Brownstein in *Becoming a Heroine: Reading about Women in Novels*, Harmondsworth, 1984. A powerful account of the problems involved for young ladies reading novels is presented in the Russian context in Pushkin's *Evgenii Onegin*.
9. J. V. Femia, *Gramsci's Political Thought: Hegemony, Consciousness, and the Revolutionary Process*, Oxford, 1981, p. 24.
10. See L. M. O'Toole, *Structure, Style and Interpretation in the Russian Short Story*, New Haven, London, 1982, and *The Structural Analysis of Russian Narrative Fiction* (Essays in Poetics Publications, 1), ed. J. Andrew, Keele, 1984.
11. For a discussion of this period and its culture, see *The Eighteenth Century in Russia*, ed. J. Garrard, Oxford, 1973, and H. Rogger, *National Consciousness in Eighteenth-Century Russia*, Cambridge, Mass., 1960.
12. For a discussion of these two terms, see H. M. Nebel, *N. M. Karamzin: A Russian Sentimentalist*, The Hague, 1967, and G. S. Smith, 'Sentimentalism and Pre-Romanticism as Terms and Concepts', in *Russian Literature in the Age of Catherine the Great*, ed. A. G. Cross, Oxford, 1976, pp. 173–89.
13. All references to this work are taken from D. I. Fonvizin, *Nedorosl'*, in *Sobranie sochinenii v dvukh tomakh*, vol. 1, ed. G. P. Makogonenko, Moscow, Leningrad, 1959, pp. 105–78. Page references are given in parentheses in the text.
14. Pushkin, *Evgenii Onegin*, chapter I, stanza xviii.
15. See D. J. Welsh, *Russian Comedy: 1765–1823*, The Hague, 1966.
16. For a discussion of the use of 'telling names', see ibid, pp. 64–6.
17. For a discussion of the schema, and other terms of narrative analysis, see O'Toole, pp. 11–36.
18. See N. K. Miller, *The Heroine's Text: Readings in the French and English Novel, 1722–1782*, New York, 1980, p. xi, for an excellent discussion of the vulnerability of the traditional heroine.
19. No distinction is made here between *syuzhet* and *fabula* (plot and fable). Any such dislocation would be extremely unusual in a play.
20. For a discussion of the overdetermination of literary characters and plots, see Miller, p. 65. On telling names, see note 16.
21. See J. Gallop, *Feminism and Psychoanalysis: The Daughter's Seduction*, London, 1982, pp. 74–5, for a discussion of the symbolic and psychoanalytical interpretation of the Father and his 'Law'.

22. See p. 140 of the text for a description of Prostakova's family background. The theme of the benighted, brutal family in rural Russia was to prove enduring: see, for example, A. N. Ostrovskii's *The Thunderstorm* (1859) and Chekhov's *The Peasants* (1897).
23. For a discussion of this model of female relationships, see S. M. Okin, *Women in Western Political Thought*, London, 1980, pp. 43–4.
24. It should be remembered that characterization, in the sense of the creation of individual, 'rounded' characters, was virtually non-existent in Fonvizin's work, as in eighteenth-century Russian literature in general.
25. See M. Ellmann, *Thinking About Women*, New York, 1968, p. 74ff.
26. M. Foucault, *Discipline and Punish: The Birth of the Prison*, New York, 1977, p. 27.
27. For a discussion of panopticon, see ibid, pp. 195–228. On the punishing Father, see Gallop, *passim*. It should be noted that the play provides an ideal, indeed idealized, version of the symbolic Father, whereas the only Mother in the work is a grotesque parody: this contrast says much for the general tendency of the play's sexual politics.
28. Much of the 'low comedy' of the play centres on linguistic distortions, especially in this scene, where the three tutors (one of whom is German) play particular havoc with the Russian language.
29. For a discussion of labelling in literature, see T. Tanner, *Adultery in the Novel: Contract and Transgression*, Baltimore, London, 1979, pp. 346–54, and M. Daly, *God the Father*, Boston, 1973, p. 47.
30. All references to this work are taken from A. N. Radishchev, *Puteshestvie iz Peterburga v Moskvu*, in *Polnoe sobranie sochinenii*, Moscow, Leningrad, 1938; reprinted, ed. I. K. Lupol et al., Vaduz, 1969, pp. 225–392. Page references are given in parentheses in the text.
31. Pushkin, 'Alexander Radishchev', in *Pushkin on Literature*, trans. and ed. T. Woolf, London, 1971, p. 390.
32. For a discussion of the depiction of women in de Sade, see A. Carter, *The Sadeian Woman*, London, 1979.
33. For a detailed discussion of childbirth in Russian literature, see Barbara Heldt's contribution to this volume, pp. 161–7.
34. For a discussion of this term, see Miller, *passim*, especially p. xi.
35. See ibid, *passim*, especially pp. 57 and 84.
36. For a discussion of a 'typical' eighteenth-century rake, see L. Stone on Boswell in *The Family, Sex and Marriage in England, 1500–1800*, London, 1977, pp. 350–78.
37. A. G. Cross, *N. M. Karamzin*, Carbondale, 1971, p. 103.
38. All references to this work are taken from N. M. Karamzin, *Bednaya Liza*, in *Izbrannye sochineniya v dvukh tomakh*, vol. 1, ed. P. Berkov, Moscow, Leningrad, 1964, pp. 605–21. Page references are given in parentheses in the text.
39. For a discussion of this term in the context of eighteenth-century literature, see Miller, especially the Introduction.
40. Not only is it tedious: even thirty years after its appearance the

narrative had taken on a rather comic coloration. Belinskii remarked: 'Now tell me frankly, *sine ira et studio*, as our true-bred scholars say, who is to blame that *Poor Liza* is now being laughed at as much as it was once cried over?' Belinskii's comment conveys more than a change in literary taste. See Nebel, p. 122.

41. Elaine Showalter, *A Literature of Their Own: British Women Novelists from Brontë to Lessing*, Princeton, 1977, p. 117. Showalter is referring to *Jane Eyre*.
42. Pechorin, an unreconstructed rake, makes the following illuminating comment about his relations with women: 'But surely there is a boundless pleasure in the possession of a young, scarcely burgeoned soul! It is like a flower whose finest aroma evaporates at the first ray of sunlight; one must pick it at this moment, and, breathing in to one's fill, cast it on the road: perhaps someone will pick it up.' (M. Yu. Lermontov, *Geroi nashego vremeni*, in *Sochineniya*, vol. 4, Leningrad, 1962, p. 401.)
43. A common trick, in that one of the usual devices of any ideology to defuse the threat of an opposing class, group or society is both to trivialize it and, simultaneously, to depict it as dangerous. See Althusser.
44. E. G. Belotti, *Little Girls*, London, 1975, p. 102, quoted in A. Oakley, *Subject Women*, London, 1982, p. 109.
45. For an extended discussion of this interconnection, see L. Fiedler, *Love and Death in the American Novel*, New York, 1960.

8
Men Who Give Birth: A Feminist Perspective on Russian Literature

Barbara Heldt

'To demonstrate the non-coincidence of woman and women'[1] in the products of all cultures has been the task of the feminist since approximately 1963. Woman, the fictional construct who is Other from man and marked (in the Jakobsonian sense) for certain characteristics useful or detrimental to him, must assiduously be kept distinct from those real beings in time and space, women. Feminists who undertake this task for Russian literature face interesting new territory dense in outgrowth of fantasy, desire and political allegory on the part of previous critics.

As Russians have always known, critics do participate in the reputation of artistic works, and cultural practice (publishing and criticism, as opposed to writing and reading) has generally been male-controlled. In Russia in the mid nineteenth century, Dmitrii Pisarev reviewed books for a female audience for the journal *Rassvet*. He told his audience of mothers and daughters what of literature – often European literature written by women – was suitable reading. His ultimate aim, as he himself wrote, was to enlighten women so as to make them better wives and mothers. Between the text and the reader, male critics of various persuasions have interposed themselves over the years. Fiction by women has not been ignored: it has in many cases (Tur, Vovchok, Verbitskaya, Nagrodskaya, Charskaya) been very popular. But it has been given a peculiar treatment. When it hasn't pandered to a popular market, women's writing has been especially vulnerable to interpreters of a different gender, as men's writing has not had to be. This creates a peculiar awareness on the part of the female writer. The author's sensitivities may become part of her writing. There is much here for the feminist critic to unravel. If self-protective irony is a constant feature of woman's prose and poetry, might this tone not be the result of the expectation of a different, gender-based reading by her male critics?[2] In Karolina Pavlova's *Double Life*, for example, the contemporary reader can uncover in the tone of the work ironic layers that protect not just poets in general against an insensitive aristocracy, but young girls against the marriage market, unhappily married or unmarried women against social scorn, and, by implication, the values of the novel and its poetry as asserted by a woman author herself vulnerable to these various female states against male critics claiming detachment from them.

A primary level of feminist awareness has already catalogued the various stereotypes of Russian literature: the radiant heroine, the female monster, the saintly old woman, the grasping materialist and all the familiar tribe. It should be clear by now that the most modernist twentieth-century Russian works as well as those imbued with Soviet self-styled humane neo-realism can contain the same old notions of sexual difference which emerged in the nineteenth century. Where is the female hero both meditative and articulate? Where is the male hero who doesn't have one or more women who love him in spite of his faults (usually more than one)?

In non-realist works, as the text fragments, as interest in word-formation and word-arrangement increases, there seems to be an increase among male authors in abuse of woman. Her body and will seemingly have to be broken along with the imagery and syntax in such authors as Mayakovskii, Babel' or Zamyatin. The Russian writers outside Russia today vie with each other in degrading women in their fiction and poetry. The radiant Russian heroine now appears only in Soviet publications; émigrés like Limonov and Maramzin have continued only half the hallowed tradition, that of the misunderstood male. Zhivago's Lara (*she* could have been published earlier in the USSR, even if *he* couldn't) and the nameless women described by these émigré writers in terms of one or two physical features none the less have more in common than meets the eye, although the latter are not expected to worship the hero-writer to quite the same degree, and he usually has less laundry for them to do.

It is not so much the image of the evil woman (the *zlaya baba*, from Daniil the Exile on down through the ages) nor that of the victimized woman, as that of her opposite number, the radiant heroine, that confirms the male dominance of Russian fiction, in my opinion. This heroine has been accepted as casually as has the glorious female nude in painting. We rejoice in the painterly beauty of her existence. She is a theme, reflecting an ideal reality that is pleasing to the male beholder. If women are good or beautiful, men can be free to seek, to make mistakes, to learn and be reformed, to remain weak or just to grow a bit older – to behave, in short, like a Jane Austen heroine, but not like a Russian one. The eye that beholds this nude, this flawless creature at the peak of her youth, is assumed to be a male eye. Generations of women, beholders and readers themselves, have been made to confirm an ideal of perfection that is not a faithful reflection of the world they belong to, less still of themselves. The most obvious instance where men have to do the same is within Socialist Realism, when male critics and readers behold the positive hero and rejoice; it would be out of line not to admire him.

Art is not a mirror. But literature does have enormous referential powers. It expects its readers and viewers to bring to it a certain understanding of its context and the means it uses to achieve its effect. The feminist critic assumes, as other critics should, that this is not necessarily the way Russian men and women really were. She or he then reflects on the question of why the persistent stereotypes are so attractive, and to whom. Do any writers, female ones in particular, sabotage these expectations while seeming to conform to them?

When the speaker of a poem or the narrator of a prose fiction is opposite in sex to its author, a different sort of rhetorical persuasion is attempted. When he used a female I-narrator in 'Family Happiness', the young Tolstoi was removing himself from the fiction while at the same time attempting to convince his readers that a man may know better and earlier than a woman what is best for her, but that her wholehearted approval must come from an understanding within herself. But when women poets or novelists use the masculine 'I', the reason is less to convince the reader of a point of view than to establish themselves within a convention where the masculine gender is the only unmarked one, the female gender being marked in various ways, autobiographically for example.

To stress difference is not always popular in the literature of a country where the writer or poet of whatever gender has been seen to perform an almost priestly function, mediating between the suffering Russian people and their ultimate Nationhood.

When the realization of a collective Self is at stake, who cares about the various expressions of the female Self? Isn't it just easier to take the male point of view as universal? But that would be to condescend to Russian literature.

Whether we choose to integrate certain rough edges of the text into an overall smooth picture that stresses complementarity between the sexes and transcendence of the dialogue between them, or whether we choose rather to stress asymmetry and disjuncture, is one major indication of the absence or presence of feminism in our critical practice.

In the most balanced and sane of Russian authors we can find evidence of verbal scar-tissue at the imperfectly healed point of dislocation between the male and female culture in Russian society as reflected in the individual voices in its literature. Consider this four-line dialogue between the narrator's mother and father in Chapter 6 of Turgenev's 'First Love', concerning Zinaida:

'... And I can't think what she has to be proud of – avec sa mine de grisette!'

'You evidently have never seen any grisettes,' father remarked to her.

'I haven't, thank God!'

'Yes indeed, thank God ... only how then can you form an opinion of them?'

In this passage the wife is actually judging her husband by denying social approval to a younger woman for whom it is possible to exert power only outside acceptable social boundaries, as a *grisette*. (This is indeed the reality of Zinaida's status.) In order to avert judgement by his wife, the husband lays claim to special knowledge available to all members of his sex but only to non-respectable members of the female sex. Conversely, the lack of this knowledge is power for women of the respectable category; but then men can use their exclusive knowledge as ultimate power because it enables them alone to make judgements about women. Only keeping to her place, which means cutting herself off from other women, even from forming negative opinions of them, ensures the married woman's status. Without this survival in her place, she meets the fate of Zinaida, the subject of the conversation. Rather than be outcast, she allows a man to mediate between the world she knows and the half-world of the other women that surrounds it. In this novella, the father's agony and, later, the son's, result from a not entirely free passage between the two worlds. This is the plot of many a male fiction where neither of the complementary pair of women is described with the inner intensity of a Zinaida. Sexual identity and social identity are synonymous with identity itself. Feminist criticism alone bridges the social, the individual and the textual without recourse to pre-established theory. Ignoring the question of the sexual identity of the text means slighting the human factor to an extent that most works of art cannot afford to bear.

The construction of sexual identity and the exercise of sexual authority within a text may be factors difficult to determine. But without a feminist criticism, the discussion of their recurring patterns and voices will continue to be haphazard, imprecise and self-indulgent. If the author mediates between the reader and her experience, the feminist critic must lay bare the mechanics of this mediation. The author's surrogate, the narrator, or his close associate, the hero, often mediate between fictional Woman and her experience, as in the Turgenev passage we have just examined. That the aim is, ultimately, to name the experience of women seems to offer some solace to men in their 'larger' pursuits of liberty and life; but we will adhere strictly to fiction in this chapter.

Of all human experiences that might be considered 'female' in a primary sense, surely childbirth would come to mind in the first instance. Men do it only as *couvade*, as surrogates. The literary depiction of childbirth, like childbirth itself, can be viewed either as a social experience or as an individual one. As the former, the entire social context of the event is paramount; as the latter, the mental/physical experience of the individual in labour, in birth and postpartum takes precedence over the immediate and distant surroundings. By the experience of the individual we mean, of course, that of the female who gives birth; we are not discussing here literary depictions of being born, as in Belyi's *Kotik Letaev*.

Until recent post-feminist writing, women authors have been reticent about describing childbirth. Perhaps women writing for a living were afraid of appealing to an exclusively female readership. Perhaps they or their public considered such scenes tasteless. As Tillie Olsen has written in *Silences*, most women authors had not given birth themselves; but if we advance this fact as a reason for the lack of extended childbirth scenes in their writing, even when (as in *Wuthering Heights*) it might have had an interesting novelistic role to play, we must surely confront the curious fact that male authors have not shrunk from the task of imagining childbirth in words. The social experience in which the male point of view could take a certain place – the difficulties peculiar to circumstance, the shared anxiety of the father or husband – do not seem to have been paramount in these descriptions; rather, the experience of the individual becomes the novelistic factor. The individual, however, is not the woman character who gives birth: she is busy with other things. The male narrator himself explains the event to the reader, occasionally under the guise of the omniscient narrator, but not always. Vicarious feelings of the male protagonist recounted in the first person often take centre-stage, to the point where childbirth becomes a male act rather than a female one.

A heroine can die in childbirth without ever being heard from. What were Zinaida's last thoughts? The narrator of Turgenev's *First Love* merely tells us in the final chapter: 'A week passed, then another; and when at last I went to the Hotel Demuth and asked for Mrs Dol'skaya I was told that she had died four days before, quite suddenly, in childbirth.' Death in childbirth, so frequent in nineteenth-century reality, is a convenient 'sudden' novelistic device usually reserved for heroines for whom life is impossible in some way. A woman character synonymous with the affirmation of life, like Tolstoi's Natasha, rarely dies in fiction; instead, in *War and Peace*, it is Princess Lise who, always described as a child, dies with no understanding at all of her brief part in life's greatest miracle. Prince Andrei is kept out of the room, and so is the reader; the two remain together and are both guilty.

Tolstoi used Anna Karenina's *not* dying in childbirth as a way of symbolizing her spiritual decline and the moral regeneration, however transient, of the two male protagonists. Expecting death as punishment, Anna is both right and wrong. She will eventually die because she intends to, but not in childbirth as other passionate heroines. Her actual childbirth scene is supplanted by her appearing 'not only fresh and well but in the best of spirits', yet saying she will die, giving her baby to a wet-nurse, and reconciling her husband and lover to the point where the one feels 'inward peace such as he had never before experienced' – a feeling perhaps akin to that following giving birth! – and the other shoots himself. The strong emotions belong to the men; Anna acts as mediator between them, enabling them to communicate, to forgive and be forgiven. When Kitty gives birth later in the novel, what we witness of that event is through Levin's consciousness, similar to the scene in *War and Peace* but with overtones of hope.

Tolstoi stands almost alone in the nineteenth century as an author who included actual details of childbirth in his fiction. In Chekhov's story of 1888, 'The Name-Day Party', the heroine Ol'ga suffers a still-birth, and the entire story is narrated from her disaffected and alienated point of view. This story would seem to stand as an exception to our argument, were it not for the fact that at the end the husband, portrayed throughout as a careerist and potential adulterer, suddenly bursts out with the words 'Why didn't we take care for our child?' The word *beregli* (look after, spare) is a strong one in Chekhov (cf. its use in 'In the Ravine'). Ol'ga's 'soul is empty' at the end. We leave her still under the effects of chloroform, silent.

The touchstone of realism in Russian writing about childbirth actually lies with another doctor/author, in a little-known work, V. Veresaev's *Physician's Notes* (*Zapiski vracha*, St Petersburg, 1901). Veresaev's reactions in his writing are of scrupulously honest subjectivity; thus we may see what other narratives lack. He remembers with horror what was considered normal childbirth: the woman 'trying to hold back her moans and none the less moaning' (p. 19), the resident-level doctor (*assistent*) asking her in a patronizing voice to be patient, the woman finally asking the doctor if she is going to die (no answer given). The husband arrives only the next morning and the baby is born that evening, with a very large skull, the mother swimming in blood. The physician's only comment: 'The birth was easy and of little interest' (p. 20). Veresaev comes closer to conveying the feelings of the woman in the reactions of the male narrator than do any of our fiction-writing authors. For them, childbirth has been raised to a conveniently symbolic level, where it doesn't really hurt so much, either because the woman is fulfilling a higher mission or because she is in the throes of primal instinct, neither state being all that painful.

In the twentieth century, as fiction becomes generally more explicit, childbirth scenes, like scenes of carnage or sex, become more extended and extensive – but not necessarily more realistic.

A story by Evgenii Zamyatin, 'The Flood' (1930), serves as an extreme example of childbirth as symbolism. The culminating event of the plot, it is conveyed to us in terms of death and deliverance – buttressed by recurring metaphors of earth, water, blood, and orifices spilling forth. The protagonist, Sof'ya, is able to conceive only when she murders her rival Gan'ka. The entire story is prolonged conception leading to childbirth. 'Hurry' is the only word Sof'ya utters as she gives birth. She knows it is a girl, for she has murdered one. Now her blood flows, but so does her confession at the end of the story and, after the doctor pronounces she will live, the police will pronounce her guilty. The inner view we have of Sof'ya is that of a murderess not a mother, though the imagery makes it clear that childbirth is the central event of her existence, that any means would have suited that end and that, once accomplished, only it has brought both womanly fulfilment and readiness for death.

If childbirth meant, for women, the risk of dying, and if Zamyatin's story can be taken as an extreme rationalization of fulfilment in birth/death, then we might view the curious preponderance of male-centred childbirth scenes in fiction as not merely the practical outcome of the fact that the authors were male and knew how they themselves felt, but as a working-out of their guilt that women were undergoing pain, of which their pleasure was the ultimate cause. The consequent literary transference of pain from female to male has never been illustrated as graphically as in Hemingway's story 'Indian Camp', where doctor/father explains to author/son that the Indian woman's screams in labour are not important. What is important for the boy and the story is that the husband has slit his own throat during the birth.

In the two best-known long novels of the Russian post-revolutionary neo-realist tradition, Sholokhov's *Quiet Don* and Pasternak's *Doctor Zhivago*, their Nobel-prize-winning authors make their heroes the centre of childbirth scenes which are not particularly central to the plot-line of the novels, but which further the characterization of their heroes. These passive heroes serve in each novel as a fulcrum for major events of history and are buttressed by contrasting female types. Both Grigorii and Zhivago transfer the birth experience to themselves: the Cossack male Grigorii does so more primitively (like Hemingway's Indian), first into anger and then into pain; the intellectual Zhivago makes the experience into a metaphor.

In *Quiet Don* (book I, part 2, chapter 20), Aksin'ya's labour and birth during the harvesting is graphically compressed. 'Biting her blackened tongue', she lies on the ground as the labourers press around her, one of them ridiculing her. Grigorii is angry at her for being there and has to drive her home in a wagon. She is compared to an animal: 'by the time he had harnessed the horse and driven up, Aksin'ya had crawled to the side of the road, struggled onto her hands and knees, and shoved her head into a pile of dusty barley, spitting out the prickly spikes she had chewed in her pain.' Sholokhov then describes her giving birth in the wagon, from an outside though very close perspective which becomes Grigorii's: 'Aksin'ya was lying, her face distorted and disfigured ... gaping like a fish flung onto the shore.' The animal metaphor has the effect of alienating the reader from her humanity. The final half of the description is from Grigorii's point of view. As he clumsily squeezes her foot, we transfer sympathy to *him*. She calls to him to stop driving and he sees her lying in a pool of blood. The birth has already occurred, unseen by both Grigorii and the reader. Aksin'ya is reduced to a disembodied voice; the completion of the birth is his: 'With trembling fingers he tore a bunch of threads from the sleeve of his own cotton shirt, and screwing up his eyes until they hurt, he bit through the cord and carefully tied up the bleeding stump with cotton.' Both the physical pain and the midwifery have been transferred to the father who trembles and cares for the child. For Aksin'ya there is no female voice from within, as Tolstoi imagined for Anna Karenina; only cries and animal suffering, followed by silence.

The ultimate transference of the childbirth experience to the male takes place in *Dr Zhivago*, whose protagonist then converts it into art, a further removal from the female realm. In the chapter entitled 'The Hour of the Inevitable', Tonia Zhivago gives birth in a Moscow hospital, attended by the head gynaecologist, who (using the Hayward/Harari translation) 'was of mammoth size, and always responded to questions by shrugging his shoulders and staring at the ceiling'. As the episode is bracketed by a successful diagnosis by Dr Zhivago himself, the reader is first led to feel some outrage that *he* (not she) is being treated with less than the respect due to his own professional status. After the birth he is prevented from seeing his wife lest he upset her.

But the indignant reader is overtaken by the saintly protagonist who, tired though he is, has very definite and characteristically modest thoughts on the meaning of the childbirth experience: 'Father–son; he did not see why he should be proud of this unearned fatherhood, he felt that his son was a gift out of the blue.'

The reader too is kept at a distance from Tonia. The closest we are admitted to her experience is when by mistake the door 'had been left half open, he heard Tonia's heart-rending screams'. She screams in Anna Karenina-like metaphor: 'like the victims of an accident dragged with crushed limbs from under the wheels of a train'. The first transference is made into male blood, that of Zhivago, though more delicately symbolic than in the famous Hemingway story: 'Biting his knuckle until he drew blood, he went over to the window.'

The second, artistic transference of the female experience to the male domain occurs a few paragraphs later, when Zhivago is allowed to see his wife *on condition that she does not see him*. Here the voyeuristic act is instantly transformed into metaphor. Tonia indeed becomes the writer's ultimate metaphor, a writing desk! 'She lay fairly high. Yurii Andreievich, exaggerating everything in his excitement, thought that she was lying, say, at the level of one of those desks at which you write standing up.' The female body, overseen, inscribed on, is next metaphorized into a ship that has just unloaded its cargo, in one of the book's many beautiful poetic digressions, an extended simile which ends with words absolving reader and husband of all guilt for their distance and self-distancing: 'And as no one had explored the country where she was registered, no one knew the language in which to speak to her.'

Zhivago's later reflections on pregnancy and childbirth, in the 'Varykino' chapter, exclude even the slightest intrusion of gross reality. The knowing husband merely writes in his journal that he feels Tonia is pregnant, though she herself 'doesn't believe it'. Tonia then becomes abstracted into 'a woman' and 'the woman': 'A woman's face changes at such a time. It isn't that she becomes less attractive, but her appearance is no longer quite under her control.' Thus deprived of choice, 'the woman' can move fully into the spiritual realm: 'It has always seemed to me that every conception is immaculate,' writes Zhivago, 'and that this dogma, concerning the Mother of God, expresses the idea of all motherhood.' Tonia/Woman has become an icon. The concept of male irrelevancy, reinforcing the main idea of the novel that Dr Zhivago's true responsibility lies elsewhere, in his artistic mission, is repeated: 'the man's part is as irrelevant as if he had never had anything to do with it, as though the whole thing had dropped from heaven.' The woman 'alone, in silence and humility, ... feeds and rears the child.' Thus the hours of childbirth are extended into a lifetime of separation of the sexes. Man the artist has been freed in this parturition of the pen. The section ends with an epiphany, Biblical quotation and Pasternakian commentary: 'all women are mothers of great men: it isn't their fault if life disappoints them later.' The circle has been closed; from an actual birth to the birth of the great man, who describes the birth process and especially its meaning to the distracted and abstracted mother and to mankind. Tonia reified becomes Woman deified under Zhivago–Pasternak's doctoring of reality and the husbandly role.

Thus, what common sense tells us is uniquely a female experience, becomes, in these works, most surely removed from the female characters who are undergoing the experience, and not only removed from them, but displaced onto the male characters, into the area of male introspection, male physical pain and, ultimately, male naming or interpretation. Feminist criticism, then, does have its task: a task of re-naming, re-interpreting women's experience as it has been portrayed in fiction. As we do so, we also interpret the interpreters that have preceded us (something all critics do). It becomes clear that we may have a quite different base of understanding, and that our experience never has been what it was named as being by those who never or only partially shared it.

NOTES AND REFERENCES

1. Teresa de Lauretis, *Alice Doesn't: Feminism, Semiotics, Cinema*, Bloomington, Indiana, 1984, p. 36.
2. This question is explored in greater detail in my book *Terrible Perfection: Women and Russian Literature*, Bloomington, Indiana, 1987.

Index

absurd, literature of the, 60, 65, 66, 70
absurdity, 64, 65, 66, 69, 70
addressee, 61, 66
addresser, 61, 66
Adorno, Theodor, 13
aesthetics
   literary, 56, 116
   and politics, 6
   pure, 14
   realist, 46 (*see also* realism)
   Soviet, 45–6, 54–5
   traditional, 16, 40, 56
Afanas'ev, Aleksandr, 117, 119, 121
   'The Vampire' ('Upyr' '), 119–22
agitation, *see* propaganda
Aikhenval'd, Yu., 125, 133n1
Al'ferov, A., 92
alienation, 13, 15
Althusser, Louis, 137, 156n43
anachronism, deliberate, 40, 58n12, 118, 133n11
Antonioni, Michelangelo, 15
Aseev, Nikolai, 58n7
Ashkenazi, S., 83
aura, breakdown of, 12
authoritarianism, 23, 24, 108
authority
   discursive, 27, 53–5, 57, 59n39, 139–45
   political, 24, 29–31, 53
   religious, 31
   see also dominance, political; oppression; power
authorship, patterns of, 31–2, 116, 157–8
avant-garde, 14, 16

Babel', Isaak, 158
Bakhtin, Mikhail, xii, 3–17, 19–35, 40–1, 44, 53, 54, 56, 57, 60, 62–5, 73, 76, 78, 84, 85, 86, 90, 92, 108, 111n81
   contradictions of, 20
   'Discourse in the Novel' ('Slovo v romane'), 20–35, 41–2, 53
   politics of, 24–5, 26
   and popular culture, 8, 15–17, 23, 24, 35, 73, 76, 78, 84, 86
   Problems of Dostoevsky's Poetics (*Problemy poetiki Dostoevskogo*), 33
   Rabelais and His World (*Tvorchestvo Fransua Rable i narodnaya kul'tura srednevekov'ya i Renessansa*), 4–5, 8, 9, 10, 11, 12, 73, 76, 78, 84, 85, 86, 90, 92, 108, 111n81
   work on, 11, 14, 16, 20, 26, 32, 33
   see also Bakhtin school; carnival; dialogism; discourse; heteroglossia; language; linguistics; monologism; novel; poetry; Voloshinov, V. N.
Bakhtin school
   authorship question, 10, 14
   communications model of, xii, 60, 62–5
balagan (Big Top), 74, 76, 77, 104
ballad, literary, 115
Baratynskii, Evgenii, 133n6
Barthes, Roland, 16
Basov-Verkhoyantsev, Sergei, 116, 133n10
Baudelaire, Charles, 6, 9, 12
Beauvoir, Simone de, 136
Belinskii, Vissarion, 156n40
belles lettres, *see* literature
Belotti, E. G., 153
Belyi, Andrei, *Kotik Letaev*, 161
Benjamin, Walter, 3–17
   Charles Baudelaire, 6
   'One-Way Street', 11
   'Weimar', 3–4
Benois, A., 75, 83, 110n36
Berkov, P. N., 83, 85, 86, 89, 92, 95
Bernstein, J. M., 14–15
Big Top (*balagan*), 74, 76, 77, 104
biography, problems of, 4–5, 7
Blue Blouse (*Sinyaya bluza*) movement, 79, 80
body
   carnival/grotesque, 86–9, 90
   of woman, xiv, 166–7
   see also physicality, distorted
Bogatyrev, P. G., 84, 92
Booth, Wayne, 14
bourgeoisie, 15, 24
Brownstein, Rachel M., 154n8
Buber, Martin, 5
Bukharin, Nikolai, 52, 53

canonical status, *see* canons
canons, xii, xiii, 14, 39–40, 46–7, 50, 53, 55, 56–7, 119, 136, 153n2

carnival, 5–6, 7, 8, 9, 11, 15, 16, Ch. 5
    passim
  Russian: general, 73–108, 109n23;
    adapted for propaganda, 78–81;
    suppressed, 78, 80–1, 108
Catherine II, 138–9
causality, absence of, 60, 65–6, 69–70,
    120–1
censorship, 39, 56, 84
  self-, 139
  theatrical, 81
centralization
  cultural, 23, 28, 29, 35
  linguistic, 23, 26, 27–8
  political, 23, 24, 28, 29, 35, 48, 50, 52
Central State Puppet Theatre (Moscow),
    81, 110n36
characterization, literary, 42, 44, 45, 48–
    50, 52, 55, 117, 121–2, 125, 140–3,
    146–7
  stereotyped, 142–3, 146–7, 148, 149,
    151, 152–3, 155n24, 158–9
  see also motivation, psychological;
    positive hero; 'telling names'
Charskaya, Lidiya, 157
Chekhov, Anton, 155n22
  'In the Ravine' ('V ovrage'), 163
  'The Name-Day Party' ('Imeniny'),
    163
childbirth, 9
  in Russian literature, xiv, 147, 161–7
  in writing by women, 161–2
circus, 75, 77, 78, 79
Civil War, 40, 75, 79, 80
Clark, Katerina, 17n3, 35n1, 46–8, 55–6
Classicism, 138
code, linguistic, 61
coherence, see text
Columbina, 83
comedy
  carnival, 88–9, 92
  linguistic, 81–2, 84, 86, 91–4, 99, 107,
    155n28
communication, xii, 27, 29, 32, 34, 60–9,
    125
  axioms of, 65–8
  models of, 60–9
  subverting conventions of, 60–9
Communist Party of the Soviet Union,
    48, 49, 50, 52
contact, linguistic, 61
content, ideological, 49–50, 51–4, 55
context, xii, 15, 26–7, 31–2, 42, 43, 50,
    53–7, 59n39, 159, 161
  linguistic: circumstances, 62, 63;
    referent, 61, 62, 65

continuity, xiii, 19–20, 35n1, 45, 46,
    49–50, 53, 55, 107–8, 115, 132
conventions
  of communication, subverted, 60–9
  literary: general, 21, 42–50, 119;
    subverted, 119, 122–32
  sexual, subverted, xii, 119, 122–32
  social: general, 29; subverted, 124–5,
    126
critic
  cultural, 3–17
  literary, see criticism, literary
criticism
  cultural, xii, 3–17
  literary: elitism of, xiv; feminist, 136–
    53, 153n1, 153n2, 157–67;
    international, 11; politics of, 25,
    34–5, 56–7, 136; practices of, xi,
    xii, xiv, 14, 19–20, 21–2, 25, 31–4,
    50, 54–5, 56–7, 136, 153n2, 157,
    160, 167; psychoanalytic, 125,
    154n21; radicalism of, xiii, xiv,
    56–7, 136–53, 157–67;
    subversiveness of, 35
  see also tradition, critical
Cross, A. G., 148
Culler, Jonathan, 57

Dal', Vladimir, 117
Dan'ko, E., 49
debauchery, 74–5, 96, 147–8
de Beauvoir, Simone, see Beauvoir,
    Simone de
deconstruction, 57
Defoe, Daniel, 9
de Lauretis, Teresa, see Lauretis, Teresa
    de
Derrida, Jacques, 13
Derzhavin, Gavriil, 138
de Sade, Marquis, see Sade, Marquis de
de Saussure, Ferdinand, see Saussure,
    Ferdinand de
dialect, 28
dialogism, xii, 5, 6–7, 8, 9, 11–12, 13–14,
    15, 19–35, 42, 44, 53–4
  ambiguity of, 24–5
  contradictory definitions of, 19
  in social relations, 19
dialogue, 19, 62
  see also dialogism
Dickens, Charles, 56
difference, sexual, 158, 159–60
  see also sexuality
discontinuity, xiii, 12–13, 19–20, 35n1,
    45, 49–50, 53, 54, 55, 60–9, 115, 118,
    122–32, 136, 157–67

Index

discourse, 21–35, 50, 61, 62, 66, 67
  authoritative, 27, 53–4, 55, 57, 59n39, 139–45
  critical, xiii, 6, 8–10
  historical character of, 21–2, 54
  literary, 42–4, 131
  official, 52–4, 55
  patriarchal, 139–45
  political effects of, 32, 143–5
  referential, 9–10
  see also dialogism; language; monologism
discursive practices, 23–34
dominance, political, 24, 29, 30, 32, 53, 137–8, 156n43
  see also authority; oppression; power
drinking, 75, 78, 90, 91, 92–4, 101, 104–5

Eagleton, Terry, 5
eating, 85, 90–1, 92–4, 101, 104–5
  and death, 92–4, 95, 105
eccentricity
  discursive, 57
  of literary character, 49, 50, 53, 55
  of scandalous figures, 6, 12–13
edinyi yazyk, *see* language, national
Emerson, Caryl, 10, 17n11
Engels, Friedrich, 154n4
Eremin, I., 87, 91, 92, 95, 97, 99
Erenburg, Il'ya, 39
eroticism, 123–4
Ershov, Petr, 'The Hunchback Horse' ('Konek-gorbunok'), 116–17, 118
evaluation, 62, 63–5
  absence of authorial, 63, 65

fairs
  British, 78
  Russian, 73–9, 81–2, 83, 94–5, 108–9n4
father, 125, 134n24, 139–45, 154n21, 155n27
  see also patriarchy
'feast of fools', the, 73
Fedin, Konstantin, 58n7
feerii (pageants), 75, 77
feminism, xii–xiv, 136–53, 153n1, 157–67
  aims of, 136, 153n2, 157, 167
  see also criticism, literary
films
  adventure, 77
  horror, 15
Five-Year Plan, 39, 45, 50–1
  novel, 39, 40, 46–55
Flaubert, Gustave, 7, 8, 9, 12–13, 56
folk culture, *see* popular culture

folk literature
  imitation of, 99, 108
  literary appropriation of: xiii, 115–18, 121–3, 125–32, 132n1, 133n10, 134n14
  poetics of, 115–18, 120–1
  style of, 118
  stylization of, 115–18, 133n10
  see also folk tale; *poema-skazka*
folklore, *see* folk literature; folk tale; popular culture
folk tale (*skazka*), 81, 115–17, 118, 133n10
  see also folk literature; *poema-skazka*
Fonvizin, Denis, xiii, 138–45
  The Minor (*Nedorosl'*), 138–45, 149, 150
form, 22
  abstract linguistic, 26, 29–30, 31–2, 34
  aesthetic, 14
  literary, 46
  see also text
formal analysis, xii, 19, 20, 25
formalism, 21, 23, 25–6, 28, 35
Formalism, xii
Foucault, Michel, 143–4, 155n27
Freud, Sigmund, 6, 15, 144
Friedberg, Maurice, 59n31

Garshin, Vsevolod, 133n10
Gel'fand, M., 45, 55, 58n7
gender, *see* sexuality
Genet, Jean, 7, 9, 13
genre, 8–9, 20, 22, 32, 33–4, 41, 42, 45, 74, 115
  carnival, 85, 104
  folkloric, 115, Ch. 6 *passim*
  see also folk tale; novel; *poema-skazka*; poetry, production novel; puppet theatre
Gladkov, Fedor, 40, 46, 47
Glagolev, A., 49
Gogol', Nikolai, 133n6, 144
Gor'kii, Maksim, 47, 83
Gouldner, Alvin, 12
Gramsci, Antonio, 137–8

Hanswurst, 82, 90
Harlequin, 83
Hebdige, Dick, 15
hegemony, 137–8, 154n4
Hemingway, Ernest, 'Indian Camp', 164, 166
heteroglossia, 13, 28, 32, 53
  repression of, 27, 28–9, 32
hierarchy, challenge to, 8, 12, 15–16, 56–7, 84
high culture, xi, xiii, 15–17, 23, 24, 76
  see also institutions, cultural and

high culture – *cont.*
    political; literature; popular culture
high literature, *see* literature
Hingley, Ronald, 39, 56
history, 8, 17, 21, 24, 31, 33–4, 54, 56–7
Hitchcock, Alfred, 15
Holquist, Michael, 4–5, 9, 10, 13–14, 17n3, 17n11, 35n1
Huston, John, 15
hysteria, 148

ideological practice, 12, 15, 16, 29, 34–5, 137–8
ideology, xi, 7, 21, 26, 32, 50
    dominant, 15, 137–8, 156n43
    middle-class, 15
Ierimii, Archbishop, 84
institutions, cultural and political, 27–35, 39, 53, 59n39, 137
intellectual, 3–17
    as observer, 3–4, 12
intellectual practice, 3–17
intelligentsia, progressive, xiii, 76, 77, 145
intention, 20, 21, 25, 26–7, 30, 32
    authorial: expression of, 21, 25, 50, 55; suspicion of, xi, xiii, 22, 45–6, 50, 55, 136
intertextuality, 25, 44, Ch. 6 *passim*
    see also quotation; representation of language
Ionesco, Eugène, 60, 65
    The Bald Prima Donna, 66
    The Lesson, 66

Jack Pudding, 90
Jakobson, Roman, 157
    communications model of, 60, 61, 62, 65
Jan Pickelhering, 90
Jay, Martin, 5

Karamzin, Nikolai, xiii, 138, 148–53
    The Island of Bornholm (*Ostrov Borngol'm*), 151
    Poor Liza (*Bednaya Liza*), 148–53
Karapet, 83
Karlinsky, Simon, 121, 135n29
Kasparek, 82
Kataev, Valentin, 39
Kaverin, Veniamin, 58n7
Kharms (Yuvachev), Daniil Ivanovich, xii, 60–70
    'Anecdotes from Pushkin's Life' ('Anekdoty iz zhizni Pushkina'), 67
    'Carpenter Kushakov' ('Stolyar Kushakov'), 67
    'The Cashier' ('Kassirsha'), 64
    'Connection' ('Svyaz''), 68–9
    'A Dream' ('Son'), 64, 67
    'The Encounter' ('Vstrecha'), 67
    'Fedya Davidovich', 65
    'The Flop' ('Neudachnyi spektakl''), 65
    letter to K. V. Pugacheva, 62, 65
    'Mashkin Killed Koshkin' ('Mashkin ubil Koshkina'), 64
    'The Old Woman' ('Starukha'), 68
    'On Phenomena and Existences No. 2' ('O yavleniyakh i sushchestvovaniyakh no. 2'), 61–2
    'The Red-Haired Man' ('Golubaya tetrad' no. 10'), 61, 67
    'Rehabilitation' ('Reabilitatsiya'), 64
    'Sonnet' ('Sonet'), 67
    'The Start to a Very Nice Summer's Day' ('Nachalo ochen' khoroshego letnego dnya'), 65
    'A Story' ('Istoriya'), 63–4
    'Symphony No. 2' ('Simfoniya no. 2'), 68
    'A Thorough Investigation' ('Vsestoronnee issledovanie'), 64
    'What Happened on the Street' ('Proisshestvie na ulitse'), 66, 67, 68
    'What They Sell in the Shops Nowadays' ('Chto teper' prodayut v magazinakh'), 64
    work on, 70–1
Khren (Horseradish), 74
Kirpotin, V., 40, 47
Kolpakova, E., 49–50
Kol'tsov, Aleksei, 117
Kremlev, A. N., 76
Kristeva, Julia, 35n5
Krupryanskaya, V., 84, 96
Kuzmin, Mikhail, 118

LaCapra, Dominick, 5–6, 14, 16
language
    dictionary meaning of, 8–9
    disruption of, 125–32
    everyday, 28, 30
    and historical change, 21
    and knowledge, 139–45
    literary, 28, 30

Index

national: formation of, 12;
   institutional character of, 27–35
   nature of, 23, 27, 34
   power of, 30
   representation of, 42, 44, 53–4, 55 (*see also* intertextuality; quotation)
   as rhetoric, 8–9
   self-consciousness of, 31, 32
   as sensual object, 125–31
   sociality of, 23
   standard, 26, 28, 30
   subversiveness of, 27
   unified, *see* national
   see also dialogism; discourse; heteroglossia; *langue*; linguistics; monologism; *parole*; speech; utterance
langue, 21–2, 26, 28, 32, 33
Lauretis, Teresa de, 157
Lavrenev, Boris, 58n7
Lenin, V. I., 52, 53–4, 59n35
Lentricchia, Frank, 17n8
Leonov, Leonid, 39, 40, 46, 56
Lermontov, Mikhail, *Hero of Our Time* (*Geroi nashego vremeni*), 156n42
Le Roy Ladurie, Emmanuel, 16
Limonov, Eduard, 158
linguistics, 23, 27, 29
   formalist, 23, 25–6, 28
   Saussurean, Bakhtinian critique of, 21–3, 25–6, 33–4
literature
   of the absurd, 60, 65, 66, 70
   carnival, 73–108
   conventions of: general, 21, 42–50, 119; subverted, 119, 122–32
   high, xiii, 8, 14, 56, 115–18
   history of, 30–1, 40
   nature of, 41, 55–7
   political functions of, 39, 45, 46–7, 55–6, 116, 133n10, 137–8, 139, 153–4n3, 159
   Russian: 18th-c., 136–53, 155n24; 19th-c., 41, 55, 115–19, 135, 153–4n3, 157–67; 20th-c., 39–50, 115–35, 157–67; émigré, 158
   self-consciousness of, 42, 43–4, 53–4, 58n7, 118, 132
   see also characterization, literary; conventions; folk literature; folk tale; high culture; metre; novel; poetics; poetry; popular culture; production; production novel; reading; reception; tradition, literary

logocentrism, 16, 108
Louis II of Bavaria, 3
low culture, *see* popular culture
Lunacharskii, A., 77–8

Malinovskaya, S., 79
Mandel'shtam, Osip, 58n7
Maramzin, Vladimir, 158
Margaryan, A., 49
market-place, 3–4, 11, 73
Markov, V., 110n28
Marshak, Samuil, 60, 103
Marxism, 4, 24
Maslyanitsa (Shrovetide), 73–4, 76
mass culture, *see* popular culture
'Master Plot' (Katerina Clark)
   functions of, 47–8
   inadequacies of, 55–6
materialism, 4, 5, 8, 11, 13, 14
Mayakovskii, Vladimir, 158
Mei, Lev, 117
Meilakh, Mikhail, 71n2
Melville, Herman, 56
message, linguistic, 61
metre, 117, 131–2, 135n28
   see also raeshnik
Mill, John Stuart, 154n4
Miryanin, Leo, 97–103
misogyny, 138, 142–3, 145–8, 152, 158–9
   see also sexism
modernism, 118, 158
modernity, 6–7, 10–11, 118
monologism, xiii, 9, 14, 16, 19–35, 53–5, 108
   see also dialogism; discourse
monologue, *see* monologism
Morson, Gary Saul, 11
motivation, psychological, 117, 121–2, 125
   see also characterization, literary
music hall, 77, 78
myth
   sexual, 119, 122
   Soviet, 47, 55, 56

Nadezhdin, N., 110n28
Nagrodskaya, Evdokiya, 157
Nakhimovsky, Alice Stone, 64, 70n2, 71n6
Napoleon III, 12
Narkompros (People's Commissariat of Education), Theatrical Department of, 80
narod, *see* people, the
narodnye gulyan'ya, *see* fairs, Russian
Narodnyi teatr, 76–7

Nekrasov, Nikolai, 116, 133n10
Nekrylova, A. F., 84, 88, 90, 91, 92
neologisms, 13, 107, 128
nesobstvenno-pryamaya rech', 53
New Criticism, 14
Nijinska, B., 75
nonsense, 69, 70
novel, 8–9, 20, 23, 30, 31, 46–7, 53
  subversiveness of, 27, 29–35, 53–4
  v. poetry, 9, 23–34, 44, 70
  see also production novel
novelistic, the, *see* novel
Novikov, Nikolai, 138

Oberiu, 60
Obraztsov, S., 81–2, 96–7, 109n18
obscenity, 10, 84–5, 86, 100–1, 103, 116, 146
official culture, *see* high culture
Olearius, Adam, 74, 81
Olsen, Tillie, 161
opposition, political, 23, 25, 33, 156n43
oppression, 25, 27, 30, 35, 148–9
  see also authority; dominance, political; power
Ostrovskii, Aleksandr, 155n22
Other, the, 5, 6–7, 157
O'Toole, L. M., 138, 145, 154n17
overdetermination, 140, 142–3, 150–1, 152–3, 154n20
oxymoron, 84, 95

pageants (*feerii*), 75, 77
parody, 10, 95
  literary, 116, 118
  of social relations, 7
parole, 21–2, 26, 33
  see also speech; utterance
Parvathi, 83
Pasternak, Boris, *Doctor Zhivago* (*Doktor Zhivago*), 158, 164, 165–7
patriarchy, 15, 136–53, 154n4
Pavlova, Karolina, *A Double Life* (*Dvoinaya zhizn'*), 158
Pêcheux, Michel, 26–7
peep-shows, 94–5
'What the Butler Saw', 94
people, the, xiii, 16, 29, 48, 80, 83, 138, 145, 159
Perlina, Nina, xii, 10
Peter I, 73, 144
Petrouchka (ballet), 75, 110n36
Petrovichev, I. F., 69
Petrushka (puppet show), 76, 79–108
  adapted: for agitation and propaganda, 79–81, 96–103, 107–8; for children, 103
  conservatism of, 95–6, 107–8
  Petrushka's Wedding (*Petrushkina svat'ba*), 87
  as socially critical, 83–4, 96
  subversiveness of, 80–1, 84, 95–6, 105–8
  texts: new, agitprop, 97–103; new, for children, 103; traditional, 81, 86–96, 103–8
  see also puppet theatre; Van'ka
  physicality, distorted, 82, 86–9, 99–100, 104
  see also body
Pisarev, Dmitrii, 157
pleasure
  linguistic, 125–31
  sexual, 124, 146
Plotkin, M. A., 104
poema-skazka
  development of, 115–19, 122–32, 133n5
  reception of, 116–17, 133n6
  see also folk literature; folk tale
poetic, the, *see* poetry
poetics
  of the absurd, 60–9
  of folk literature, 115–18, 120–1
poetry, 23, 26, 27
  v. novel, 9, 23–34, 44, 70
Polichinelle, 82
politics, xi, 6, 57
  of Bakhtin, 24–5, 26
  conservative, xi, 20, 55
  of criticism, 25, 34–5, 56–7, 136
  sexual, 136–53, 155n27, 157–67
  utopian, 7, 15
  see also subversiveness, political
polyphony, 125–6, 129–30
Pomorska, K., 78
popular culture, xiii, 8, 14–17, 24, 35, 73–108
  adapted: for agitation and propaganda, 79–81, 96–103, 107–8; for children, 103
  conservatism of, 15, 95–6, 107–8
  manipulation of, 78–9
  subversiveness of, 15–16, 23, 35, 80–1, 84, 95–6, 105–6, 108
  suppressed, 78, 80–1, 108, 109n18
  see also folk literature; folk tale; Petrushka; *poema-skazka*; puppet theatre; Van'ka
Popular Theatre (*Narodnyi teatr*), 76–7

pornography, *see* obscenity
positive hero, 48–50, 52, 55, 81, 96–7, 140–5, 159
   see also characterization, literary
power
   cultural, 23, 137–8
   of institutions, 25, 27–35, 53, 137
   and knowledge, 143–5, 160
   of language, 30
   patriarchal, 139–45
   political, 12, 16, 24, 27, 32, 53, 137–8
   sexual, 122, 160–1
   of tradition, 55
   see also authority; dominance, political; oppression
pre-Romanticism, 138, 154n12
Prishvin, Mikhail, 58n7
production
   cultural, 6, 31
   literary, xi, xii
production novel, 39, 40, 46–55
proletariat, 6, 13, 52
propaganda
   carnival adapted for, 78–81
   live theatre used for (Blue Blouse movement), 79, 80
   puppet theatre adapted for, 79–81, 96–103, 107–8
Propp, Vladimir, 47
prostitution, 146–8, 151–3
provisionality
   of authoritative discourse, 53–4, 57
   of critical positions, 57
   of representation, 42, 43–4, 54
   see also relativism
Pugachev, Emel'yan, 138
Pulcinella, 82, 83
pulp novels, 77
Punch, 82, 83, 84, 93–4
Punch and Judy, 78, 82, 91, 93–4
   see also puppet theatre
punk rock, 15
puns, 92
   see also comedy, linguistic
puppet theatre
   Chinese, 79
   Czech, 84
   English, 78, 82, 91, 93–4
   European: heroes of (Pulcinella etc.), 82, 83, 90; successful modernization of, 107–8
   Russian: general, xiii, 74–108; adapted for propaganda, 79–81, 96–103, 107–8; agitprop puppet groups ('Red Petrushka', etc.), 79–81;

professionalization of, 78, 81; suppression of, 78, 80–1, 108, 109n18
   see also Petrushka; Punch and Judy; Van'ka
Pushkin, Aleksandr, 67
'Alexander Radishchev' ('Aleksandr Radishchev'), 145
Evgenii Onegin, 139, 154n8
poemy-skazki, 116–17, 118, 133n6, 133n7, 133n10
The Prisoner of the Caucasus (*Kavkazskii plennik*), 44
vampire tales, 119
Putintsev, A. M., 103

quotation, 52, 53–4
   see also intertextuality; representation of language

Rabelais, François, 8, 9, 10, 11, 12, 13, 73, 85
   see also Bakhtin, Mikhail
radicalism
   of criticism, xiii, xiv, 56–7, 136–53, 157–67
   of intellectual, 3–17
   Russian, xiii, 76, 77, 145
   see also subversiveness, political
Radishchev, Aleksandr, xiii, 138, 145–8, 150
   Journey from St Petersburg to Moscow (*Puteshestvie iz Peterburga v Moskvu*), 145–8
raeshnik (doggerel), 82, 117, 133n8
   see also metre
rape, *see* violence
rap music, 16
reader, *see* reading
reading, 25, 31–2, 39–57, 61, 62–5, 68, 69–70, 130–2, 137–8, 153, 161–2
   gender-based, 157–67
   as writing, 4–5, 9
   see also reception
realism, 14–15, 46, 78, 85, 120, 146, 158, 163
   see also Socialist Realism
reception, xi, xii, 6, 31–2, 54–7
   see also reading
Red'ka (Radish), 74
referent, 61
   dismantling of, 61–2
Reiss, Timothy, 8
relations, social, 6–7, 8, 13, 16, 20, 22, 24, 31, 63–4, 151, 160–1

relations, social – *cont.*
  dialogism in, 19
  parody of, 7
relativism, 33–4
  see also provisionality
religion, 96, 107
religious authority, 31
religious rites, Greek and Roman, 73
Remizov, Aleksei, *By the Course of the Sun (Posolon')*, 118, 122–3
representation
  of language, 42, 44, 53–4, 55 (*see also* intertextuality; quotation)
  provisionality of, 42, 43–4, 54
  of reality, 41–2, 44, 66, 67–8, 70
  of women: general, xiii–xiv, 119, 122–32, 136–53 (*esp.* 142–3, 146–7, 152–3), 155n32, 157–67; idealized, 139–40, 143, 144–5, 158–9, 163, 166–7
revision of literary works, 51–4, 58n12, 59n31
Revzina, O. G. and Revzin, I. I., communications model of, 60, 65–8
Richardson, Samuel, 146
  Clarissa, 146, 147
romanticism, 42, 44, 119
Rousseau, Jean-Jacques, 145, 147
ruling class, 24–8, 33, 137
Russian Enlightenment, 138, 144, 154n11
Russian literature, *see* literature
Russian Revolution, 4, 58n12, 75, 77, 78–9, 80, 96
Russian studies, xi, xii, xiii, 56
Ruthven, K. K., 153n2

Sade, Marquis de, 146–7, 155n32
Said, Edward, 11
Saltykov-Shchedrin, Mikhail, 133n10
Sartre, Jean-Paul, 3–17
  Critique de la raison dialectique, 12
  L'idiot de la famille, 7, 8, 10
  Les Mots, 15
  'Sur "L'idiot de la famille"', 2
satire, 44–5, 64, 83–4, 139
Saussure, Ferdinand de, 21–3, 25–6, 33–4
seduction, 141, 147–8, 149–53
Segal, D., 58n7
self-consciousness
  of language, 31, 32
  of literature, 42, 43–4, 53–4, 58n7, 118, 132

self-criticism, 52, 54
  see also self-consciousness
Selivanovskii, A., 45, 55, 58n7
Sel'vinskii, Il'ya, 58n7
Sentimentalism, xiii, 136–53, 154n12
sexism, 136–53, 157–67
  see also misogyny
sexuality, xiii, xiv, 52, 160–1
  female, xiii, xiv, 122–32, 146–8, 153
  male, 122, 146–8
  see also pleasure, sexual
Shaginyan, Marietta, xii, 39–57
  Hydrocentral (Gidrotsentral'), 39–40, 46–55, 56, 57
  Kik, 40–6, 54–5, 56, 58n6, 58n7
  Mess-Mend, or A Yankee in Petrograd (Mess-mend, ili yanki v Petrograde), 39, 46
  My Work on 'Hydrocentral' (Kak ya rabotala nad 'Gidrotsentral'yu'), 49, 59n29
  'On Socialist Realism' ('O sotsialisticheskom realizme'), 46
Shane, A., 123
Shcheglov, L., 76
Shiva, 83
Sholokhov, Mikhail, 39
  The Quiet Don (Tikhii Don), 164–5
Showalter, Elaine, 152
Shrovetide *(Maslyanitsa)*, 73–4, 76
Simonovich-Efimova, N., 75–6, 85, 103, 109n23
Sinyaya bluza (Blue Blouse) movement, 79, 80
skazka (folk tale), 81, 115–17, 118, 133n10
  see also folk literature; *poema-skazka*
Skorino, L., 44, 46, 54–5
Slavic studies, xi, xii, xiii, 56
Smirnova, N., 80, 84, 109n23, 109n25
Socialist Realism, 45, 46–7, 54–5, 56, 159
  see also realism
society, *see* relations, social
Sologub, Fedor, 133n10
  Night Dances (Nochnye plyaski), 118, 133n11
Soviet literature, *see* literature, Russian: 20th-c.
speech, 21, 28
  another's, 42
  indirect free, 53
  see also parole; utterance
speech act, *see* utterance
Stalin, I. V., 52, 53–4, 56, 57, 82, 111n81
stereotype
  literary, 42, 44, 45, 122, 142–3, 146–7,

Index 177

148, 149, 151, 152–3, 155n24, 158–9
sexual, xiii, xiv, 122
Stravinsky, I., 75, 110n36
style, 20–34, 53
 critical, 8–10, 13
 of folk literature, 118
 as social and historical, 22–3
stylistics, *see* style
stylization, 42
 of folk literature, 115–18, 133n10
subjectivism, 21, 22, 25, 26
subversion of conventions
 of communication, 60–9
 literary, 119, 122–32
 sexual, xii, 119, 122–32
 social, 124–5, 126
 see also subversiveness, political
subversiveness, political
 of criticism, 35
 of language, 27
 of novel, 27, 29–35, 53–4
 of popular culture, 15–16, 23, 35, 80–1, 95–6, 105–8
 of texts, xiii, 12, 31, 53–4, 57
 see also radicalism

'telling names', 140–2, 154n16
text, xii, xiii, 6, 9, 16, 21–2, 25, 31, 32, 34, 40, 53, 56–7, 66, 67–8
 coherence of, xiii, 49, 53, 55, 60, 66, 68–9, 70, 116, 125–33, 158
 formal qualities of, 19–20, 22, 25, 116, 139–40, 150–1
 sexual identity of, 159–61
 subversiveness of, xiii, 12, 31, 53–4, 57
textual analysis, xii, 19, 25, 35
theory, literary-critical, xi, xiv, 3–17, 19–35
Todorov, Tzvetan, 5
Tolstoi, Lev, 133n10
 Anna Karenina, 162–3, 165, 166
 'Family Happiness' ('Semeinoe schast'e'), 159
 War and Peace (*Voina i mir*), 162, 163
tradition
 critical: maintenance of, 14, 19–20; re-evaluation of, xi, xiii–xiv, 8, 16–17, 20, 22, 34–5, 56–7, 136, 157–67
 literary: maintenance of, 14, 55, 65, 115, 118, 119; re-evaluation of, xiii, xiv, 11–12, 65, 118, 119, 132, 136–53, 157–67
 power of, 55

Tsar Maksimilian (*Tsar' Maksimilian*) (play), 79, 85, 95, 96
Tsvetaeva, Marina, 115–32
 'Egorushka', 119, 121, 134n15
 Juvenilia (*Yunosheskie stikhi*), 119
 'A Poet on Criticism' ('Poet o kritike'), 121–2
 'Sidestreets' ('Pereulochki'), 119, 134n15
 The Swain (*Molodets*), 115–32, 132–3n1
 Tsar-Maiden (*Tsar'-Devitsa*), 119, 121
Tur, Evgeniya, 157
Turgenev, Ivan, 41
 'First Love' ('Pervaya lyubov''), 160–1, 162

upyr', *see* vampire tales
uslovnost', *see* convention; provisionality
Utenkov, M. D., 97–103
utterance, 6, 9, 13–14, 24, 26, 27, 62, 63
 historical character of, 22
 see also parole; speech

Vaginov, Konstantin, 58n7
value
 aesthetic, xi, 40
 cultural, xiii
 literary, 56, 57
values
 cultural, 63–5
 interrogation of, 63–5, 70
 moral, 63–4
 social, 63
vampire tales, 119–32, 134n17
Van'ka (puppet show), 81, 90, 103–7
 see also Petrushka; puppet theatre
Verbitskaya, Anastasiya, 157
Veresaev, V. *A Physician's Notes* (*Zapiski vracha*), 163
verisimilitude, *see* realism
versification, 117, 131–2, 135n28
 see also raeshnik
violence, 85, 92, 139–40, 163
 carnival, 84–5, 86, 89, 104
 sexual, 146–8, 158
 textual, 125–32
Voloshinov, V. N., 4, 14, 60, 62–5
 see also Bakhtin school
Vol'pin, M., 97–103
Vovchok, Marko, 157
Vsevolodskii-Gerngross, V. N., 76, 96
vulgarity, *see* obscenity

Warner, Elizabeth, 90
Watt, Ian, 9

Wolin, Richard, 14
Wollen, Peter, 16
women
　representation of: general, xiii–xiv,
　　119, 122–32, 136–53 (*esp*. 142–3,
　　146–7, 152–3), 155n32, 157–67;
　　idealized, 139–40, 143, 144–5,
　　158–9, 163, 166–7
　sexuality of, xiii, xiv, 122–32, 146–8,
　　153
　writing by, 157–9, 161–2
Wood, Robin, 15
word, 31
　father's, 139–45
　as unit of sound, 129
　see also discourse; *parole*; speech;
　　utterance

writing, 41, 44, 54, 157
　effects of, 8, 30
　and history, 17
　minimalist, 60, 67–8
　modernity of, 10–11
　by women, 157–9, 161–2

Yazykov, Nikolai, 116
Yuvachev, Daniil Ivanovich, *see*
　　Kharms, Daniil Ivanovich

Zaitsev, I., 96
Zamyatin, Evgenii, 158
　'The Flood' ('Navodnenie'), 163–4
Zhukovskii, Vasilii
　poemy-skazki, 116–17, 118, 133n6
　'Svetlana', 119

GPSR Compliance

The European Union's (EU) General Product Safety Regulation (GPSR) is a set of rules that requires consumer products to be safe and our obligations to ensure this.

If you have any concerns about our products, you can contact us on

ProductSafety@springernature.com

In case Publisher is established outside the EU, the EU authorized representative is:

Springer Nature Customer Service Center GmbH
Europaplatz 3
69115 Heidelberg, Germany

www.ingramcontent.com/pod-product-compliance
Lightning Source LLC
Chambersburg PA
CBHW031541230426
43749CB00025B/439